SCHOLAR Study Guide

Higher Economics

CW00616216

Authored by:

Colin Spence (Culloden Academy)

Reviewed by:

Wilson Turkington (Edinburgh Academy)

Previously authored by:

Bill McFarlane

Tommy Stewart

Heriot-Watt University

Edinburgh EH14 4AS, United Kingdom.

Distributed by the SCHOLAR Forum.

SCHOLAR Study Guide Higher Economics

Higher Economics Course Code: C822 76

ISBN 978-1-911057-40-6

Print Production and Fulfilment in UK by Print Trail www.printtrail.com

Acknowledgements

Thanks are due to the members of Heriot-Watt University's SCHOLAR team who planned and created these materials, and to the many colleagues who reviewed the content.

We would like to acknowledge the assistance of the education authorities, colleges, teachers and students who contributed to the SCHOLAR programme and who evaluated these materials.

Grateful acknowledgement is made for permission to use the following material in the SCHOLAR programme:

The Scottish Qualifications Authority for permission to use Past Papers assessments.

The Scottish Government for financial support.

The content of this Study Guide is aligned to the Scottish Qualifications Authority (SQA) curriculum.

Contents

Unit 1: Economics of the Market

Unit 1 Topic 1

The economic problem

Contents

Prerequisites

The topic builds on and expands the concept of scarcity studied in National 5 Economics. Prior knowledge of the concept of scarcity, although useful, is not essential.

Learning objective

By the end of this topic you should:

- understand the basic economic problem of unlimited wants in relation to limited resources;
- be able to explain the difference between needs and wants;
- be able to explain what is meant by scarcity in Economics;
- know what is meant by free goods;
- understand the difference between scarcity and shortages;
- understand how the basic economic problem forces choices on individuals, firms and government;
- understand what is meant by rational behaviour;
- know how choices are made;
- be able to explain the concept of opportunity cost;
- know the relationship between scarcity, choice and opportunity cost;
- know what is meant by resources, mobility and substitutability.

1.1 Introduction

The starting point for economic courses is the basic economic problem. To understand this universal problem you will first have to understand the relationship between the following concepts:

- *Limited resources* - The world has a finite amount of resources, such as coal and oil that must run out at some point. There is also a limited amount of skilled and unskilled labour and a limited amount of machinery. The resources of the world are limited or scarce relative to the potential demand for them.

- *Unlimited wants* - Sometimes humans are described as greedy. It is kinder to say that they are always striving to better themselves and this often involves obtaining life's material comforts and luxuries. Humans want to consume more and more goods and services and have a higher standard of living. Consider the life that a king had several centuries ago: no central heating, no plumbed toilet, no vacation in a hotspot, no car, no television or mobile phone, etc. Most citizens of the UK can now exceed the lifestyle of this monarch.

- *Scarcity* - The two terms, limited resources and unlimited wants, are a mismatch. Resources will always be scarce relative to the unlimited wants. Scarcity can never be solved. It will continue to exist because even people in rich countries will continue to demand more and better goods and services. New technology will also give them new wants. This forces individuals (consumers), businesses (producers) and governments to make choices.

- *Choice* - Individuals make choices they think will maximise their satisfaction (or utility). They do this by comparing prices with the level of satisfaction that purchasing one more of a product will give them. Which product gives them the most "bang for their buck"? This product is the rational consumer's choice and will be purchased. The next best alternative that has not been purchased - the second on the consumer's order of preference - is called the *opportunity cost*.

- *Opportunity cost* - A product has a price tag, but an alternative way of looking at the purchase of a product is to consider what you have gone without. If a government uses its resources to fund a bypass, then a hospital might not be built. These difficult decisions and how we make them are the study of Economics.

The world faces a multitude of economic problems, from a global level to an individual level. Although some of these problems are relatively trivial, e.g. how much money should I spend on sweets?, others are of crucial importance, e.g. how can we best reduce climate change?

Economic problems

Q1: Complete the following table by entering at least three economic problems faced by each group. One example for each group has been added for clarity.

No.	Consumers	Producers	Governments
1	Spend or save	What to produce	Increase or decrease taxation
2			
3			

1.2 Needs and wants

Our basics needs for survival are food, water, clothing and shelter. The poorest in the world struggle even for needs. For the affluent, choices are about wants; for example, which of the latest electronic devices they should choose?

The starting point is to realise that every person has **needs** and **wants**. A want is simply something that we would like to have that we do not have at the moment. A need is a special type of want - one that, if we cannot satisfy, will make life very difficult or even impossible.

Human needs are the basic requirements for life such as food, water and shelter. There remain many places on the planet where even these cannot be taken for granted. Wants include holidays, cars, and fashionable clothes and are not a matter of survival.

The reasons why our wants are unlimited   Go online

For each of the following statements, state whether they are true or false.

Q2: It is human nature to be content with what one already has.

a) True
b) False

....

Q3: Some of the goods we buy wear out and have to be replaced.

a) True
b) False

....

Q4: We do not have enough money to buy all the things we want.

a) True
b) False

....

Q5: New goods are continually coming on to the market.

a) True
b) False

Needs   Go online

Q6: Choose from the following goods those which can be regarded as needs. Explain why you made your choice.

TV	Car	Clothing
Fridge	Food	Computer
Shelter	Newspaper	Washing machine

. . . .

Q7: Imagine you were given £1,000 on the strict condition that you had to spend it. Write down how you would spend it, listing the wants you would satisfy. Study your answer and then answer the question below.

Having spent the £1,000 would you now be completely satisfied, i.e. would you want nothing else - ever?

1.3   Factors of production

In order to produce the goods and services that we want, we require resources or inputs. The limited resources that were mentioned earlier can be placed in one of the four **factors of production**:

- **Land** (all natural resources);
- **Labour** (all human resources);
- **Capital** (the produced means of production, all man-made resources);
- **Enterprise** (the organising factor that also takes business risks).

Factors of production   Go online

Complete the gap with the most appropriate factor of production:

- Land;
- Labour;
- Capital; or
- Enterprise.

Q8: . . . . is man-made resources (such as factories, plant, machinery, offices, roads, schools, hospitals) which are used to produce goods or services.

. . . .

Q9: .... is the active factor which organises and controls the other three passive factors. It is carried out by entrepreneurs. The basic entrepreneurial functions are decision-making and risk-taking.

....

Q10: .... is the human effort (manual or mental) for which payment is made, which is directed to the production of goods and services.

....

Q11: .... refers to all the gifts of nature. It therefore includes not only land itself, but also all the minerals in and on the land, the sea and everything in the sea, the air, sunlight, etc.

Q12: Choose the correct word, *limited* or *unlimited*, to complete the following sentence.

The combination of .... wants for goods and services but .... resources to make the goods and services, creates the basic economic problem.

The problem is that, unlike wants, these resources are limited in supply. Although it may appear that there are plenty of them, there is not an unlimited supply of them.

Economists call this problem *scarcity* and believe that it is faced by everyone.

1.4   Scarcity

Scarcity is the basic economic problem and applies to all countries - rich and poor (although the results of scarcity vary greatly from country to country). Scarcity is a relative problem in that nothing is scarce in itself, only in relation to the desire for it.

The basic economic problem of scarcity does not have a solution. Economists can only seek to minimise waste by creating an economy that works at maximum efficiency. This would allow the maximum number of needs and wants to be satisfied.

Scarcity	Go online

Q13: Complete the following sentence by replacing the gaps with the most appropriate word - goods, resources, services, or wants.

No country in the world has enough .... to produce enough .... and .... to satisfy completely all the .... of its people.

Scarcity must not be confused with shortages. Scarcity involves wants whereas shortages involve demand.

Q14: Which of the following statements is correct?

a) If a good is limited in supply, it must be scarce.
b) If a good is scarce, it must be limited in supply.
c) Both of the above.
d) Neither of the above.

1.5   Scarcity versus shortage

Shortages occur when the demand for a product is greater than the available supply of it. Shortages do not usually last very long as they tend to push up the price of the good and this increase in price usually persuades producers to supply more.

Scarcity, on the other hand, occurs when the wants for a product are greater than the available supply of it. Scarcity can never be eliminated because our wants for goods will always be greater than the amount our resources can produce.

Complete the following sentences:

Q15: Demand is the want for a product backed by the ability to buy it with ....

....

Q16: Although our wants are unlimited, our demand is limited by ....

Defining the economic problem	Go online

Complete the following sentences by replacing the gap with the most appropriate word (please note that words can be used more than once):

- goods;
- limited;
- resources;
- services;
- scarcity;
- unlimited;
- wants.

Q17: The basic economic problem is .... This comes about because our ....
for .... and .... are .... but the .... we need to produce the ....
and .... are ....

Scarcity forces us to make choices. As scarcity is universal, so is choice.

Complete the following sentences:

Q18: Consumers must choose what to .... because their .... is limited.

....

Q19: Producers must choose what to .... because their .... are limited.

....

Q20: Governments must choose what .... to provide because their .... are limited.

....

Q21: Every choice is the result of ....

....

Q22: In the following statement choose the correct option.

"Therefore scarcity .... the same as being limited in supply."

a) is
b) is not

1.6   Free goods

To the economist, all things are scarce, the only exception being **free goods**. These are goods of which there are enough to satisfy everyone's desire for them at a zero price. Just because a good does not cost anything to buy, it does not necessarily make it a free good as far as Economics is concerned.

For example, "free air" for tyres, advertised at a garage is not really a free good. The garage has incurred costs in providing it, but has chosen to absorb these costs and provide it at no charge. Examples of free goods include sunshine and wild brambles.

Identifying free goods   Go online

Q23: Read the following passage and list any of the bold words/phrases that you think are free goods.

John Smith took his two sons to the seaside for the day. The boys had a great time. They made castles out of *sand*, paddled in the *sea* and spent an hour on the swings and roundabout in a nearby *swing park*.

In the afternoon a young lad walked along the beach selling *ice-cream*. The boy was offering them three for two i.e. if you bought two, you got the *third cone free*. John took the boy up on his generous offer and bought three ice-cream cones. Later on, another lad came along

---

handing out *free small tubes of sun-tan lotion*. John took one, promising he would try it out later.

As they left the beach, John and the boys picked and ate some *strawberries that were growing wild* and washed them down with some water they got from a *water fountain*. On the way home, John stopped for petrol and as he spent more than £20, he was given a *free wine glass*. The boys had a great day out and John, being a typical Scot, was delighted with all his free goods.

1.7 Opportunity cost

Every choice involves a sacrifice, i.e. what we could have chosen instead. Therefore the real cost, as opposed to the monetary cost, of any choice is the next best alternative choice that we have sacrificed. If resources are used to build a bridge then the same resources cannot also be used to build a school.

This real cost is known as **opportunity cost** and is one of the most fundamental concepts in Economics.

Opportunity cost Go online

Choose the most appropriate item from the list to complete each sentence:

- building a school;
- employing more workers;
- buying a toffee crisp;
- buying a packet of crisps;
- cutting the rate of income tax;
- buying a tractor.

Q24: The opportunity cost to a consumer of buying a Mars bar might be ....
or ....
....
Q25: The opportunity cost to a farmer of buying a combine harvester might be
.... or ....
....
Q26: The opportunity cost to the government of building a hospital might be
.... or ....

Q27: Complete the following sentence by replacing the gap with the most appropriate words:

- a free good;
- choice;
- scarcity.

Opportunity cost is the direct result of .... and occurs every time a .... is made. All economic goods therefore have opportunity costs as something has to be sacrificed to produce and/or consume them. If a good has no opportunity cost it must be ....

....

Q28: A clothing firm can produce any one of the following combinations of shorts and t-shirts per week.

Shorts	T-shirts
1,000	8,000
2,000	6,500
3,000	5,000
4,000	3,500

What is the opportunity cost of producing one pair of shorts?

a) 1

b) 1.5

c) 2

d) 8

1.8 Rational economic behaviour

Although scarcity explains why we have to chose, it does not explain how we choose, i.e. why do we chose one alternative over another? To answer this question we need to examine the aims of consumers, producers and governments.

Aims of consumers	In Economics it is assumed that consumers are "rational" as, when faced with a choice, they will always choose the alternative that gives them the greatest satisfaction. This implies that consumers have a scale of preferences, i.e. a list of unsatisfied wants arranged in order of preference. Rational behaviour means that we will always satisfy our most pressing wants first.
Aims of producers	Economists assume that producers aim to maximise profit. When deciding what to produce they will therefore choose the option which will give them the most profit.
Aims of governments	Governments aim at maximising the economic welfare of society and will therefore spend their taxation revenue on the goods and services which will achieve this. For example, if the government believes that society will benefit more from having more hospitals than having more schools, it will increase its spending on the NHS rather than on education.

When faced with any choice it is important to weigh up all the possible alternatives and use the concept of opportunity cost to determine which is the best one.

Correct choice Go online

Q29: Complete the following sentence.

To make a correct choice, consumers, producers and governments must weigh up all the alternatives and then choose the one that has the .... opportunity cost.

1.9 Factor mobility

Factor mobility is the speed and ease with which a factor can move - either from place to place (geographical mobility) or from job to job (occupational mobility). Although it is economically important for factors to be mobile, in practice there are many obstacles to factor mobility.

Land and specialised capital, e.g. oil rigs, are obviously immobile and little can be done to change this, however much can be done to overcome and remove the obstacles to labour mobility. Labour mobility can be improved by more re-training and re-education, reform of the housing market, more job information, help with removal costs and shorter apprenticeships.

Resources, to a certain extent, can be substituted for each other and this can result in cost savings. The trend in modern economies is for industries to become more capital intensive, i.e. to replace some labour with machinery. Although this can result in greater profits and higher wages, it can also lead to more redundancies and therefore an increased need for labour to be mobile.

Obstacles to labour mobility   Go online

For each of the following obstacles to labour mobility, state whether they refer to geographical or occupational mobility.

Q30: Family ties?

a) Geographical
b) Occupational

....

Q31: Cost of moving?

a) Geographical
b) Occupational

....

Q32: Lack of qualifications?

a) Geographical
b) Occupational

....

Q33: Different school systems?

a) Geographical
b) Occupational

....

Q34: Age?

a) Geographical
b) Occupational

....

Q35: Obsolete skills?

a) Geographical
b) Occupational

....

Q36: Housing costs?

a) Geographical
b) Occupational

1.10   The three basic questions

All countries are faced with the basic economic problem of scarcity, i.e. they do not have enough resources to produce all the goods and services that their citizens want. This means that every country has to decide what to produce, how to produce and for whom to produce.

These are the problems of *resource allocation*.

Q37: Looking at these questions in more detail, the same three words are missing from each of the following bullet points. What are they?

- What .... will be produced?
- How will these .... be produced, i.e. what methods of production will be used?
- To whom will the .... be distributed? In other words, who will get the .... once they have been produced?

Every country must devise a method or system of how to allocate its scarce resources and distribute the goods and services it has produced. There are basically three types of economic system:

- the command or planned economy;
- the market economy;
- the mixed economy.

Each system answers the resource allocation questions in different ways. Planned economies replace the market with political value judgements on what is best to produce and the consumer is not sovereign in a planned economy. Market economies allocate resources to the areas that are most profitable and this reflects the consumer demand. Mixed economies involve the government intervening in areas where the market fails such as public, merit and demerit goods (this is dealt with in a later topic).

1.11   The position of Economics on the subject map

Having learned something about Economics, you may be able to consider which other subjects are its neighbours. Economics is about how people make choices and decisions in the use of limited resources. History could be described as people and their past. Geography may deal with people and their environment.

Spot the common factor - people. These are all social sciences, and close neighbours on the subject map. When history is not about wars and battles, it is often about social and economic change. Hardly surprising that there is a subject called economic history.

Economics looks at the behaviour of consumers - so might a psychologist!

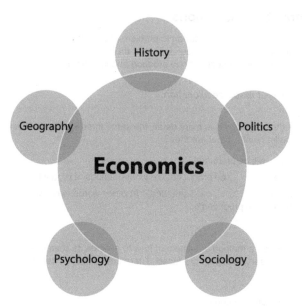

The position of Economics on the subject map

1.12 Summary

The basic economic problem is scarcity. It is universal and cannot be solved. Scarcity means that choices have to be made by consumers, producers and governments. Each choice will have an opportunity cost - the second choice that can longer be done because resources have been allocated to the first choice.

Economics studies how to minimise opportunity costs so that as many choices as possible can be satisfied with our limited resources.

Summary

Having completed this topic you should:

- understand the basic economic problem of unlimited wants in relation to limited resources;
- be able to explain the difference between needs and wants;
- be able to explain what is meant by scarcity in Economics;
- know what is meant by free goods;
- understand the difference between scarcity and shortages;
- understand how the basic economic problem forces choices on individuals, firms and government;
- understand what is meant by rational behaviour;
- know how choices are made;
- be able to explain the concept of opportunity cost;
- know the relationship between scarcity, choice and opportunity cost;
- know what is meant by resources, mobility and substitutability.

1.13   End of topic test

End of Topic 1 test   Go online

Q38: In the UK economy today, which of the following would an economist regard as being scarce?

a) Milk only
b) Milk and Museums with no admission charge
c) Museums with no admission charge and NHS hospitals
d) All of the above

....

Q39: Jane Smith is standing in the queue for the Scottish cup final between Rangers and East Fife when someone offers her £500 for her ticket. If the ticket cost Jane £100, what is the opportunity cost of her now going in to see the final?

a) £0
b) £100
c) £400
d) £500

....

Q40: A vehicle manufacturing firm can use its resources to produce any one of the following combinations of car and motorbikes per day.

Cars	Motorbikes
10	16
20	12
30	8
40	4

What is the opportunity cost of producing one motorbike?

a) 1.6 cars
b) 2.5 cars
c) 5 cars
d) 10 cars

....

Q41: Enter the correct word or words missing from the following paragraphs from the following list:

- land;
- scarce;
- capital;
- choices;
- free;
- second;
- social;
- resources;
- labour;
- an opportunity;
- wants;
- enterprise.

Economics is a .... science. The basic economic problem arises because of the mismatch between the unlimited .... of people and society and the limited .... available. As a result .... must take place. This applies to all .... goods, but a few .... goods are excluded because they have no opportunity cost to produce.

The four factors of production are .... (natural resources), ... (human resources), ... (man-made resources) and .... (the organising and risk-taking factor). When one item is selected, then there is .... cost. This is the .... preference that cannot now be achieved.

Unit 1 Topic 2

Production possibility curves

Contents

Prerequisites

The topic builds and expands on topics studied at National 5 Economics. However, prior knowledge of this concept, although useful, is not essential.

Learning objective

By the end of this topic you should:

- know how production possibility curves are constructed and what they show;
- understand the distinction between shifts of and movements along the production possibility frontier;
- know the relationship between technical efficiency and economic efficiency.

2.1 Efficiency

Efficiency comes in more than one form, as defined below:

- **technical efficiency** is the maximum output from minimum inputs;
- **economic efficiency** is when the most valued goods and services are produced and no one can be made better off by transferring resources. Resources have to be used in the most technically efficient way before economic efficiency can happen.

The basic purpose of Economics is to show how we can make the best use of our scarce resources, i.e. how to use our resources in a way which satisfies as many wants as possible. This is known as economic efficiency.

Economic efficiency requires that:

1. All resources are fully employed, i.e. there are no unemployed resources.

2. We are getting the maximum output from our resources. This means that the goods are being produced at the minimum unit cost and minimum opportunity cost. This is known as technical efficiency.

3. The goods that are produced are those most wanted by consumers or society.

Economic efficiency = technical efficiency + the goods and services being produced must be those which society most wants.

Economic and technical efficiency   Go online

Q1: Complete the following sentence.

Although scarcity can never be eliminated, because resources will always be ...., and wants will always be ...., its effects can be reduced by making full use of our ....
.

....

Q2: Select the activities, from those listed below, which are likely to result in greater technical efficiency.

a) Greater specialisation by workers

b) Increased mechanisation

c) Employing more workers

d) Improved education and training

e) Cutting workers wages

f) Increasing the length of the working day

2.2 Equity

The aim of efficiency can often conflict with the aim of equity or fairness. For example, most advanced economies base production decisions on demand. They could therefore achieve economic efficiency by satisfying the demands of a few rich people at the expense of the demands of a large number of poor people. This could mean that the economy was efficient but not equitable.

Efficiency is concerned with maximising satisfaction, whereas equity concerns social justice or fairness.

Scales of Justice
(*3D Scales of Justice* (http://bit.ly/2r6wNZ0) by *ccPixs.com* is licensed under *CC BY 2.0*)

2.3 Expanding and declining industries

In a modern dynamic society where demand and production methods are continually changing, some industries and occupations will be expanding because demand for their products is increasing while others will be declining because demand for their products is falling.

If economic efficiency is to be achieved it is vital that resources move in response to changes in demand. If this does not happen, our economy will not achieve its full productive potential.

Expanding and declining industries	Go online

For each of the following industries, state whether they have expanded or declined *in the UK* in the last twenty years.

Q3: Finance?

a) Expanded
b) Declined

....

Q4: Electronics?

a) Expanded
b) Declined

....

Q5: Shipbuilding?

a) Expanded
b) Declined

....

Q6: Coal?

a) Expanded
b) Declined

....

Q7: Leisure?

a) Expanded
b) Declined

....

Q8: Textiles?

a) Expanded
b) Declined

2.4   Resource substitution

Resources, to a certain extent, can be substituted for each other and this can result in cost savings.

The trend in modern economies is for industries to become more capital intensive, i.e. to replace some labour with machinery. Although this can result in greater profits and higher wages, it can also lead to more redundancies and therefore an increased need for labour to be mobile.

2.5   Consumer and capital goods

The economic goods produced in an economy will fall into one of two categories:

- *consumer goods* that are used up by consumers for the satisfaction they give;
- *capital goods* that are used for the production of more goods.

Consumer goods are "jam today" whereas capital goods are used to create a richer future - "more jam tomorrow". Consumer goods provide benefits today but, by investing in capital goods, increased production and improved efficiency will be possible in future expanding the economy. Consider a basic choice that faces all economies - producing consumer goods or producing capital goods.

In a centrally planned economy such as the old Soviet Union, resources were directed by government into the production of capital goods. As a result, an economy which could not feed its population in the 1930s was able to put the first man in space only 30 years later, such was the pace of advance. The lack of consumer goods meant a substantially poorer lifestyle for the average citizen compared to their western counterparts.

This process cannot continue as citizens are given more freedom and the profit motive, rather than threats from the state, is then needed to encourage efficient production. Move on another 30 years and it became clear that centrally planned economies were unable to keep up with the profit-driven market economies of the west.

The centrally planned system could not push the production possibility curve outwards and generate economic growth as quickly as the capitalist, market system could.

Consumer and capital goods	Go online

Q9:   Put the following ten items under the correct heading of consumer goods or capital goods in the table below:

- apple
- supertanker
- private plane
- work uniform
- factory machine
- television
- taxi
- personal computer
- hard hat
- casual clothes

Consumer good	Capital good

Q10: Explain how a company car can be both a consumer good and a capital good.

. . . .

Q11: Complete the following sentence.

It is how a good is . . . ., that determines whether it is a consumer or capital good.

2.6   Constructing a production possibility curve (PPC)

The concepts of technical efficiency and opportunity cost can be shown diagrammatically by constructing production possibility curves (PPCs). These can be drawn, in theory, for an individual, a firm or a country. They show the possible combinations of goods that can be produced. Assume there are only two goods or two categories of goods.

The PPC joins all the possible combinations of consumer and capital goods that the economy can produce provided all resources are being fully and efficiently employed. If more capital goods are produced then the opportunity cost will be the consumer goods that have to be given up, as resources move over to the production of these extra capital goods. Indeed, any change in the combination of goods produced will incur an opportunity cost.

Production possibility curve (PPC)	Go online

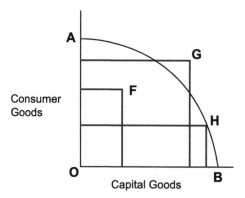

In the above diagram, point A represents the maximum quantity of consumer goods that the country could produce provided that all its resources are being fully and efficiently employed in the production of consumer goods.

Point B represents the maximum quantity of capital goods that the country could produce provided that all its resources are being fully and efficiently employed in the production of capital goods.

Point F and any other points inside the curve show combinations of consumer and capital goods which the economy is capable of producing. These points indicate that some resources are either unemployed or inefficiently employed.

Point G and any other points outside the curve show combinations which the economy cannot produce because it does not have the productive capacity to do so.

Point H and any other points on the curve are just attainable - provided all resources are being fully used.

Q12: Complete the following sentence:

If the economy is producing at a point on the curve, its production must be ....

.

If the economy is producing at a point inside the curve then it is producing less of both goods than it could. Its production is therefore technically inefficient. This can be caused by some resources lying idle, e.g. unemployed labour, and/or some resources being used inefficiently, e.g. six workers doing a job that could equally well be done by four (known as over-manning).

The downward slope of the curve shows that there is an opportunity cost of producing more than one type of good.

Q13: What will happen to the curve if there is a sudden large increase in the level of unemployment in the economy?

....

Q14: Complete the following sentences:

If an economy is currently producing at a point on the curve, the only way it can produce more capital goods is by .... A PPC is simply a diagrammatic representation of ....

The diagram below shows the PPC for an economy demonstrating the opportunity cost of producing consumer goods and capital goods.

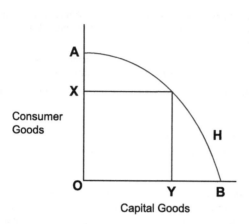

Q15: In the above diagram, what is the opportunity cost of producing 0Y capital goods?

....

Q16: In the above diagram, what is the opportunity cost of producing YB more capital goods?

The usual PPC curves outwards from the origin as the opportunity cost of producing one good, in terms of the other, usually increases as more of it is produced. The example below shows the opportunity cost of producing carrots and sprouts.

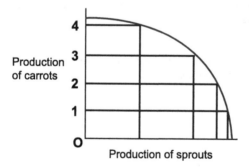

The opportunity cost of producing carrots, i.e. the amount of sprouts sacrificed, increases as more carrots are produced. This is because some resources are more suitable for the production of one good rather than another, e.g. in order to grow more and more carrots the farmer will have to grow carrots on land that would be much more suitable for growing sprouts.

2.7 Economic growth

If the economy's productive capacity, i.e. its ability to produce, increases, the PPC will be pushed outwards and more of both goods can now be produced. This is known as economic growth.

Economic growth

Q17: Draw a diagram to show what happens to a country's PPC when it experiences a period of economic growth.

Economic growth can only occur when:

- there has been an increase in the quantity and/or quality of a country's resources, e.g. the discovery of North Sea oil or increased training;

- the country has experienced an advance in technology, e.g. the microchip. Although the microchip may seem to have been a great step forward, at least one economist has suggested that labour-saving household devices had a greater benefit because they released a vast mainly female workforce to increase production. Historically there are many examples of dramatic leaps in technology, e.g. canals.

Economic growth is covered in more detail in CfE Higher Economics Unit 2.

2.8 Summary

Summary

Having completed this topic you should know that:

- production possibility curves (PPCs) can be used to illustrate the concept of opportunity cost. If an economy is directed towards the production of capital goods then this will be at the cost of some consumer goods as the same resources cannot be used twice;

- the concept of economic growth can also be illustrated with the curve moving further from the origin;

- technical efficiency is maximum output from minimum inputs. Economic or allocative efficiency means that there is technical efficiency plus no one can be made better off by transferring resources because the most valued goods and services are being produced.

2.9   End of topic test

Q18: Which of the following is an example of a firm experiencing an increase in technical efficiency?

a) Increasing its profit by selling more goods.
b) Reducing its price by 10% but its profit level falling by only 5%.
c) Reducing its total cost by closing one of its factories.
d) Producing its normal output but with fewer factors.

....

Q19: The following table shows those combinations of tables and chairs which a firm can produce per day.

Tables	0	6	12	18	24	30
Chairs	60	48	36	24	12	0

As the output of tables rises, what happens to the opportunity cost of producing tables in terms of chairs?

a) It rises then falls.
b) It remains constant.
c) It falls continuously.
d) It rises continuously.

....

Q20: The following production possibility curve relates to an economy.

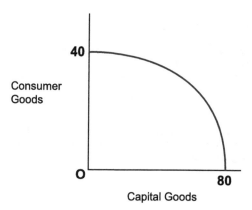

For this economy, what happens to the opportunity cost of producing capital goods as it increases its production of capital goods?

a) It increases.
b) It decreases.
c) It does not change - it is always half a unit of consumer goods.
d) It does not change - it is always two units of consumer goods.

. . . .

Q21: The following table shows how the factors of production may be combined to produce 100 units a day of a certain good.

	Land	Number of workers	Capital
A	20	30	5
B	20	40	3
C	20	50	3
D	20	60	2

From the information in the table, which combination must be technically *inefficient*?

a) A
b) B
c) C
d) D

. . . .

Q22: The following statements refer to efficiency. Which of the following is correct?

a) If a production process is technically efficient, it must also be economically efficient.
b) If a production process is economically efficient, it must also be technically efficient.
c) Both of the above
d) None of the above.

. . . .

Q23: The following production possibility curve AB relates to an economy.

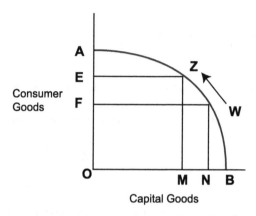

Capital Goods

Production possibility curve showing points W and Z on the curve. Point W on the curve has capital goods equal to ON and consumer goods equal to OF. Point Z on the curve has lower capital goods equal to OM and higher consumer goods equal to OE.

For this economy, what is the opportunity cost of changing production from point W to point Z?

a) FA consumer goods
b) MN capital goods
c) MB capital goods
d) FE consumer goods

Unit 1 Topic 3

Theory of demand

Contents

Prerequisites

The topic builds on and expands the concept of demand studied at National 5 Economics. However, prior knowledge of this concept, although useful, is not essential.

Learning objective

By the end of this topic you should:

- know the definition of demand and what is meant by effective demand;
- know the difference between individual and market demand;
- know the law of demand;
- know the shape of a normal downward sloping demand curve;
- understand the income and substitution effects and how they affect demand curves;
- know the reasons why some demand curves are unusual;
- know what is meant by total, marginal and diminishing utility;
- understand the law of diminishing marginal utility;
- understand the derivation of a demand curve using marginal utility.

3.1 Theory of demand and supply

Economics is known as a behavioural science because it attempts to explain how people behave in an economic situation, i.e. when they have to make choices.

The theory of **demand** attempts to explain consumer behaviour.

Theory of supply   Go online

Q1: Complete the following statement:

The theory of supply attempts to explain .... behaviour.

3.2 Utility

When consumers consume goods and services they obtain satisfaction. Economists call this satisfaction **utility**. Utility is therefore defined as the amount of satisfaction a consumer gains from consuming a good or service at any moment in time.

Utility can be expressed in two ways - total or marginal.

- **Total utility** is the total amount of satisfaction a consumer gains from consuming a good or service.

- **Marginal utility** is the extra satisfaction, i.e. the increase in the total amount of satisfaction, a consumer gains from consuming one more of a product.

Total and marginal utility   Go online

The figures in the following table represent the amounts of utility a consumer receives from consuming various amounts of packets of crisps per day. In practice utilities cannot be measured accurately, although they can be compared, but the price consumers are willing to pay for a product does give some indication of the amount of utility they think they will receive from consuming it.

Q2: Study the table and then complete the last column.

Number of packets per day	Total utility	Marginal utility
1	100	100
2	180	
3	250	
4	300	
5	320	

From the answer to the above activity you can see that as a person consumes more of a good or service per unit of time, total utility increases but marginal utility decreases. For example, if on a warm day you are thirsty enough for one glass of lemonade then a second one shortly afterwards is unlikely to give you quite as much satisfaction. The second glass has less marginal utility than the first, although the total utility of the two glasses added together is higher than the total utility of one glass.

You could also consider the efforts made by supermarkets with offers such as 'buy three for two'. In effect they realise that the extra item of the same gives less marginal utility than the earlier ones, so a price reduction or offer is needed to persuade you to buy it. By matching up the reduced marginal utility with a reduced price they may keep the item high enough in your preferences to persuade you to buy a further one.

3.2.1   Plotting total and marginal utility

Plotting total and marginal utility

Q3:   Using the figures in the table below, plot marginal utility on a graph. Join the points and label the curve 'marginal utility'.

Number of packets per day	Total utility	Marginal utility
1	100	100
2	180	80
3	250	70
4	300	50
5	320	20

3.2.2   The law of diminishing marginal utility

The fact that marginal utility decreases as consumption increases is known as 'the law of diminishing marginal utility'. This law (or theory) states that "the more of a good a consumer consumes, the less utility he/she will get from each extra unit". In simple terms, this means that the more we have of a good, the less we want one more.

The law of diminishing marginal utility   Go online

Q4:   Complete the following sentence.

In money terms, the law of diminishing marginal utility states that "the more we have of a good, the less we are willing to .... for one more".

3.3   Rational consumers

Economists assume that consumers are rational, i.e. they assume that consumers will spend their money in a way which gives them maximum satisfaction (the greatest amount of total utility). When considering buying a good, a consumer will compare the expected marginal utility with the price of the good.

Rational behaviour results when consumers buy the goods which give them the greatest marginal utility for the money they spend. In economic terms, consumers will achieve maximum satisfaction when the ratio of the marginal utility to the price of every good they buy is equal. When one good has a higher marginal utility per pound spent than others, then it is the first preference for purchase. The act of buying it means that another of the same would have less marginal utility. In this way all goods and services are continually returned to an equality of marginal utility.

In simple terms, consumers achieve maximum satisfaction when they spend their money in a way which gives the best value for their money or maximises their utility.

Rational behaviour   Go online

Q5: Fill in the missing word.

A consumer spends all his money on two goods - cans of juice, which cost £1 each, and packets of crisps, which cost 50p each. He will maximise his total utility when he buys the goods in such amounts that the satisfaction he gets from the last can of juice is .... the satisfaction he gets from the last packet of crisps.

3.4 Effective demand

In Economics, demand always means **effective demand**, i.e. the desire for a good backed by the ability to get it using money. Therefore demand is not the same as wants. Our wants are unlimited but our demand is limited by the amount of money we have.

Effective demand   Go online

Q6: Does a starving man who has no money have a demand for food?

a) Yes
b) No

3.5 Individual and market demand

Individual demand is the demand by one person for a product. Market demand is the sum of all the individual demands for a product (the total demand for a product).

An individual's demand for a product is determined by the following:

- the price of the product;
- the level of disposable income;
- tastes and preferences;
- the price of other goods.

The price of the product   Go online

Q7: In the following sentences, when given a choice, select the correct option.

For most goods, the higher the price the (*greater/lower*) the quantity demanded. When price rises some consumers will regard the good as being too expensive and so will buy (*more/less*) of it. If the price falls some people will regard it as a "good buy" and therefore the quantity demanded of it will (*rise/fall*). Price and quantity demanded therefore are therefore (*directly/inversely*) related.

There are many factors other than the price of a product that influence demand. The factors other than price will be dealt with in Unit 1 Topic 4.

3.6   The law of demand

The law of demand states that "the quantity demanded of a good will tend to increase if its price falls and decrease if its price rises - *ceteris paribus*."

Ceteris paribus means other things remain unchanged, and is an assumption that is generally made in economic theory. Obviously in the real, non-theoretical world, many other factors would be changing all the time. However economists cannot create controlled laboratory conditions and must therefore create their theories in a theoretical world, where conditions other than those being studied are assumed to be stable.

These theories are then carried out into the real and ever-changing world to provide an improved understanding of how the economy works.

The law of demand   Go online

Q8: Choose the correct option in the following sentence.
There is (*an inverse/a direct*) relationship between price and quantity demanded.

The law of demand can be illustrated in two ways:

1. by constructing a demand schedule, i.e. a table;

2. by drawing a demand curve, i.e. a graph.

Price (p)	Demand (per week)
50	100
40	150
30	250
20	350
10	500

A demand schedule

The above figures can be plotted on a graph.

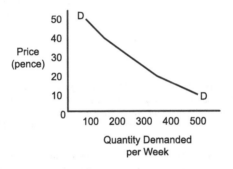

A demand curve

3.6.1 The shape of the demand curve

The normal demand curve slopes from top left to bottom right (a negative slope) showing that more is bought at a low price than a high price. This happens for two main reasons:

- the income and substitution effects, and
- marginal utility.

The income and substitution effects

If a good falls in price, existing consumers of that good will experience a rise in their real income and purchasing power. Real income refers to the comparison of actual money income with changing prices. As prices fall, the same actual money income will buy more and we say that real income (or the purchasing power of money) has risen.

Consumers might use this extra purchasing power to buy more of other goods, but some consumers might use it to buy more of the good whose price has fallen. This is known as the **income effect**.

If a good for which there are close substitutes falls in price, then it becomes "a better buy" than its substitutes. Some consumers might therefore switch their spending from the dearer to the cheaper substitute. This is known as the **substitution effect**.

Distinguishing between the income effect and the substitution effect when asked for an explanation of the shape of a normal demand curve will be important - you will get marks for it.

Income and substitution effect   Go online

Q9:   If a good increases in price, what happens to the money incomes of consumers of the good?

....

Q10: If a good increases in price, what happens to the real incomes of consumers of the good?

Marginal utility

In order to maximise satisfaction, consumers will buy those goods which give them the best value for their money. If one of the goods they buy falls in price it will now give them more marginal utility relative to the price, i.e. it becomes a better buy as they are getting the same amount of utility for less money. They can now increase their total utility by buying more of it and less of another good.

A demand curve is simply a curve which plots marginal utilities and it is downward sloping because marginal utility diminishes as quantity increases i.e. consumers will only buy more of a good if its price falls.

Marginal utility curves and demand curves   Go online

Q11: Why do marginal utility curves and demand curves have the same shape?

Remember, the price consumers are willing to pay for a good is one way of measuring the utility they will receive from consuming it.

3.6.2 Exceptions to the law of demand

There are some exceptions to the law of demand when a rise in the price of a good results in more of it being demanded. In these situations the demand curve will slope upwards from left to right, for example:

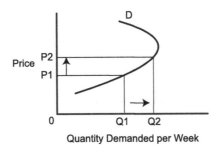

Quantity Demanded per Week

Note how the demand curve eventually resumes its normal shape as consumers cannot continue buying more of a product as its price rises - the income effect.

Upward sloping demand curves are known as *unusual or regressive demand curves.*

The following are situations where the law of demand might not apply.

- *Articles of ostentation* - some goods have a lot of prestige or social status attached to them. These goods are valued as a status symbol because their price is well known, therefore if their price rises, they may become even more attractive. They are known as 'goods of ostentation' or 'Veblen goods'.

- *Speculative buying* - when there is an expectation of a further rise in price, consumers might buy more when the price rises because they think that the price will rise again. Speculators in capital markets often respond to a rise in the price of a good by buying more of it, in anticipation of further price rises.

- *Giffen goods* - named after Sir Robert Giffen a 19th century economist who reported that, during the Irish potato famine, the rise in the price of potatoes caused poor people to buy more as they could no longer afford to supplement their diet with better foods. Although his findings are debatable, a recent study showed that households in the Hunan province of China bought more of their staple food when they had to buy it at a higher price, and less when the price they paid was subsidised.

Categorise the goods   Go online

Q12: Place the goods given in the following list into the most appropriate column of the table:

- rice;
- Rolex watch;
- shares;
- bread;
- fine wines;
- oil;
- Rolls Royce.

Ostentatious goods	Speculative goods	Giffen goods

It is also true that when the quality of a good cannot easily be judged, the price is often taken as an indication of quality. Consumers might therefore associate a rise in price with a rise in quality and buy more at the higher price.

There is an example of this referred to in some business texts where the price of a shampoo was increased and sales increased because the price change inferred a higher quality. Similarly the average consumer does not examine the insides of a wrist watch before buying it. The quality is inferred from the price and the brand image.

3.7 Summary

Summary

Having completed this topic you should:

- understand the concepts of utility and rational behaviour;
- understand the importance of *ceteris paribus*;
- be able to explain and account for the shape of a normal demand curve;
- be able to draw and explain unusual (or regressive) demand curves;
- know the law of demand (how demand changes inversely with price).

3.8 End of topic test

End of Topic 3 test   Go online

Q13: When deciding whether or not to buy a good, which of the following will a rational consumer compare?

a) Total utility and price
b) Marginal utility and price
c) Marginal utility and their income
d) Total utility and their income

....

Q14: Last week John Smith consumed six apples. This week he consumed seven apples. As far as apples are concerned, which of the following is correct?

a) John's marginal has increased but his total utility has decreased.
b) John's marginal has decreased but his total utility has increased.
c) John's marginal and total utility have both increased.
d) John's marginal and total utility have both decreased.

....

Q15: The following table shows the amount of total utility a consumer receives from consuming oranges.

Number of oranges per week	Total utility
0	0
1	6
2	11
3	14
4	16
5	16

What happens to this consumer's marginal utility as the number of oranges consumed increases from zero to five?

a) It increases and then remains constant.
b) It increases continuously.
c) It decreases continuously.
d) It decreases and then remains constant.

....

Q16: When the price of apples increases from 20p each to 25p each, Jane Smith buys six per day, rather than her usual seven. How would this change appear on Jane's demand curve?

a) By the curve moving to the right.
b) By a rightwards movement down the demand curve.
c) By the curve moving to the left.
d) By a leftwards movement up the demand curve.

....

Q17: Which of the following statements is correct?

a) A rational consumer will continue consuming a free good until its total utility is at a maximum.
b) A rational consumer will continue consuming a free good until its marginal utility is zero.
c) Both of the above.
d) Neither of the above.

....

Q18: "The more cream crackers I eat, the more I want to eat one more."

The above consumer is claiming that as his consumption of cream crackers increases:

a) his marginal utility increases.
b) his total utility increases.
c) both his marginal and total utility increase.
d) neither his marginal and total utility increase.

....

Q19: Match the following four terms with the following four scenarios in the table below:

- Speculative buying;
- Article of ostentation;
- Price assumed to indicate quality;
- Giffen good.

Scenario	Term
The demand for Bentley cars rises with an increase in their price.	
More people rush to buy houses as prices begin to increase rapidly.	
As the price of rice rises, more is bought.	
A cheap brand of tea sees its sales (demand) rise when it increases price	

Unit 1 Topic 4

Determinants of demand

Contents

Prerequisites

The topic builds on and expands the concept of demand studied at National 5 Economics. However, prior knowledge of this concept, although useful, is not essential.

Learning objective

By the end of this topic you should:

- understand the determinants of demand;

- understand the conditions of demand;

- know what causes an increase and a decrease in demand;

- know what is meant by *ceteris paribus* and understand its importance;

- know the difference between a change in demand and a change in the quantity demanded;

- be able to illustrate changes in the conditions of demand diagrammatically.

4.1   Determinants and conditions of demand

The key understanding in this section is that only a change in the price of the product will lead to a movement along the demand line.

Look at the axes labels in the example demand curve below. Price is on the vertical. This means that the line plots only changes in demand resulting from a change in this very product's price.

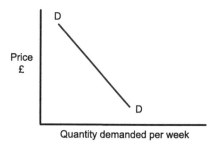

A demand curve

When factors other than the price of the product alter, then the demand line will move rightwards or leftwards. Typically we show this with a "before and after" diagram showing the original line labelled D1 D1 and the after line labelled D2 D2. This is the result of a change in the conditions of demand.

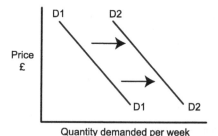

Demand curve illustrating an increase in demand

The fact that there is more than one determinant of demand creates a major problem. How do we isolate the effect on demand of a change in any *one* of the determinants? For example, if we are trying to establish the effect on the demand for tennis balls of a reduction in their price, we will have to isolate this one change. If, at the same time, incomes rose, the price of tennis rackets doubled and Andy Murray won Wimbledon - it would be impossible to isolate the effect of cheaper tennis balls.

Determinants of demand   Go online

Choose the correct option, either increase or decrease, to show how the demand for tennis balls would be affected by each of the changes mentioned below.

Q1: Incomes rose.

a) Increase
b) Decrease

....

Q2: The price of tennis rackets doubled.

a) Increase
b) Decrease

....

Q3: Andy Murray won Wimbledon.

a) Increase
b) Decrease

4.1.1 Conditions of demand

As we are mainly interested in price, we simplify matters by assuming that all determinants other than price are not changing. This enables us to identify and isolate the effect of price changes on the demand for any good.

Economists refer to this assumption as the **ceteris paribus** assumption. *Ceteris paribus* is a Latin phrase which means "other things remaining the same".

The determinants of demand, other than price, are known as **the conditions of demand**.

Conditions of demand   Go online

Q4: Complete the following sentence:

The conditions of demand are the factors which may cause the demand for a product to change other than ....

....

Q5: Fill in the blanks in the following sentence:

In order to isolate the effect on the demand for a good of a change in its price, we assume that all other influences, i.e. ...., are not changing and we assume ....

4.2   Changes or shifts in demand

Once we have drawn our demand curve we must examine how it would be affected by a change in any of the factors we assumed were constant, i.e. the conditions of demand.

Changes or shifts in demand   Go online

Place the following words into the correct place in the sentences below:

- new

- price

- prices

- quantity

Q6: By a change or shift in demand we mean that demand has changed at all .... - resulting in a .... demand curve. A movement along a demand curve indicates that a different .... is being demanded because the .... of the good has changed.

Changes in demand   Go online

Q7:   Fill in the missing word from the following sentence:

The conditions of demand are the factors, other than the .... of the good, which may cause demand to change.

4.3   An increase in demand

An increase in demand is where more is demanded at each price. On the demand curve, demand moves rightwards at each and every price creating a new and parallel line to the right of the original.

Increase in demand   Go online

Q8:   Draw a demand curve and label it D1 D1.

On the same graph draw another demand curve labelled D2 D2.

Curve D2 D2 should represent an increase in demand from curve D1 D1.

Compare your graph with the answer given.

....

Q9: Complete the following sentence:

If the demand for a good increases, the demand curve will shift ....
.

4.3.1 Definitions of types of goods

Complementary goods go together such as fish and chips. A fall in the price of fish would increase the demand for chips (without a price change for chips). In effect the combination has become cheaper and demand for chips rises as a result.

Substitutes are alternatives such as tea and coffee. If the price of coffee rises, then some will switch to tea, increasing the demand for tea although its price has not changed.

Inferior goods are bought less as real incomes rise. If you can now afford steak, you may buy less mince.

Giffen goods are staple goods and a fall in your real income may make you more dependent on them. Poverty may cause you to buy more potatoes and less meat, even if the potatoes went up in price in the first place.

4.3.2 Causes of an increase in demand

The demand for a good will increase if there is:

- an increase in consumers' real income;
- a change in taste or fashion towards the good;
- an increase in the price of a substitute good;
- a decrease in the price of a complementary good.

Causes of an increase in demand	Go online

Q10: For the demand for a good to increase, the conditions of demand must either increase or decrease. Place each of the following conditions under the correct heading:

- Income
- Fashion
- Price of a substitute
- Price of a complement

Increase	Decrease

Causes of an increase in demand

Go online

Q11: Why is one cause of an increase in demand *not* a decrease in the price of the good?

....

Q12: Draw a demand diagram to show what happens when the price of a good decreases. Compare your graph with the answer given.

The decrease in price results in an increase in the quantity demanded (Q1 to Q2) but does not result in a new demand curve.

4.4   A decrease in demand

A decrease in demand is where less is demanded at each price. On the demand curve, demand moves leftwards at each and every price creating a new and parallel line to the left of the original.

Decrease in demand

Go online

Q13: Draw a demand curve and label it D1 D1. On the same graph draw another demand curve labelled D2 D2. Curve D2 D2 should represent an decrease in demand from curve D1 D1.

Compare your graph with the answer.

....

Q14: Complete the following sentence:

If the demand for a good decreases, the demand curve will shift ....
.

4.4.1   Causes of a decrease in demand

Causes of a decrease in demand

Go online

Select the correct alternative. The demand for a good will decrease if there is:

Q15: .... in consumers' income.

a) an increase
b) a decrease

....

Q16: a shift in tastes .... the good.

a) against
b) in favour of

. . . .

Q17: .... in the price of a substitute good.

a) an increase
b) a decrease

. . . .

Q18: .... in the price of a complement.

a) an increase
b) a decrease

Q19: Why is one cause of a decrease in demand *not* an increase in the price of the good?

Increased price   Go online

Q20: Draw a demand diagram to show what happens when the price of a good increases. Compare your diagram with the answer.

The increase in price results in an decrease in the *quantity* demanded (Q1 to Q2) but does not result in a new demand curve.

4.5 Summary

Summary

Having completed this topic you should:

- be able to explain the determinants of demand;

- understand the conditions of demand;

- understand the importance of *ceteris paribus*;

- know how and why demand can change;

- know the difference between a change in demand and a change in the quantity demanded;

- be able to illustrate changes in the conditions of demand diagrammatically.

4.6   End of topic test

Q21: The following diagram shows the weekly demand for Esso petrol.

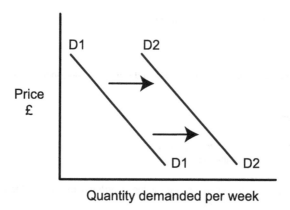

Quantity demanded per week

Which of the following could have caused the shift in demand from D1 D1 to D2 D2?

a) An increase in the price of cars.
b) A decrease in the price of Esso.
c) An increase in the price of Shell Petrol.
d) A decrease in the price of public transport.

....

Q22: Which of the following might explain why, when the price of a good falls, more of it is demanded?

a) New consumers of the good experience a rise in their real income.
b) Existing consumers of the good experience a rise in their money income.
c) New consumers of the good experience a rise in their money income.
d) Existing consumers of the good experience a rise in their real income.

....

Q23: When the price of apples increases from 20p each to 25p each, Jane Smith buys six per day, rather than her usual seven. How would this change appear on Jane's demand curve?

a) By the curve moving to the right.
b) By a rightwards movement down the demand curve.
c) By the curve moving to the left.
d) By a leftwards movement up the demand curve.

....

Q24: An increase in the price of good A causes an increase in the demand for good B. What conclusion can be drawn from the above statement?

a) Goods A and B are complementary goods.
b) Goods A and B are substitute goods.
c) Good B is an inferior good.
d) Good B is a Giffen good.

. . . .

Q25: Which of the following factors could *not* cause a rightward shift in the demand curve for fish?

a) A decrease in the price of chips.
b) An increase in the price of pizzas.
c) A decrease in the price of fish.
d) A government report stating that fish is good for you.

. . . .

Q26: Which of the following factors would cause a leftward shift in the demand for coffee?

a) An increase in the price of tea.
b) A decrease in the price of milk.
c) A decrease in the price of tea.
d) An increase in the price of coffee.

. . . .

Q27: Which of the following factors would cause a rightward shift in the demand for new cars?

a) An increase in the price of new cars.
b) A decrease in the price of new cars.
c) A decrease in disposable incomes.
d) An increase in disposable incomes.

. . . .

Q28: Which of the following factors would cause a leftward shift in the demand for ice cream?

a) An increase in the price ice lollies.
b) An increase in the price of ingredients.
c) A rainy day.
d) A sunny day.

. . . .

Q29: Which of the following factors would cause a rightward shift in the demand for haggis?

a) A health scare about the ingredients.

b) The anniversary of Robert Burns.

c) A decrease in the price of the ingredients.

d) An increase in the price of turnips.

. . . .

Q30: Which of the following statements is true? You may choose more than one option.

a) If a substitute good increases in price, then demand moves rightwards.

b) If disposable incomes increase, then demand moves rightwards.

c) If a complementary good decreases in price then demand moves rightwards.

Unit 1 Topic 5

Price elasticity of demand (PED)

Contents

Prerequisites

The topic builds on and expands the concept of demand studied at National 5 Economics. However, prior knowledge of this concept, although useful, is not essential.

Learning objective

By the end of this topic you should:

- know what is meant by elasticity of demand;
- be able to define price elasticity of demand (PED);
- know and understand the formula for PED;
- know and understand that demand can be:
  - perfectly price elastic;
  - price elastic;
  - unitary price elastic;
  - price inelastic;
  - perfectly price inelastic;
- be able to draw demand curves for all of the above;
- know and understand the factors that affect PED;
- know and understand the importance of PED.

5.1   Elasticity

In Economics, elasticity is a measurement of the extent to which the demand for a good, or the supply of a good, responds to certain changes.

Elasticity   Go online

Q1: Complete the following sentence by adding one word.

Elasticity is a measure of ....

Elasticity can therefore be defined as "the extent to which the demand for a good will change in response to either a change in the price of the good or a change in the incomes of consumers."

There are two types of elasticity of demand:

- price elasticity of demand (PED);

- income elasticity of demand (note that income elasticity is not covered in the Higher course).

Price elasticity of demand (PED)   Go online

Q2: Complete the following definition.

Price elasticity of demand is a measure of the extent to which the demand for a good changes when there is a change in ....

5.2   Price elasticity of demand (PED)

Price elasticity of demand (PED) measures the reaction of consumers to a change in the price of the good. PED is calculated by comparing the percentage change in *price* with the percentage change in *demand*.

The formula is:

$$PED = \frac{\text{the \% change in the quantity demanded of good X}}{\text{the \% change in the price of good X}}$$

The value of PED is usually negative because price and quantity demanded usually move in opposite directions, i.e. an increase in price usually results in a fall in the quantity demanded and *vice versa*.

Example : PED - coffee example

The price of a brand of coffee increases from £4 to £4.40, i.e. by 10%. Sales of this brand reduce from 10,000 jars a day to 9,500 jars, i.e. by 5%.

PED for this brand can be calculated as: -5% / +10% = -0.5 .

Economists often ignore the negative sign and call it 0.5, which may annoy mathematicians!

Any answer of less than one indicates an *inelastic* demand. Demand has been relatively taut (or inelastic) when compared to the price change. As the price rise more than compensates for the loss of some sales, it follows that the revenue gained from selling the coffee has increased.

Increased revenue tells us nothing about profit. For all we know, the costs of producing the coffee may have risen significantly.

Q3: In example 1, how much has the revenue increased by?

Example : PED - petrol example

The price of Esso petrol increases from £1.40 to £1.47, i.e. by 5%. Sales of Esso reduce from 10 million litres to 9 million litres i.e. by 10%.

PED for this brand can be calculated as: -10% / +5% = -2.

Any answer of more than one indicates an *elastic* demand. Demand has been relatively flexible (or elastic) when compared to the price change. As the price rise does not compensate for the loss of some sales, it follows that the revenue gained from selling Esso has decreased.

Decreased revenue tells us nothing about profit. For all we know, the profit margin per litre sold have increased significantly.

Q4: In example 2, how much has the revenue decreased by?

Theoretically the price elasticity of demand could equal one. This is termed *unit elasticity*. It is often said that the revenue should not be affected, but when this assertion is checked with some figures, the revenue can be seen to have moved slightly.

Example : PED - unit elasticity

Price down from £10 to £9 (-10%). Demand up from 100 to 110 (+10%).

+10% / -10% = -1 (typically described by economists as one or unit elasticity).

Has revenue changed?
Before: £10 x 100 = £1,000
After: £9 x 110 = £990

So, despite what even some texts will claim, there is a slight change in revenue at unit elasticity. However, candidates who assert that at unit elasticity, the revenue is unaffected have been marked correct - close enough and they clearly understand the broad concept.

PED calculations

Q5: When the price of good X increased from 50p to 55p, the quantity demanded of it fell from 100 a week to 95 a week. What therefore is the PED of good X?

....

Q6: The demand for good Y is currently 200 per week. If the PED of good Y is -2, what will be the new quantity demanded if its price falls from 20p to 18p? Enter a number.

....

Q7: What must have happened if the result of the PED equation is:

1. greater than one?
2. less than one?
3. equal to one?

Price elasticity   Go online

Select from the following words to correctly finish the sentences:

- price inelastic;
- unitary price elastic;
- price elastic.

Q8: If price elasticity of demand is greater than one, demand is ....

....

Q9: If price elasticity of demand is less than one, demand is ....

....

Q10: If price elasticity of demand is equal to one, demand is ....

5.3   PED effects on the demand curve

PED affects the slope of the demand curve.

There are two extreme cases of PED:

1. When the quantity demanded of a good does not change when its price changes. In this case demand is not just price inelastic it is **perfectly price inelastic**.

---

2. When the quantity demanded of a good falls to zero when its price changes. In this case demand is not just price elastic it is **perfectly price elastic**.

Diagrams 1 and 2 (below) show the typical way of expressing elasticity using the gradient of the demand line. It assumes that the price and quantity demanded axes are to the same scale.

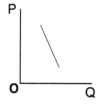

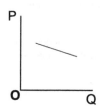

1 *Inelastic*: (less than one) because demand alters less as price changes significantly.

2 *Elastic*: (more than one) because demand alters more as price changes slightly.

Diagrams 3 and 4 (below) show theoretical positions of total inelasticity and infinite elasticity.

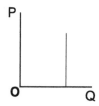

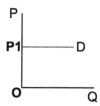

3 *Perfectly inelastic*: (zero) because demand does not alter at all when price changes.

4 *Perfectly elastic*: (infinity) because demand varies without a price change.

Unit elasticity (one): It would be easy to assume that unit elasticity could be represented by a straight line at 45 degrees. However the elasticity of such a line would very at different points on the line. Unit elasticity is therefore shown using a curve.

PED effects on the demand curve   Go online

Q11: Study the following two demand curves, X and Y, and state which one is price elastic and which one is price inelastic (assume they are drawn to the same scale).

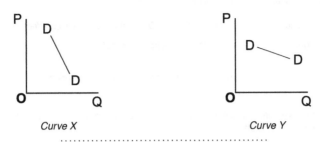

Curve X   Curve Y

Q12: If demand is perfectly price inelastic what would be the result of the equation?

Q13: If demand is perfectly price elastic what would be the result of the equation?

Q14: Using the following graph as a template, draw a perfectly price elastic demand curve *and* a perfectly price inelastic demand curve.

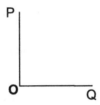

Although no goods have demand curves like the two above, the demand for cheap, essential goods might be perfectly inelastic around the prevailing price. For example, if the price of salt rose or fell by 1p, the quantity demanded by consumers is unlikely to change.

5.4   Factors which affect PED

Factors which affect PED are:

1. the closeness and amount of available substitutes;

2. the degree of necessity or habit of consuming the good;

3. fashion;

4. the relationship between the price of the good and average income;

5. frequency of purchase;

6. if a product is a relatively small but vital part of something else.

Please note - do not confuse factors which affect PED with the factors which affect demand.

Complete the following sentences using either *elastic* or *inelastic*.

Q15: If a good has many close substitutes, the demand for it will be price ....

....

Q16: The more essential or habit forming a good is, the more price .... the demand for it will be, e.g. salt, cigarettes.

....

Q17: If it is fashionable to consume a particular good the demand for it will not only be high, it will also be price ....

....

Q18: If a good is very cheap, relative to average incomes, the demand for it will tend to be price .... , e.g. the demand for bread is much more price .... than the demand for cars.

....

Q19: The more frequently something is bought, the more price .... demand will be.

....

Q20: The demand for a pot of glue is likely to be price .... because it tends to be bought infrequently.

....

Q21: If a product is a relatively small but vital part of something else the demand for it will be price ....

5.4.1   Determinants of PED

The factors which affect the PED for a good do not always "pull" in the same direction. For example, there are some factors that make the demand for bread price inelastic and others that might make it price elastic.

Determinants of PED   Go online

Decide how the following determinants of PED will affect the price of bread.

Q22: Available substitutes?

a) Price elastic
b) Price inelastic

....

Q23: Degree of necessity?

a) Price elastic
b) Price inelastic

. . . .

Q24: Price relative to income?

a) Price elastic
b) Price inelastic

. . . .

Q25: Frequency of purchase?

a) Price elastic
b) Price inelastic

Q26: Explain why the demand for petrol is price inelastic but the demand for Shell petrol is price elastic.

5.5   Effect of PED on total revenue (TR)

Total revenue (TR) is the amount of money a seller receives from selling a product in a specific time. It is calculated by multiplying the price of the product by the amount sold:

$$TR = price \times quantity\ sold$$

If we know what the demand for a good will be at various prices, we can work out the TR from the sale of that good at various prices.

Key point

It will depend on the PED of the good whether TR rises or falls when the price of a good changes.

Study the graph and answer the questions which follow.

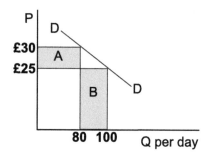

Demand for Good X

Q27: When the price rises from £25 to £30, what does rectangle A represent?

a) The revenue gained from selling 80 goods at £30 rather than £25.
b) The revenue lost from selling 80 goods at £30 rather than £25.

....

Q28: When the price rises from £25 to £30, what does rectangle B represent?

a) The revenue gained from only selling 80 goods instead of 100.
b) The revenue lost from only selling 80 goods instead of 100.

....

Q29: What is the total revenue in £ when P = 25 and when P = 30?

Consider the following two diagrams. Both goods have experienced a similar increase in price but the demand for Good X is price inelastic whereas the demand for Good Y is price elastic.

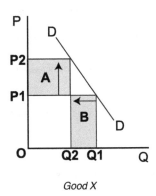

Good X

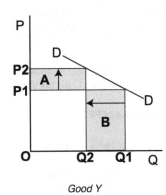

Good Y

Q30: When price increases from P1 to P2, what happens to the TR received from the sale of Good X and from the sale of Good Y?

....

Q31: Explain why TR increases for Good X.

....

Q32: Explain why TR decreases for Good Y.

....

Q33: Choose the word which correctly completes the following sentences:

If the demand for a good is price inelastic, producers of the good will gain revenue if its price (*increases/decreases*). If the demand for a good is price elastic, producers of the good will (*gain/lose*) revenue if its price increases.

If the demand for a good is price inelastic, price and TR move in the same direction, i.e. an increase in price leads to an increase in TR and vice versa.

Q34: Complete the following sentence, taking into account the conclusion above.

If the demand for a good is price elastic, price and TR move in ...., i.e. an increase in price leads to a .... in TR and vice versa.

5.6   The importance of PED

Much of the importance of PED stems from its influence on TR. Firms will want to know how their TR will change when they change their price - this will help them to decide whether to increase or decrease their price.

The government will also want to know how TR will change if they change the rate of tax on expenditure, e.g. VAT. The purpose of expenditure taxes is to raise revenue for the government, but taxes such as VAT raise the price of goods. This explains the high level of tax on tobacco, alcohol and petrol.

The government will raise most revenue if sales do not fall much as the result of increasing tax. This means they would be wiser to put tax up when price elasticity is low.

The importance of PED   Go online

Complete the following sentences.

Q35: Firms will tend to increase the price of goods whose demand is price .... and reduce the price of those goods whose demand is price ....

....

Q36: This helps explain why holidays, travel, etc. are cheaper at off-peak times - demand is not only smaller, it is also more price ....

....

Q37: It also helps explain why firms spend so much money on advertising. The aim is not only to increase demand, but also to make it more price .... This will enable them to increase price without losing too many ....

....

Q38: The demand for all of these goods (tobacco, alcohol and petrol) is highly price ....
.

5.7   Summary

Summary

At the end of this topic you should know that:

- elasticity is a measure of responsiveness;

- PED measures the extent to which the quantity demanded of a good changes when its price changes:

  ◦ if PED = 0, demand is perfectly price inelastic;
  ◦ if PED is > 0 but < 1, demand is price inelastic;
  ◦ if PED = 1, demand is unitary price elastic;
  ◦ if PED is > 1 but < ∞ (infinity), demand is price elastic;
  ◦ if PED = ∞, demand is perfectly price elastic;

- price elastic demand curves are flatter than price inelastic demand curves;

- the PED of a good is influenced by:

  ◦ the availability of substitutes;
  ◦ how essential it is;
  ◦ how fashionable it is;
  ◦ how often it is bought;
  ◦ how expensive it is relative to average income;
  ◦ whether or not it is a vital part of an expensive good;

- total revenue (TR) = price × quantity sold;

- the PED of a good determines what will happen to TR when its price changes:

  ◦ if demand is price elastic, price and TR move in opposite directions;
  ◦ if demand is price inelastic, price and TR move in the same direction;
  ◦ governments heavily tax goods which have price inelastic demands in order to gain revenue.

5.8   End of topic test

End of Topic 5 test   Go online

Q39: A golf club maker is currently selling 100 clubs a week at a price of £200 each.
Given that the price elasticity of demand for golf clubs is -0.8, how many would he sell per week if he reduced the price to £160?

   a) 108
   b) 125
   c) 140
   d) 116

....

Q40: A cabinet maker is currently selling 100 tables a week at a price of £250 each.
Given that the price elasticity of demand for tables is -0.7, how many would he sell per week if he reduced the price to £200?

....

Q41: When the price of a national newspaper increased from 50p to 60p, sales of the paper fell by 40%. What, therefore, was the price elasticity of demand for the newspaper for the given price change?

   a) -0.5
   b) -2.5
   c) -0.25
   d) -2.0

....

Q42: A firm which is operating at full capacity and is selling all it produces wants to increase its total revenue.
Which of the following suggestions, given to the firm by four young economists, is correct?

   a) If the demand for your product is price elastic, you should reduce the price.
   b) If the demand for your product is price inelastic, you should reduce the price.
   c) If the demand for your product is price elastic, you should increase the price.
   d) If the demand for your product is price inelastic, you should increase the price.

....

Q43: If the demand for a product is *price inelastic*, which of the following statements concerning the product is correct?

a) An increase in its price will result in fewer of the good being sold but its sales revenue rising.

b) A decrease in its price will result in more of the good being sold but its sales revenue rising.

c) An increase in its price will result in more of the good being sold but its sales revenue falling.

d) A decrease in its price will result in more of the good being sold but its sales revenue falling.

....

Q44: Which of the following would tend to make a product price elastic? You may choose more than one option.

a) A large number of substitutes.

b) Brand loyalty has been secured through successful marketing.

c) The product is habit-forming.

....

Q45: Which of the following would tend to make a product price inelastic? You may choose more than one option.

a) No close substitute exists.

b) The product costs just a few pence.

c) The product is a luxury.

....

Q46: From the following list of products select the ones that are likely to show price elasticity greater than 1. You may choose more than one option.

a) BP petrol.

b) The Guardian newspaper.

c) A box of matches.

....

Q47: If the price of a good increases from £5 to £6 and sales drop from 1,000 per day to 900 per day, then the price elasticity of demand is:

a) 2 and the revenue will fall;

b) 2 and the revenue will rise;

c) 0.5 and the revenue will fall;

d) 0.5 and the revenue will rise.

....

Q48: If the price of a car decreases from £20,000 to £19,000 and sales increase from 100 per day to 110 per day, then the price elasticity of demand is:

a) elastic and the revenue increases;

b) elastic and the profit increases;

c) elastic and the profit falls;

d) inelastic and the revenue increases.

Unit 1 Topic 6

Production

Contents

Prerequisites

This topic assumes no previous knowledge and is intended to be accessible for those studying Economics for the first time. However, if you have already completed National 5 Economics, you will be familiar with some of the concepts outlined.

Learning objective

By the end of this topic you should be able to explain:

- what is meant by specialisation and the division of labour;

- what is meant by productivity;

- the returns to the factors of production;

- the returns to the variable factor.

6.1   The factors of production

Production can be divided into three sectors:

- Primary production which involves the extraction of resources, e.g. farming, fishing, forestry, mining and quarrying;

- Secondary production which involves manufacturing and construction, e.g. all industrial production processes and all building and engineering;

- Tertiary production which includes all services. This is the largest employer and covers areas such as retailing and transport and many professions such as doctors and teachers.

The following images illustrate the production process. The inputs are the four **factors of production**, production then takes place and the output is the finished product (either a good or service).

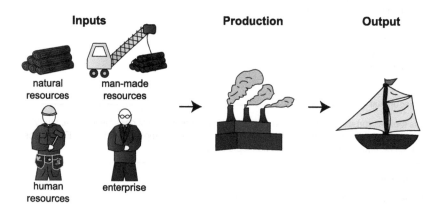

The production process

In the above process each factor of production receives a return for its efforts. The **returns** are outlined in the table below.

Factors of production	Returns
Land (natural resources)	Rent
Capital (man-made resources)	Interest
Labour (human resources)	Wages
Enterprise	Profit

Note that rent and interest cannot be paid to inanimate objects and are in fact paid to the owners of the land and capital. All returns go to households in one way or another.

The returns received by offering up the factors of production go to the owners of the factors of production.

After completing the following activity to confirm your understanding, we will move forward to a more detailed explanation of costs in a later topic.

The factors of production Go online

Choose the correct return for the factor of production given.

Q1: Land

a) Wages
b) Profit
c) Rent
d) Interest

....

Q2: Labour

a) Wages
b) Profit
c) Rent
d) Interest

....

Q3: Capital

a) Wages
b) Profit
c) Rent
d) Interest

....

Q4: Enterprise

a) Wages
b) Profit
c) Rent
d) Interest

6.2 The difference between short-run and long-run

If asked to guess the meaning of the terms **short-run** and **long-run**, the usual response is to talk vaguely of dates and time-scales. This response is entirely ***wrong***. Banish all concern with dates and time-scales from your mind.

The only definition of short-run and long-run for Economics is the one below:

- In the short-run, at least *one factor* of production is in *fixed supply* and cannot be changed.
- In the long-run, *all factors* of production can be changed.

There is absolutely no reference to dates and time-scales because these will vary enormously depending on the particular production process.

The fixed factor could be land and/or capital, making you unable to extend your shop or factory in the short-run. It might involve choosing a new location, talking to architects, obtaining planning permission, dealing with building delays. Land and capital are quite often fixed factors in the short-run.

If you are running the National Health Service and it takes six years to train doctors, you may regard labour as a fixed factor in the short-run. There can be more than one fixed factor, but in the short-run there is *at least* one factor of production that is fixed and restraining your expansion.

Short-run and long-run   Go online

As an example, let's consider a workshop producing coffee tables. We used to produce 100 tables a week. This employed the following inputs: five workers, two machines, one workshop, and one manager. After expanding output to 200 tables a week we now require ten workers, four machines, one workshop and one manager. It is not possible to extend the workshop or train up another manager.

Using the information in the above paragraph, you should be able to infer which factors are variable and which factors are fixed.

Decide which factors are fixed and which are variable.

Q5: Workers

a) Fixed
b) Variable

....

Q6: Workshop

a) Fixed
b) Variable

....

Q7: Manager

a) Fixed
b) Variable

Q8: Machines

a) Fixed
b) Variable

6.3 Short-run average cost curves

The relationship between average cost, i.e. average total cost, and marginal cost can be shown on the following diagram.

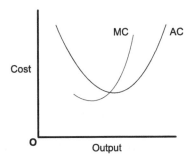

The relationship between average cost (the cost per unit of output) and marginal cost (the addition to total costs resulting from the production of one more unit)

Each additional (marginal) unit that costs less than the average pulls the average cost downwards. The optimum (lowest average cost and most efficient) output is passed when an additional (marginal) unit costs more than than the average, thus beginning to pull average cost upwards.

The short-run average cost curve first falls because of increasing returns. This means that the fixed factor is used more and more efficiently until it best combines with the number of variable factors used.

For example, a machine now has enough workers to make sure it is continuously running. Reaching the lowest point in the average cost curve is the **optimum output** level and represents technical efficiency, i.e. maximum output from minimum input.

6.4   The law of diminishing returns

The law of diminishing returns explains that short run average cost will ultimately rise because adding more variable factors to one fixed factor eventually reduces productivity. Continuing to add variable factors will not increase efficiency beyond the optimum point.

For example, adding even more workers to the one machine may increase output a bit more. However, the wages of the added workers who make such a small contribution to output will force up average costs.

The solution is usually to expand to new premises or to buy more machines. This can only happen in the long-run when all factors can be varied.

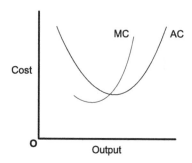

The relationship between average cost and marginal cost

There are three stages to drawing the above diagram successfully:

1. Draw the axes and label them;

2. Draw the u-shaped average cost curve;

3. Carefully add the marginal cost curve, which must cut across the lowest point on the u-shaped average cost curve.

Better than memorising the above, you should try to understand the mathematical reason why marginal cost must cut average cost at the lowest point.

Suppose in a classroom there are four pupils with an average height of 160 cm. The next pupil to enter (the marginal pupil) is 135 cm tall. If you re-calculate the average now that a short pupil has entered the room, the average will have decreased to 155 cm. If the marginal cost is below the average cost, it pulls the average cost **downwards**.

However, suppose in the classroom there are four pupils with an average height of 160 cm and the next pupil to enter (the marginal pupil) is 185 cm tall. If you re-calculate the average now that a tall pupil has entered the room, the average will have increased to 165 cm. If the marginal cost is above the average cost, it pulls the average cost **upwards**.

It follows from this that marginal cost will always cut average cost at its lowest point. As soon as a marginal cost is above average cost, the average cost will start heading upwards.

The law of diminishing returns Go online

Q9: *Without looking at the diagram above*, draw the diagram showing the relationship between average cost and marginal cost.

....

Q10: Fixed costs of production include:

a) piece-rate wages paid to factory workers.
b) the cost of machinery repairs other than regular maintenance.
c) the rent paid for the use of the factory.
d) the cost of raw materials used by a manufacturer.

....

Q11: As a manufacturer increases his output, so that it approaches the volume for which his factory was designed, the average total cost per unit tends to fall mainly because:

a) variable cost per unit cannot rise.
b) increased wages are always paid in proportion to output.
c) fixed cost per unit becomes less.
d) marginal costs are rising.

6.5 The division of labour

The famous Scottish economist, Adam Smith, first explained the efficiency gains resulting from the **division of labour** using a study of a pin making factory in Fife. You can use the internet to obtain the original text.

Adam Smith's text

Use a search engine to find the relevant page section in Adam Smith's famous text 'An Enquiry into the Nature and Causes of the Wealth of Nations' published in 1776. Read the original pages that deal with this important concept.

The division of labour (or **specialisation**) involves each worker taking one part of the manufacturing process and repeating this single task.

The advantages of specialisation are:

- workers become more skilled at a particular process by concentrating on it;
- speed increases and therefore output;
- less skilled workers can be employed because only a routine task has to be learned;
- they can be paid less than craftsmen;
- expensive machinery can be fully utilised in a well-organised production line and rarely lies idle;
- workers do not travel between work stations and are not constantly setting up for different processes.

Taken together this creates increased **productivity** (output per worker hour) and lowers average costs. The factory jobs thus created were a feature of the industrial revolution. Economic growth increased rapidly and living standards steadily improved.

However, the jobs were often dull and repetitive. Workers were forced to work at a machine's pace. They were detached from the end product of their work and therefore unable to take pride in their work or obtain the job satisfaction that a craftsman would have enjoyed.

The division of labour   Go online

If you want to find out more about the development of the division of labour into mass production then enter something like the following into your search engine "mass production henry ford model T rouge river".

6.6 Summary

Summary

At the end of this topic you should be able to explain:

- that, in the short run, average cost falls because of increasing returns, and then rises because of ultimately diminishing returns;
- that productivity is output per input, e.g. output per worker hour;
- the returns to the factors of production are wages, profits, rent and interest;
- the division of labour explains how output can be dramatically increased if workers specialise in one particular task.

6.7 End of topic test

End of Topic 6 test Go online

Q12: Increased specialisation takes place when:

a) a football team employs its first goalkeeping coach.
b) office staff rotate between jobs such as photocopying and reception work.
c) sales rise in do-it-yourself shops.
d) additional cleaners are taken on in schools.

. . . .

Q13: A short-run variable cost of production for a baker would be:

a) the cost of flour.
b) the rates paid on the premises to the local authority.
c) the rental charge for a security system for the bakery.
d) the depreciation in the value of machinery due to its age.

. . . .

Q14: When, in the short-run, a firm's marginal cost of production is greater than its average cost then the firm is:

a) experiencing diminishing returns.
b) experiencing increasing returns.
c) suffering losses.
d) benefiting from economies of scale.

. . . .

Q15: The law of diminishing marginal returns states that:

a) an additional unit of capital always produces less than the last unit, no matter what the present output.
b) irrespective of present output, an additional unit of labour always produces less than the last unit.
c) high profits will eventually decline because competition will increase.
d) as the quantity of one of the factors employed is increased, eventually the output ceases to rise in proportion.

. . . .

Q16: Explain why short-run average total cost curves are usually U-shaped.

(9 marks)

Unit 1 Topic 7

Costs

Contents

Prerequisites

This topic assumes no previous knowledge and is intended to be accessible for those studying Economics for the first time. However, if you have already completed national 5 Economics, you will be familiar with some of the concepts outlined.

Learning objective

By the end of this topic you should:

- explain the term, costs of production, and the relationship between the various costs of production, and be able to calculate costs;

- draw and explain the shape of a long-run average cost curve and explain how it derives from economies and diseconomies of scale;

- explain the relationship between costs, revenues and profit.

7.1   Fixed costs, variable costs and total costs

Fixed costs do not vary with the level of output and exist even at zero output. Even if you chain the factory gate, you will still be paying items such as fire insurance on the building. Whether output is zero or you are working flat out, fixed costs by definition in economic theory, will stay the same.

Variable costs vary with the level of output and will not exist if you chain the factory gate. Your workforce will go unpaid and you will need no raw materials or components. Variable costs are zero when output is zero. Variable costs grow as output levels grow - you will need more raw materials and more workers in proportion to your output.

Total costs are the total costs after adding fixed costs and variable costs together. The entire universe of costs is included within the terms fixed and variable. This means that when you add them together you get total costs. Total costs at zero output must be the same as fixed costs. This is because only fixed costs exist at zero output. There are no variable costs such as labour, when nothing is being produced.

The relationship between fixed cost, variable cost and total cost (FC + VC = TC) can also be shown diagrammatically (see below).

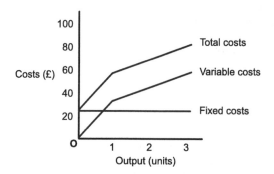

The relationship between fixed cost, variable cost and total cost

Minimising losses by staying open

If a loss making firm's revenue from sales exceeds its variable costs (wages, materials, etc.), then it may continue to trade in the short run. This is because it will at least make some contribution to paying the fixed costs. This will minimise losses, when compared to shutting down and still having all the fixed costs to pay.

This is one reason why administrators of failing businesses may decide to keep a firm open in the short run. Losses are still increasing, although at a slower rate, and the firm will in the future close unless changes are made.

Fixed and variable costs   Go online

Q1: Deciding which costs are fixed and which are variable, complete the table using the following words:

- workers' wages;
- manager's salary;
- designer royalties;
- wood for tables;
- factory rent;
- fire Insurance.

Fixed	Variable

Fixed, variable and total costs   Go online

Q2: Complete the table with the correct figures.

Output (units)	Fixed costs (£)	Variable costs (£)	Total costs (£)
0		0	25
1	25	30	
2			70
3	25		85

7.2 Average cost

Average cost (AC) is sometimes termed average total cost (ATC); both mean the same. It is the cost of producing one unit (or batch). Note that if you are making small mass-produced items then the unit of account will be a batch rather than a single unit.

To calculate average cost, divide total cost by the number of items made. If the total cost of producing two units is £80 then the average cost is £40. The formula for this can be given as:

- Average cost = total cost ÷ output

Now try the following activity to check that you understand average cost.

Average cost   Go online

Q3:   Complete the table with the correct figures.

Output (units)	Fixed costs (£)	Variable costs (£)	Total costs (£)	Average costs (£)
0	100	0	100	-
10		90	190	19
20	100		260	
30	100	230		

7.3   Marginal cost

The **marginal cost** is the cost of producing the marginal unit. Just as "the margin" means at the edge, if you lined up all the units you have manufactured in order, the marginal unit would be the one at the end.

If you are looking forward, the marginal unit could be the next one you are about to produce. If you already have a complete set of cost figures to consider, the marginal unit is the final unit. Having two options might sound confusing but the question always makes it obvious whether the marginal unit in question is the last one or the next one.

Total cost increases step by step as output increases. The size of each step is the marginal cost of each extra unit. As output increases unit by unit, a new marginal cost is established with each step. The example in the table below illustrates this:

Output (units)	Fixed cost	Variable cost	Total cost	Marginal cost
0	100	0	100	n/a
1	100	40	140	40
2	100	75	175	35
3	100	105	205	30

Marginal cost relative to total cost and output

To understand how the marginal cost is calculated, look at the relationship between successive total cost figures:

- The marginal cost of the first unit is the difference between the total cost of producing zero units and the total cost of producing one unit (£140 - £100 = £40).

- The marginal cost of the second unit is the difference between the total cost of producing one unit and the total cost of producing two units (£175 - £140 = £35).

- The marginal cost of the third unit is the difference between the total cost of producing two units and the total cost of producing three units (£205 - £175 = £30).

Marginal cost   Go online

Q4: Complete the table with the correct figures.

Output (units)	Fixed costs (£)	Variable costs (£)	Total costs (£)	Marginal costs (£)
0	200	0	200	-
1	200	120	320	
2	200	210	410	
3	200	290	490	
4	200	360	560	

7.4   Summary of costs

Summary of costs   Go online

Q5:   Complete the table by entering the correct figures.

Output (units)	Fixed cost (£)	Variable cost (£)	Total cost (£)	Marginal cost (£)	Average cost (£)
0	20	0	20	n/a	n/a
1	20	18			
2	20	34			
3	20	46			
4	20	56			
5	20	65			
6	20	70			
7	20	92			
8	20	124			

7.5   Average fixed cost

Average fixed costs are calculated by dividing fixed costs by output. As you already know, average cost (average total cost) = total cost ÷ output. The process of calculating average fixed costs is shown in the table below.

Output (units)	Fixed cost (£)	Average fixed cost (£)
0	120	n/a
1	120	120
2	120	60
3	120	40
4	120	30
5	120	24

Calculating average fixed costs

Note that dividing by zero is not sensible. Hence there is no entry for average fixed costs at zero output.

If you were to draw a diagram for average fixed costs it would fall continuously but never quite reach the horizontal axis. The diagram below illustrates this using the figures above extended to 10 units of output.

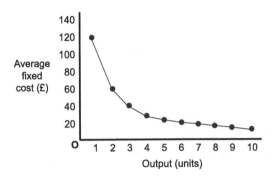

Average fixed costs

Average fixed costs

Q6: Draw a diagram for average fixed costs based on the figures in the table below and compare your diagram to the answer.

Output (units)	Fixed cost (£)	Average fixed cost (£)
0	720	n/a
1	720	720
2	720	360
3	720	240
4	720	180
5	720	145
6	720	120

7.6 Average variable costs

Average variable costs are calculated by dividing variable costs by output, as shown in the table below.

Output (units)	Variable cost (£)	Average variable cost (£)
0	0	n/a
1	40	40
2	70	35
3	90	30
4	100	25
5	115	23

Calculating average variable costs

The formula for this can be given as:

* Average variable cost = variable cost ÷ output

Remember that when output is zero there are no wages or raw materials to pay for. Therefore variable cost is always zero when output is zero. The efficiency of most operations is greater as the output increases so the average variable cost does tend to fall as output increases. Note that in many texts, the variable cost is shown as entirely proportionate to output and is diagrammatically a rising straight line from left to right. The more realistic figures chosen above mean that the rate at which the total variable cost line rises will taper off.

Setting aside what happens to total variable cost, here is an example of a diagram for average variable cost, using the figures above.

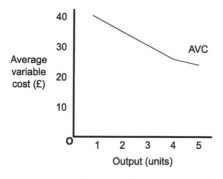

Average variable cost

As you already know, average total cost = total cost ÷ output.

Average total cost can also be obtained by adding average fixed cost and average variable cost together so:

* Average total cost = average fixed cost + average variable cost

Go online

Average variable costs

Q7: Complete the bottom two rows of the table with the correct figures.

Output (units)	Fixed cost (£)	Average fixed cost (£)	Variable cost (£)	Average variable cost (£)	Total cost (£)	Average total cost (£)
0	24	n/a	0	n/a	24	n/a
1	24	24	16	16	40	40
2	24	12	30	15	54	27
3	24		42			
4	24		48			

7.7 Long-run average cost curves

If you remember earlier sections of this topic you will recall that the long run is defined as that period of time when all factors can be varied. For a firm this may mean finding new land and building a bigger factory, for example. Typically, land is fixed in the short run.

As a firm grows, it will move to an entirely new short run average cost curve. This happens as it increases the scale of production, having been able to change a fixed factor in the long-run. Indeed, as the firm grows it will move on to successive new short-run average cost curves. Each curve will represent a new lower cost position than the previous one. This is shown diagrammatically below.

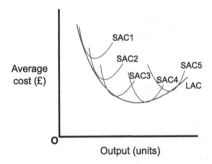

Long-run and short-run average cost curves

As you see in the diagram above, all these successive short-run average cost curves, labelled SAC1 to SAC5, can be linked together with a single envelope curve which represents long-run average cost (LAC).

We have already established that for the short-run cost curves the fall is due to increasing returns to the fixed factor and the rise is due to the law of diminishing returns which must eventually take hold.

In the long-run the most significant causes of the fall and then rise of the curve are called economies and diseconomies of scale. Diminishing returns to the variable factor can be ruled out as a cause of the rise in the long-run average cost curves because in the long-run all factors are variable.

7.8   Economies of scale

Economies of scale come in two categories:

- **internal economies of scale** - the advantages that large firms enjoy over smaller competitors. Mostly these are reductions in average cost (cost per unit).

  In some cases there is a quality improvement that leads to lower average costs, e.g. the use of specialist managers leading to better decision making;

- **external economies of scale** - the result of the concentration of firms in one area enjoyed by the firm and its neighbours.

7.8.1   Internal economies of scale

The main kinds of internal economies of scale are outlined below.

- *Technical economies* - Many processes are more efficient as size increases. Consider a large articulated truck that carries as much stock as ten vans:

  ○ it will require one driver, not ten;

  ○ it will use more diesel but not as much as ten vans;

  ○ the driver will be paid less than ten individual van drivers.

  Many aspects of large-scale production offer technical economies such as this, cutting cost per unit.

- *Marketing economies* - Advertising is more effectively spent when there are many outlets for customers to buy in. If you advertise expensively on television, it is important that all the viewers can easily reach your product in local shops otherwise a portion of your advertising spending is wasted. Hence one pound spent on advertising by a small firm can be less effective than one pound spent by a large firm.

- *Administrative economies* - Large orders involve similar procedures and paperwork to small orders. Per unit sold, the cost will be less. This is one factor leading to purchasing economies.

- *Purchasing economies* - Big orders are cheaper to process and when batched for transport further savings in average cost may be obtained. These savings can be passed on by suppliers to large firms as a discount. It will also be important to obtain a large order to maintain the continuous output of a supplier's production line and ensure that labour and expensive capital equipment are fully used. For these reasons the large firm is likely to receive favourable treatment.

- *Managerial economies* - Employing specialist managers may initially add to the wage bill, but the quality of output from specialists, e.g. in marketing, should generate additional revenues and profits for large firms that far outweigh the costs.

- *Research and development economies* - Large firms tend to devote more funds to research. The initial costs of this are more than recouped by sales of new and improved products.

- *Risk-bearing economies* - Small firms may have one or few products and are often very dependent on sales in one area. This is a riskier position than a large, diversified company which spreads risk over many products and markets. They have many baskets and it is unlikely all will drop at the same time. This is one of the factors that gives rise to financial economies of scale.

- *Financial economies* - Large 'blue-chip' companies operating in diverse markets with many products are less risky for banks to lend to. Banks compete for these less risky loans by offering lower interest rates to large firms.

Internal economies of scale	Go online

Q8: Match the following types of internal economy of scale with the descriptions in the table below:

1. Technical;
2. Risk-bearing;
3. Financial;
4. Marketing;
5. Purchasing;
6. Administrative;
7. Research and Development;
8. Managerial.

Description	Internal economy of scale
Merging a hotel chain with an airline	
Obtaining a 15% discount on an order for 100,000 televisions	
Replacing two small secondary schools with one larger one	
Advertising on local radio for a local chain of bakers with ten retail shops	
Employing a Human Resource Manager to take care of hiring staff	
Receiving a favourable interest rate on a loan from a bank	
Processing a single order for the sale of 100,000 televisions	
Developing an ironing machine to reduce ironing time by 50%	

. . . .

Q9: An example of a technical economy of scale is:

a) diversifying into a foreign market.
b) negotiating a discount on a big order for stock.
c) replacing three smaller ships with a super tanker.
d) employing a specialist engineering manager.

. . . .

Q10: Economies of scale are best described as:

a) increases in profits as a firm grows.
b) reductions in total costs as a firm grows.
c) increases in total costs as a firm grows.
d) reductions in average costs as a firm grows.

7.8.2 External economies of scale

Internal economies come about inside your firm as a result of your management activity and decisions you make. External economies involve the decisions of competitors that have a favourable impact on your company. They also cut your average costs.

Typically external economies of scale arise from the concentration of firms in one area. If the firms are all in the same industry then the effect can be even greater.

The main kinds of external economies of scale are outlined below.

* *Local suppliers* - Suppliers or component firms spring up locally to supply all the firms in the local industry. It is clearly their most efficient location to be next to where their customer firms are. If you are isolated from the rest of your industry you may incur cost-raising transport costs for supplies and components. A car transporters firm would locate next to the car industry.

* *College courses* - The local colleges are keen to train people for major local industries and services. Training costs for the companies are reduced. As a small or isolated company you may not be significant enough to the local economy to justify the creation of a college course.

* *Research centres* - As an industry becomes concentrated in one region it becomes the best place to site research facilities. Companies benefit from the work of scientists and academics.

* *Locally skilled labour force* - When an industry is concentrated in one region, the necessary skills are present in the local labour force. Many will have been employed in the industry at one time or another or have been trained at the local college. In contrast, an isolated company will exist in a region where relevant local skills are more limited.

* *Infrastructure improvements* - As an area's industry and commerce grows, the local infrastructure develops. Government spends on road improvements, airports expand and leisure facilities grow. These facilities help to attract workers and managers to the town and retain them. The transport improvements make connections to head office easier. Faster journey times reduce transport costs for business.

External economies of scale   Go online

Q11: Match the following types of external economy of scale with the descriptions in the table below:

- Infrastructure improvement;
- Locally skilled labour;
- Local suppliers;
- College courses;
- Research centres.

Description	External economy of scale
Tyre manufacturer sites nearby	
Local university obtains grant to research crash safety	
Places on engineering courses available	
Many qualified applicants for vacancies	
Local council improves road linking to nearby motorway	

7.8.3 Internal and external diseconomies of scale

Very large firms can suffer from **diseconomies of scale**. In the long-run, average costs begin to increase. The firms become slow-moving, lumbering giants. Encumbered by bureaucracy and layers of middle management, they respond more slowly to changing market conditions than their smaller rivals.

Internal diseconomies of scale

Internal diseconomies of scale are:

- **Slow decision-making** - There are many staff to involve, meetings to convene, departments to consult, and reports to write. Remember the saying that a camel is a horse drawn up by a committee. The final decision may be a weak compromise;

- **Communication problems and delays** - Within the layers of management, good ideas can be diluted or lost entirely. Somewhere in the bureaucracy an idea can be altered as if in a Chinese whisper;

- **Labour problems** - The workers can feel isolated from the final product, a process known as alienation. A "them and us" attitude between workers and management may leave the company prone to low motivation, poor quality output, and high labour turnover.

There are good examples of very large firms being overtaken by enterprising small upstarts. IBM once dominated the international computer market. However Bill Gates's Microsoft, reputed to have started in his garage, went from start-up to overtaking the computing giant in a relatively short time. Microsoft was innovative and quick to respond to changing market conditions.

Logo on front of Microsoft building
(Microsoft sign outside building 99 (http://bit.ly/1FJ7onj) by Robert Scobie (http://bit.ly/1rO2 OMh) is licensed under CC BY 2.0)

There are also examples of large firms that re-invent their management structures to stay at the top so rising long-term average costs are not as inevitable in reality as the theory would have us believe.

There are several ways in which very large firms can try to avoid internal diseconomies, i.e. rising long-term average costs, or at least postpone such an event.

- Companies can be sub-divided into medium-sized divisions (or cost centres) that make most decisions independently of Head Office. Head Office can then be massively reduced in size and bureaucracy shrinks. An example would be the firm General Electric, which runs as a group of independent units with their own profit and loss.

- Management can be delayered. The management structure can be simplified by taking out a whole tier of middle management, with tasks delegated to lower levels.

- Companies can be de-merged. They are split into two or more smaller companies to increase efficiency and give greater returns to shareholders.

- Rationalisation involving the concentration of output in the most efficient plants and the closing of less efficient production units.

External diseconomies of scale

These are closely linked to the concept of negative externalities, the details of which are outside the scope of this topic. As they can also be thought of as consequences arising from the over-concentration of industry they could be considered external diseconomies. This is because they add to costs and problems faced by firms and their employees.

There are disadvantages to being clustered in the same region as other firms. Consider the reputation for congestion and delays of the M25 motorway around Greater London. Heavily populated areas can have issues with pollution (air, visual and noise) and can be stressful places to live. In densely populated areas, soaring land and property prices and lengthy commuting times can all add to the costs of business and the individual. The cost of transport infrastructure in these areas increases, e.g. underground railways are needed.

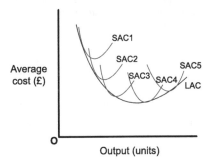

Long-run and short-run average cost curves

You saw the above diagram previously in this topic. Note that the long-run average cost curve first falls because of economies of scale. The long-run average cost curve then begins to rise because of diseconomies of scale.

The long-run average cost is composed of a sequence of short-run curves. You can draw a curve that runs tangential to the lowest point on the short-run curves.

7.9   Revenues

Amidst all this detail about costs we should not forget the opposite side of the coin. You will remember that in order to calculate profit, we will need total revenue as well as total cost. This is because profit can be defined as total revenue minus total cost.

Normal profit is the return to the factor "enterprise" and is therefore within total cost. If we accept this definition then total revenues exceeding total costs means an above-normal profit has been made. A normal profit is a profit that is neither so high that it attracts new entrants into an industry, nor is so low that firms begin to leave.

Revenues can be thought of as the opposite of costs. They provide income to a company whereas costs are expenses for a company. There are three revenues to understand:

- total revenue = sales × price per unit sold;

- average revenue = total revenue ÷ quantity sold;

- marginal revenue = the addition to total revenue from selling one more unit.

If you only sell one type of product and it is priced at £100, then your average revenue is the price per item which is £100. If you sell one more unit, your marginal revenue will be the £100 you will add to total revenue. In these circumstances, price is the same as average revenue and marginal revenue.

However, if you have to reduce your price to £95 in order to increase demand and sell more units then your average revenue will start falling. In these circumstances, your marginal revenue will fall faster than the average revenue. The table below illustrates this.

Units sold	Sales price	Total revenue	Marginal revenue	Average revenue
1	£100	£100	£100	£100
2	£100	£200	£100	£100
3	£100	£300	£100	£100
4	£100	£400	£100	£100
5	£95	£495	£95	£99

Marginal and average revenue

Revenues   Go online

Q12: Complete the following table.

Units sold (£)	Sales price (£)	Total revenue (£)	Marginal revenue (£)	Average revenue (£)
1	20			
2	20			
3	20			
4	20			
5	15			

7.10   Summary

Summary

At the end of this topic you should know that:

- total costs of production can be sub-divided into fixed costs and variable costs;

- average cost is cost per unit and can be worked out by dividing total cost by the number of units;

- marginal cost is the addition to total costs as a result of making one further unit;

- marginal cost cuts the U-shaped average cost curve at its lowest point;

- in the long-run, average cost falls because of economies of scale, and then rises because of diseconomies of scale.

7.11   End of topic test

Q13: The marginal cost of production for a firm is the:

a) extra cost of employing one more worker.
b) addition to total cost caused by producing one more unit.
c) difference between total cost and variable cost.
d) total cost divided by the number of units produced.

....

Q14: Which one of the following is a fixed cost?

a) Wages paid to production line staff.
b) The cost of components for building into the final product.
c) The managing director's salary.
d) The electricity bill for running factory machinery.

....

Q15: A firm produces 1,000 units of output per month and its costs of production per month are:

- Interest to bank on a loan: £2,000;
- Wages to workers: £10,000;
- Raw materials: £8,000;
- Managers' salaries: £5,000.

The average variable cost of production is:

a) £10
b) £18
c) £23
d) £25

....

Q16: In Economics it is usual to assume that commercial firms want to:

a) maximise profits.
b) maximise output.
c) maximise total revenue.
d) maximise employment.

....

Q17: Profits of a firm (all figures in thousands) are shown in the table below.

Output	Average costs	Average revenue
100	£80	£60
200	£60	£60
300	£40	£50
400	£45	£50

At what level of output does the firm make the greatest total profit?

a) 100
b) 200
c) 300
d) 400

. . . .

Q18: External economies of scale can be enjoyed by manufacturers when:

a) nationwide advertising brings benefits to a large firm.
b) larger delivery vans are bought to replace small ones.
c) a specialist website designer is used to set up a website for the firm.
d) several firms in the industry benefit from being located near to each other.

. . . .

Q19: The following cost figures relate to a firm's hourly production:

- Total fixed costs £400;
- Total variable costs £350;
- Marginal costs £85;
- Number of units produced 10.

Its average total cost is:

a) £35
b) £40
c) £75
d) £85

. . . .

Q20: Explain why long-run average total cost curves are usually U-shaped.

(9 marks)

Unit 1 Topic 8

Supply

Contents

Prerequisites

The topic builds on and expands the concept of supply studied in National 5 level Economics. However, prior knowledge of this concept, although useful, is not essential.

Learning objective

By the end of this topic you should:

- be able to define supply;

- know the difference between supply and output;

- know the factors which cause movement along the supply schedule;

- understand the law of supply;

- be able to draw a supply curve.

8.1   A behavioural science

Economics is known as a behavioural science because it attempts to explain how people behave in an economic situation, i.e. when they have to make choices.

The theory of supply attempts to explain producer behaviour.

> **Q1:**   Complete the following sentence by adding the missing word.
> The theory of demand attempts to explain .... behaviour.

Supply is the quantity of a good or service that firms are willing and able to offer for sale per unit of time at a given price.

As with demand, we make a distinction between individual supply and market supply:

* Individual supply is the supply of a particular firm;

* Market supply is the total supply of all the firms in the industry.

> **Q2:**   Complete the following sentence.
> To go from individual to market supply, we .... all the individual supplies.

8.2   Supply and output

Supply is not the same as output.

* **Output** is the amount of a good that a firm produces.

* **Supply** is the amount of a good that a firm puts on the market.

Supply and output can differ because of the existence of stocks. Some firms hold stocks of goods which they can use to meet sudden increases in demand. If output:

* exceeds supply then some of the output will be added to stock because not all of it is going on to the market;

* is less than the amount supplied to the market, then the stocks are being reduced.

Q3: Complete the following sentences by using the words *greater than* or *less than*.

When a firm adds to its stock of goods, output will be (*greater than / less than*) supply. When a firm uses its stock of goods to help meet demand, output will be (*greater than / less than*) supply.

8.3   The law of supply

The law of supply states that "the quantity of a commodity produced and offered for sale will tend to increase if its price increases and decrease if its price falls - *ceteris paribus.*"

There is a direct relationship between price and the quantity supplied, i.e. when the price of a good increases its supply increases and vice versa.

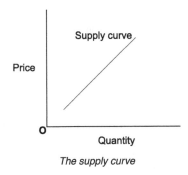

The supply curve

This is because:

- existing producers seeking to maximise their profits will move as many resources as possible into this good. For example, if red t-shirts are fashionable (and obtaining higher prices) and blue ones are not, then workers and machines will be directed towards increasing the supply of red t-shirts.

- existing producers may be able to overcome additional overtime costs and increase the level of profitable production.

- less efficient (higher cost) producers will enter or re-enter the market as they can now make a profit by producing the good.

- entrepreneurs (new suppliers) will move into the production of goods that now offer above normal profits.

Q4:   Complete the following sentence.

There is .... relationship between price and quantity supplied.

a) an inverse
b) a direct

8.3.1   Illustrating the law of supply

The law of supply can be illustrated in two ways:

1. by constructing a *supply schedule* i.e. a table;

2. by drawing a *supply curve* i.e. a graph.

Supply curve

Q5:   Draw a supply curve using the data given in the table below.

Price (£)	Supply per week
50	400
40	350
30	300
20	250
10	200

A supply curve shows the quantity of a product producers will wish to make and offer for sale at different prices.

Q6:   Complete the following sentence.

Supply curves, like demand curves, are drawn on the basis of ....

Once we have drawn our supply curve we can examine how it would be affected by a change in any of the factors we assumed were constant, i.e. the determinants of supply, apart from the price of the good (covered in the next topic).

8.4 Summary

Summary

At the end of this topic you should know that:

- supply is the amount of a good produced and offered for sale;
- when a firm adds to its stocks, its supply will be less than its output;
- when a firm dips into its stocks, its supply will be greater than its output;
- price and supply are directly related;
- supply curves slope upwards from left to right;
- when price increases existing producers are willing and able to produce more because their profit per good will have increased. In addition, new producers might now be able to make a profit by producing the good.

8.5   End of topic test

Q7:   Select the normal supply curve from the options below.
(2 marks)

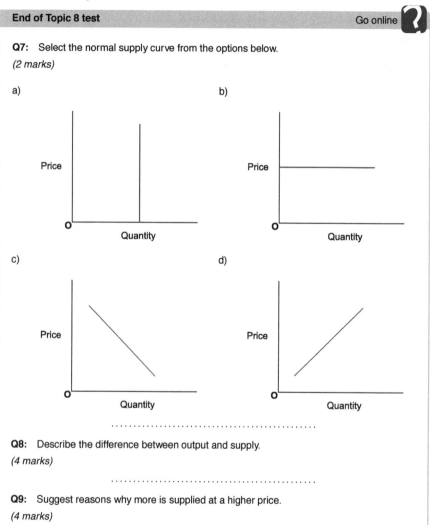

a)

b)

c)

d)

....

Q8:   Describe the difference between output and supply.
(4 marks)

....

Q9:   Suggest reasons why more is supplied at a higher price.
(4 marks)

Unit 1 Topic 9

Determinants of supply

Contents

Prerequisites

The topic builds on and expands the concept of supply studied in National 5 level Economics. However, prior knowledge of this concept, although useful, is not essential.

Learning objective

By the end of this topic you should:

- know the factors which affect supply and cause shifts in the supply schedule;
- know how and why supply can increase;
- know how and why supply can decrease.

9.1   Determinants of supply

Determinants of supply are the factors which affect supply.

The major determinants of supply are:

- changes in profit;
- the costs of production;
- the prices of other goods;
- government intervention;
- increases in productivity;
- the weather.

Determinants of supply   Go online

Q1:   Complete the following sentence by adding the correct phrase.

In order to isolate the effect on supply of a change in price, we must again assume that all other determinants, i.e. the conditions of supply, are not changing. Therefore we must assume ....

9.1.1   Change in profit

As producers are motivated by profit, anything which increases profit will increase supply and anything which reduces profit will reduce supply.

Increase in profit

Change in profit   Go online

Q2:   Select the two phrases which correctly complete the following sentence.

As profit = revenue - costs, it will increase if something happens which results in (*an increase/a decrease*) in revenue or (*an increase/a decrease*) in costs.

9.1.2 The costs of production

If the costs of production increase then supply is less profitable at each and every price. The supply curve moves to the left.

If the costs of production decrease then supply is more profitable at each and every price. The supply curve moves to the right.

The costs of production

Effect of changes in costs   Go online

Q3: In the following table, say whether the effect (direction) of the following changes in costs on supply schedules is towards the *left* or *right* of the supply curve.

Change in costs on supply schedules	Effect on supply curve
Efficiency gains due to new technology	
Higher wages	
Rising price of components	

There is an inverse relationship between costs and supply, i.e. an increase in the cost of any factor of production will lead to a decrease in supply and *vice versa*.

Relationship between costs and supply   Go online

Q4: Choose the word which correctly completes the following sentence.

A decrease in the cost of wood will increase the supply of wooden tables because the profit made on each table will ....

9.1.3   The prices of other goods

The prices of other goods that the producer is making, or could make, have an inverse relationship.

For example, an increase in the price, and therefore the profit, of potatoes might persuade some farmers to grow more potatoes and fewer cabbages.

The prices of other goods

The prices of other goods   Go online

Q5:   What might a manufacturer of t-shirts do if red ones were in fashion and selling for higher prices than blue ones?

9.1.4   Government intervention

Government intervention concerns expenditure taxes and subsidies.

Government intervention
(UK Parliament (http://bit.ly/1y9JzTI) by Alan Cleaver (http://bit.ly/1yCrOfi) is licensed under CC BY 2.0)

Government intervention   Go online

Select the phrase which correctly completes the following sentences.

Q6: Expenditure taxes, such as VAT, impose extra costs on producers and will therefore result in .... in supply.

a) a decrease
b) an increase

....

Q7: When a good is subsidised, the government gives the producer a certain amount of money for each good supplied. A subsidy therefore increases the producer's revenue and will therefore result in .... in supply.

a) a decrease
b) an increase

9.1.5   Increases in productivity

Increases in productivity will lead to an increase in supply as they reduce average costs (due to advances in technology, improved working practices, etc.).

Increases in productivity
(Wolfsburg VW-Werk (http://bit.ly/1rNuyGo) by Andreas Praefcke (http://bit.ly/11JKj51) is licensed under CC BY 3.0)

Increases in productivity   Go online

Q8: Which of the following three options is an example of the highest productivity (output per worker)?

a)   100 units, 10 workers
b)   180 units, 15 workers
c)   300 units, 26 workers

9.1.6   The weather

Although the weather does not affect the supply of most goods, it can influence the output of the agricultural and construction industries.

The weather
(NASA satellite shot of UK snow (http://bit.ly/1u0JRLv) by Phil Plait (http://bit.ly/11JLIOt) is licensed under CC BY-SA 2.0)

The weather   Go online

Q9: Why might the weather influence the output of the agricultural and construction industries?

9.2   An increase in supply

An increase in supply is where more is supplied at each price (and the same amount will be sold at a lower price).

An increase in supply   Go online

Q10: Draw a supply curve and label it S1 S1.

On the same graph draw another supply curve labelled S2 S2.

Curve S2 S2 should represent an increase in supply from curve S1 S1.

. . . .

Q11: Complete the following sentence.

If the supply of a good increases, the supply curve will shift . . . .

9.2.1 Causes of an increase in supply

Causes of an increase in supply   Go online

Select the correct phrase in each of the following sentences about causes of an increase in supply.

Q12: The supply of a good will increase if there is .... in productivity.

a) an increase
b) a decrease

....

Q13: The supply of a good will increase if there is .... in the costs of producing the good.

a) an increase
b) a decrease

....

Q14: The supply of a good will increase if there is .... in the price of other goods the producer is making.
Hint: think of the idea of "relative profit," i.e. the amount of profit a producer can make from one good relative to another. In Economics it is assumed that producers are in business to make as much profit as they can.

a) an increase
b) a decrease

....

Q15: The supply of a good will increase if there is .... in the tax placed on the good.
Hint: when a good is taxed, the producer (seller) receives the market price less the tax.

a) an increase
b) a decrease

....

Q16: The supply of a good will increase if there is .... on the subsidy producers receive for producing the good.
Hint: when a good is subsidised, the producer (seller) receives the market price plus the subsidy.

a) an increase
b) a decrease

....

Q17: Why is one cause of an increase in supply *not* a decrease in the price of the good?

....

Q18: Draw a supply diagram to show what happens when the price of a good decreases.

9.3   A decrease in supply

The factors that can cause a decrease in supply are the *opposite* of the factors that can cause an increase in supply.

A decrease in supply   Go online

Select the words which correctly complete the following two sentences.

Q19: A decrease in supply means that, at any price, ... is supplied than previously.

a) more
b) less

....

Q20: A decrease in supply means that the same amount will be supplied at a .... price than previously.

a) lower
b) higher

....

Q21: List five causes of a decrease in supply.

9.4 Summary

Summary

At the end of this topic you should know:

- the supply of a good is affected by:
  - the cost of producing it;
  - other prices;
  - the availability of its inputs;
  - taxes and subsidies;
  - productivity;
  - the weather;
- when the supply of a good increases, its supply curve shifts to the right;
- the supply of a good will increase if:
  - the cost of producing it falls;
  - the price (and profitability) of producing other goods falls.
  - it is subsidised;
  - the tax on it is reduced;
  - productivity increases;
- when the supply of a good decreases, the opposite happens.

9.5   End of topic test

End of Topic 9 test   Go online

Q22: Plastics are made from crude oil components. Explain how the recent increases in the price of oil are likely to affect the supply of plastics.

You should explain what will happen to the supply curve and you should include a diagram in your answer.

(3 marks)

. . . .

Q23: If the government gives a producer a subsidy for producing a good, the supply of that good will increase.

a) True
b) False

. . . .

Q24: If the government place a tax on sugar, the supply curve for sugar will move to the right.

a) True
b) False

. . . .

Q25: If the wages paid to teachers in private schools are increased, the supply curve for private education will move to the right.

a) True
b) False

. . . .

Q26: If frost hits the orange crop in Florida then the supply curve for oranges will move to the right.

a) True
b) False

. . . .

Q27: If new technology improves the efficiency of car production then the supply curve for new cars will move to the right.

a) True
b) False

. . . .

Q28: If the price of fashionable purple t-shirts increases then the supply curve for pink t-shirts will move to the right.

a) True
b) False

....

Q29: When good management increases productivity in bakers then the supply curve for cakes will move to the right.

a) True
b) False

....

Q30: If the weather in Scotland is perfect for growing raspberries then the supply of raspberries will move to the right.

a) True
b) False

....

Q31: A rise in the price of raspberries will move the supply curve to the right.

a) True
b) False

Unit 1 Topic 10

Markets

Contents

Prerequisites

The topic builds on and expands the concept of markets studied at National 5 Economics. However, prior knowledge of this concept, although useful, is not essential.

Learning objective

By the end of this topic you should know:

- what is meant by "a market";
- why markets are important;
- the conditions necessary for a market to be free;
- what is meant by equilibrium or market clearing price;
- how to show equilibrium price (EP) and equilibrium quantity (EQ) diagrammatically;
- how to explain how EP and EQ is established in a free market;
- how to show effects of shortages and surpluses diagrammatically;
- how price (P) and quantity (Q) will change if either demand (D) or supply (S) change;
- how to show the effects of changes in D and S diagrammatically;
- the effects of simultaneous changes in D and S;
- the inter-relationships of D and S;
- why changes in one market can affect the price in a related market;
- diagrams of how changes in a market affect another related market.

10.1   Markets

Demand and supply operate in markets. In Economics, the term "market" is given a wide meaning.

A **market** occurs when buyers and sellers come into contact in some way in order to agree a price and exchange a good or service.

Some examples of markets are:

- shops;

- telephone shopping;

- eBay;

- mail-order catalogues;

- an auction;

- the stock market (for shares in public limited companies);

- Forex - the foreign exchange market for currencies;

- commodity markets, e.g. oil, rice, cocoa.

Markets can be worldwide, e.g. the market for oil, or very local, e.g. a car boot sale.

Markets exist for:

- goods;

- services;

- resources;

- currencies.

Goods, services, resources and money   Go online

Q1:   Place the following under the correct heading:

- cars;
- education.
- foreign currency;
- haircuts;
- labour;
- raw materials;
- sweets;

Goods	Services	Resources	Money

10.2   Market price

All markets have three things in common. They have:

- **buyers** (consumers/demand);
- **sellers** (producers/supply);
- **something to be exchanged**.

The buyers and sellers must be in contact with each other. It could be on market day in the town square, or it could be internationally on computer. Negotiation occurs and market prices are the outcome. The "forces of the market" are simply the forces of demand and supply.

The main importance of a market is that it is where *price* is determined. However, price can take various forms.

Forms of price   Go online

Q2:   Complete the sentences below by using one of the following words:

- rent;
- wages;
- interest;
- exchange rate.

- The price of labour is ....
- The price of foreign currency is its ....
- The price of land is ....
- The price of borrowing money is ....

Q3:   What is the "price" of getting a place at a particular university?

10.3   Market equilibrium

In economic theory some markets can be described as "free markets".

A free market is one in which:

- there is no government intervention;

- there are a great many competing firms;

- the firms are price takers (not price makers), i.e. they must sell at the price set by the market. This is because the output of one firm is just a tiny part of overall supply, so no matter how much they increase supply the effect on the market supply (and price) is negligible.

In a free market, the price that will eventually be established will be where the demand for the good equals the supply of that good. This price is known as the **equilibrium price**.

The equilibrium price (EP) is also known as **the market clearing price**, i.e. the price which "clears the market". This is because, at that price, there will be no unsatisfied demand (everyone who wants the good, and is willing to pay the market price, will get the good) and no unsold supplies (all the goods put on the market will be sold).

Equilibrium price (EP)   Go online

Q4:   Complete the following sentence.

At   the   equilibrium   price,   the   amount   consumers   wish   to   buy   equals
....

Q5: Complete the following sentence by using two words.

At the equilibrium price there are neither .... nor ....

Hint: think of one word for "unsatisfied demand" and one word for "unsold supplies".

The equilibrium price can be illustrated by using a diagram.

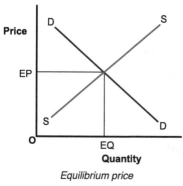

Equilibrium price

Although, in a free market, the equilibrium price will eventually be established, at any moment in time, the actual price may be above or below the equilibrium price.

In the following diagram the market price is above the equilibrium price.

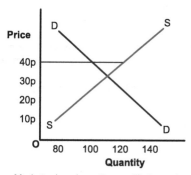

Market price above the equilibrium price

Market price   Go online

Q6: What will be the result of the market price being 40p?

Hint: compare the amount demanded at 40p with the amount supplied at 40p.

....

Q7: How will sellers get rid of a surplus?

....

Q8: Draw a diagram to show what will happen if the market price is *below* the equilibrium price. Explain what will happen to the market price.

10.4   Causes of movement in equilibrium

Once the equilibrium price has been established it will remain - unless there is a change in either demand or supply (or both).

Example : Increase in demand

What happens to the equilibrium price and equilibrium quantity (EQ) when there is an increase in demand?

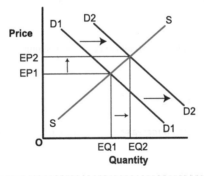

Changes in supply or demand 1

Use the following diagram as a template:

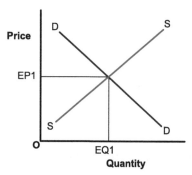

Hint: *when demand or supply change, the curve will shift - either to the right or to the left.*

Q9: Show what happens to the equilibrium price and equilibrium quantity (EQ) when there is a decrease in demand.

....

Q10: Show what happens to the equilibrium price and equilibrium quantity (EQ) when there is an increase in supply.

....

Q11: Show what happens to the equilibrium price and equilibrium quantity (EQ) when there is a decrease in supply.

Changes in supply or demand 2

Choose either '*a decrease*' or '*an increase*' to complete the following sentences.

Q12:
An increase in demand will cause .... in the equilibrium price and .... in the equilibrium quantity.

....

Q13: A decrease in demand will cause .... in the equilibrium price and .... in the equilibrium quantity.

....

Q14: An increase in supply will cause .... in the equilibrium price and .... in the equilibrium quantity.

....

Q15: A decrease in supply will cause .... in the equilibrium price and .... in the equilibrium quantity.

Changes in supply or demand 3

Sometimes the demand for a good and the supply of it change at the same time. The final outcome is complicated as the change in demand might outweigh the change in supply and vice versa. If we do not know the relative size of the changes, we can only predict what will happen to the equilibrium price (EP) or the equilibrium quantity (EQ) but not both.

Example : Increase in demand and decrease in supply

What will happen in the market for a good when the demand for it increases and the supply of it decreases?

The EP will rise but the EQ might rise, fall or stay the same. On both sides, this creates the conditions for an increase in market equilibrium price, which must happen. However the equilibrium quantity could change either way depending on the gradient (elasticity) of the demand and supply lines.

See the two possibilities illustrated below.

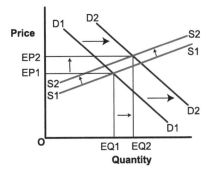 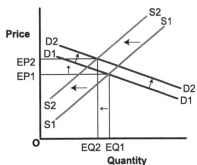

State what will happen in the market for a good in the following circumstances.

Hint: think of the effects of each change in isolation and then put them together.

Q16: The demand for it decreases and the supply of it increases.
....

Q17: The demand for it and the supply of it both increase.
....

Q18: The demand for it and the supply of it both decrease.

10.5   Demand and supply relationships

When the demand for different goods or the supply of different goods are linked is some way, changes in the market for one of the goods can bring about changes in the market for the other good.

We will consider three types of relationship:

- *joint or complementary demand;*
- *competitive demand;*
- *joint supply.*

10.6   Joint or complementary demand

Joint or complementary demand is when two goods tend to be demanded together, e.g. fish and chips, strawberries and cream. An increase in the demand for one will tend to lead to an increase in the demand for the other.

Joint or complementary demand

Use the following diagram as a template:

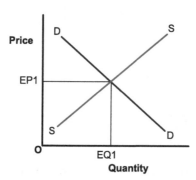

Hint: On the first diagram show an increase in the supply of cars and notice how the quantity of cars moves. On the lower diagram show how demand for petrol will move in response to increased sales of cars. Notice what happens to the price of petrol.

Q19: Show how the demand for cars will be affected by an increase in the supply of cars.

Hint: Show an increase in the supply of cars and notice how the quantity of cars moves.

. . . .

Q20: Show how the demand for petrol will be affected by an increase in the supply of cars.

Hint: Show how demand for petrol will move in response to increased sales of cars. Notice what happens to the price of petrol.

....

Q21: Explain what these graphs show about the increase in the supply of cars and what the effect will be on the demand for petrol.

10.7 Competitive demand

Competitive demand is when the goods are close substitutes, e.g. Shell petrol and Esso petrol. An increase in demand for one usually results in a fall in demand for the other.

Competitive demand

Q22: Draw *two* graphs to show how an increase in the supply of butter will affect the market for butter and margarine.

Explain what these graphs show about the effect of the increase in the supply of butter.

10.8 Joint supply

Joint supply is when two or more goods are produced together, i.e. when one is produced so, automatically, is the other.

An example of this is an increase in the demand for mutton, which would result in an increase in the supply of wool and, therefore, a fall in the price of wool.

Joint supply   Go online

Q23: Explain how an increase in the demand for milk is likely to affect the price of meat.

10.9   Summary

┌─ Summary ───

At the end of this topic you should know that:

- a market is any situation where buyers and sellers come into contact;

- the prices of goods, services, and resources are determined in markets;

- a free market has no government intervention and the competing firms sell the good at the price set by the market;

- the equilibrium price is the price where demand and supply are equal;

- the equilibrium price is the price which "clears the market", i.e. at that price there is neither a shortage nor a surplus;

- if the price is above the equilibrium price then the sellers will not be able to sell all they have produced and will have to reduce their price to get rid of surplus stock;

- if the price is below the equilibrium price then there will be a shortage and the buyers will bid up the price;

- although the price can be above or below the equilibrium price, in a free market the equilibrium price will eventually be established;

- an increase in demand will increase price and result in more being bought and sold (and vice versa);

- an increase in supply will result in a decrease in price and more being bought and sold (and vice versa);

- changes in one market can affect the equilibrium price in related markets.

10.10   End of topic test

End of Topic 10 test   Go online

Q24: If the demand for a good increased by 5% and, at the same time, the supply of the good decreased by 5%, what would happen to its price?

a) It will stay the same.
b) It may rise, fall or stay the same.
c) It will rise.
d) It will fall.

. . . .

Q25: Good X and good Y are substitutes for each other. If the cost of producing good X fell and, at the same time, the price of good Y fell, what would happen?

a) The quantity sold of good X would decrease.
b) The price of good X would increase.
c) The price of good X would decrease.
d) The quantity sold of good X would increase.

. . . .

Q26: If the government were to double the VAT on new cars, how would this affect the average price of second-hand cars?

a) It would stay the same.
b) It might increase, decrease or stay the same.
c) It would decrease.
d) It would increase.

. . . .

Q27:

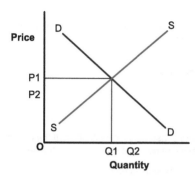

In the above diagram the equilibrium price is P1 and the equilibrium quantity is Q1. Which of the following could cause the equilibrium price and quantity to change to P2 and Q2?

a) An increase in the demand for good X.
b) A decrease in the demand for good X.
c) A decrease in the supply of good X.
d) An increase in the supply of good X.

. . . .

Q28:

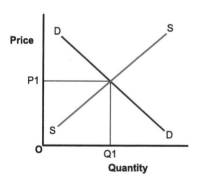

If the price of good Y is P1, which of the following is correct?

a) There will be no unsatisfied demand.
b) Producers will be able to sell all they wish to supply.
c) Both of the above.
d) None of the above.

. . . .

Q29:

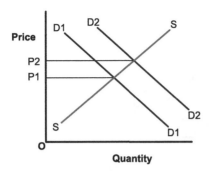

Which of the following could have caused the change in price from P1 to P2?

a) A decrease in the price of golf clubs.
b) An increase in the productivity of the workers who are making the golf balls.
c) An increase in the cost of playing golf.
d) A decrease in the cost of making golf balls.

. . . .

Q30: More and more people are switching from personal computers to laptops.

From the following four diagrams, choose which diagram shows the likely effect of an increase in demand for laptops on the price of personal computers.

a)

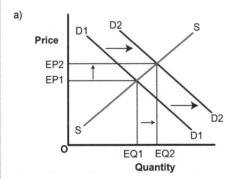

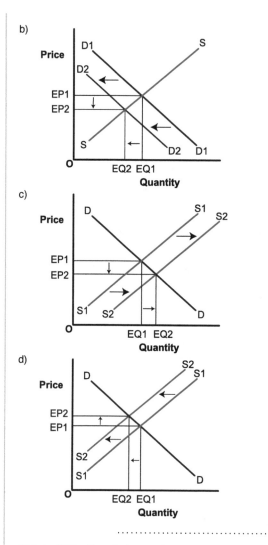

b)

c)

d)

. . . .

Q31: In 2008, although the supply of oil increased, the price of oil rose dramatically. Explain how the price of a good can increase despite a rise in its supply.

(2 marks)

Unit 1 Topic 11

Market intervention

Contents

Prerequisites

The topic builds on and expands the concept of markets studied at National 5 Economics. However, prior knowledge of this concept, although useful, is not essential.

Learning objective

By the end of this topic you should know:

- and understand the causes of market failure;
- the reasons for market intervention by government;
- the different ways in which government can intervene in markets;
- the effect on markets of taxes, subsidies and quotas;
- the effect that maximum and minimum prices have on markets;
- and understand the characteristics of perfect competition compared to those of monopoly;
- what is meant by the terms:
  - public good;
  - merit good;
  - demerit good;
- the significance that externalities have in the understanding of markets;
- how government can act to alter the income distribution that markets create.

11.1 Market failure

In a market failure, the market fails to allocate goods efficiently. Market prices only reflect the business costs in producing, e.g. wages, materials. They ignore wider social costs or social benefits. The market price then sends the wrong signal to the market and factors of production are allocated to make too much or too little of a product, because the price does not reflect the entire costs. In some cases the market will fail to provide altogether.

Market failure leads to market intervention.

Five examples of market failure

1. **Public goods**, e.g. street-lighting, lighthouses, public parks, defence. The market fails totally and they would not be supplied. Non-payers (free riders) cannot be stopped from accessing the good or service. This makes it impossible to sell them at a profit, so entrepreneurs in the market place will not supply them at all. They are also non-rival, in that when one consumer uses them, they still exist for the next consumer.

2. **Merit goods**, e.g. education, health care, housing. The market will under-provide these. The market will provide merit goods only up to the point that they are profitable. Therefore your education will depend on your parent's income - only private fee-paying schools would exist.

3. **Demerit goods**, e.g. alcohol, tobacco, (perhaps sugar in the future). The market will over-provide these. The private business costs of production are low, but the wider costs for the community arising from alcohol misuse are not built into this price.

4. **Externalities**, e.g pollution, congestion, noise. Factory costs will not reflect the impact on third-parties, such as when the soot and pollution from the chimney causes an increase in asthma attacks. Note that some products may have wider benefits for the community which are not charged for in the ticket price. For example, there is a case for subsidising public transport.

5. *Monopolies*, e.g. Microsoft Windows. When one firm dominates a market, then it may be able to exploit consumers by charging higher prices, confident that consumers have no close substitute. Market price no longer reflects the true costs of production, with a knock-on effect on the allocation of resources by the market.

What policies does the government have at its disposal to deal with market failure?

Market failure   Go online

Q1: In the table below, place each of the following market failures next to the appropriate government action.

- Merit good;
- Monopoly;
- Public good.
- Demerit good;
- Externalities (negative);
- Externalities (positive);

Government action	Market failure
Use tax revenue to pay completely for the good or service	
Use high taxes to discourage excess consumption and production.	
Introduce strict laws and regulations covering the industry	
Subsidise the companies to cover the losses made	
Supply some of the good or service, paid from taxes	
Create a Competition Commission to monitor mergers and take-overs	

11.2   Maximum price

Governments sometimes set a legally imposed **_maximum price_** in a market that suppliers cannot exceed. To be effective the maximum price must be set below the equilibrium price (EP).

Maximum prices are often imposed to protect low income consumers.

Let us take as an example a product such as sausages in a communist country. As the maximum price is below the EP, demand will be greater than supply, i.e. there will be a shortage of the good in the market. As the price is not allowed to rise, the shortage will be permanent and will result in long queues and, possibly, black markets. This situation occurred in the former communist countries where the price of some essential commodities was fixed by the government.

Maximum price   Go online

Q2: Select the word which correctly completes the following sentence.

The government will set a maximum price when they feel that the EP is too ....

a) low
b) high

....

Q3: Draw a diagram to show the effect a maximum price has on the market for a good. Briefly explain what the diagram shows about the effect of a maximum price.

Hint- fix the maximum price below the EP.

11.3   Minimum price

Sometimes a legally imposed *minimum price* is set in a market. The good cannot be sold for less than the minimum price.

Minimum prices are imposed in order to encourage production or to give producers (or workers) a guaranteed income. That is why a minimum price is sometimes known as a "guaranteed price" - it is the minimum price a producer will receive for his product. As the minimum price is above the EP, supply will be greater than demand, i.e. there will be a surplus of the good in the market.

The Common Agricultural Policy (CAP) set minimum prices on farm products in the European Union (EU), e.g. beef and butter, which created massive surpluses. The EU bought the surpluses and stored them (hence the various food mountains and wine lakes). The surplus produce was routinely destroyed or dumped very cheaply on markets outside the EU, mainly in developing countries, which had the effect of putting farmers in these countries out of business.

Another example of minimum pricing was created in 1999 when the government introduced a minimum wage of £3.60 per hour for all workers aged 22 and over. Wages are the price of labour.

The minimum wage and unemployment   Go online

Q4: Some critics of the minimum wage argued that it would lead to an increase in unemployment.

Explain how a minimum wage might lead to an increase in unemployment. In the following paragraph, when given a choice, select the correct option.

"A minimum wage set (*above/below*) the equilibrium wage in an industry would (*increase/reduce*) the (*demand/supply*) for workers in that industry. Although more people would now be (*unwilling/willing*) to work in the industry, i.e. the (*demand/supply*) of workers would (*increase/decrease*), employers (*would/would not*) be willing to employ as many as before, i.e. there would be a (*shortage/surplus*) of workers."

Please note that the above theory is a simple one. In the real world there is little evidence that unemployment is increased by the current minimum wage. These workers are also consumers and have a high marginal propensity to consume. Their wage rise becomes an increase in aggregate demand in the economy and thus maintains employment.

Minimum price

Q5: Select the word which correctly completes the following sentence.

To be effective the minimum price must be set .... the EP.

a) above
b) below

....

Q6: Draw a diagram to show the effect a minimum price has on the market for a good.

Briefly explain what the diagram shows about the effect of a minimum price.

Hint - fix the minimum price above the EP.

11.4   The effect of taxes on markets

Sometimes governments impose expenditure taxes, e.g. VAT, in order to raise revenue or to discourage consumption. When a good is taxed, the producers receive the market price less the tax which will have the effect of reducing supply. The tax acts like an increase in costs, i.e. supply falls and the EP rises.

The incidence of the tax, i.e. who bears the burden of the tax, is determined by price elasticity of demand (PED). The producer will wish to pass all the burden on to the consumer but the responsiveness of demand will limit his ability to do so.

Imposing expenditure taxes Go online

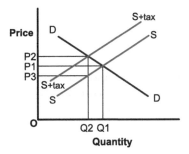

The amount of the tax is represented by the vertical distance between the two supply curves. The cost of the tax is equal to P2 to P3. Although the producers will increase the price to recover the cost of the tax they will probably have to bear some of the burden of the tax themselves, i.e. they will have to take a cut in profit.

Using the above diagram answer the following questions.

Q7: What is the amount of the tax per good?

a) P1 to P2
b) P1 to P3
c) P2 to P3

....

Q8: What is the EP after the imposition of the tax?

a) P1
b) P2
c) P3

....

Q9: What price do producers receive after the tax is imposed?

a) P1
b) P2
c) P3

....

Q10: What part of this tax is borne by the consumer?

a) P1 to P2
b) P1 to P3
c) P2 to P3

....

Q11: What part of this tax is borne by the producer?

a) P1 to P2
b) P1 to P3
c) P2 to P3

....

Q12: Which word correctly completes the following sentence?
The more price .... the demand, the more of the tax burden the producer can pass on.

a) elastic
b) inelastic

11.5   The effect of subsidies on markets

Subsidies to producers have the opposite effect to taxes. When the government places a subsidy on a good, the producers receive the market price plus the subsidy. This will have the effect of increasing supply. The subsidy reduces the producer's cost so supply is increased and price falls.

PED will determine who benefits more from the subsidy.

Governments grant subsidies to encourage production and keep prices low, e.g. EU subsidies to sugar producers.

Granting subsidies   Go online

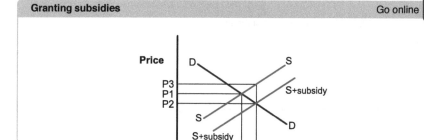

The amount of the subsidy is represented by the vertical distance between the two supply curves. Producers may pass on some of the reduction in cost to the consumers. The amount of the subsidy is equal to P2 to P3.

Using the above diagram answer the following questions.

Q13: What is the EP after the granting of the subsidy?

a) P1
b) P2
c) P3

....

Q14: What is the amount of the subsidy per good?

a) P1 to P2
b) P1 to P3
c) P2 to P3

....

Q15: What price do producers receive after the subsidy is granted?

a) P1
b) P2
c) P3

....

Q16: What part of this subsidy is received by the consumer?

a) P1 to P2
b) P1 to P3
c) P2 to P3

....

Q17: What part of this subsidy is received by the producer?

a) P1 to P2
b) P1 to P3
c) P2 to P3

....

Q18: Which word correctly completes the following sentence?
The more price elastic the demand, the more the .... will benefit from a subsidy.

a) consumer
b) producer

11.6   The effect of quotas on markets

Governments sometimes place a quota, which puts a limit on the amount of a good which producers can supply to a market. Once the quota has been reached the supply is fixed, i.e. perfectly price inelastic.

If the quota is placed below the equilibrium quantity (EQ), the EP will rise. For example in the diagram below:

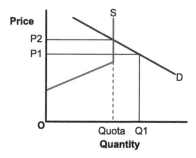

The UK government placed a quota on the amount of white fish (cod and haddock) UK fishermen were allowed to catch per year. This was done to try to conserve the stocks of fish. The most famous quota is that set by OPEC (the oil producing exporting countries). It sets a limit on the amount of oil each member country is allowed to produce. By so doing, OPEC can influence the world price of oil.

11.7   Barriers to entry in markets

Barriers to entry are factors which make it difficult for new firms to enter an industry, for example:

- **Capital costs** - The vast amount of capital required to set up a car or oil firm, for example, can prevent new firms from entering.

- **Economies of scale** - Where these are large, new firms (which are likely to be small to begin with) will find it difficult to compete on price.

- **Legal barriers** - Patents (given to, for example, drug companies) and copyrights (given to, for example, software publishers) give certain firms exclusive rights to produce or publish certain products.

- **Advertising** - Can create brand loyalty, e.g. breakfast cereals, making it difficult for new firms to compete.

- **Sunk costs** - Costs which cannot be recovered if the firm closes, e.g. marketing and R and D, may deter new firms from entering.

11.8   Types of market

There are basically only two types of market: *perfect* and *imperfect*. Perfect markets are a theoretical extreme, but they are studied in Economics to help us fully understand the behaviour of markets. Although perfect markets do not exist, some markets come close, e.g. the Stock Exchange.

Types of market Go online

Q19: Complete the following sentence.
In the real world, all markets are, to a greater or lesser extent, ...

11.9   Perfect markets

A perfect market has the following characteristics:

- **A large number of firms (sellers)** - There are so many firms that none is big enough to have any influence on the market price. The firms are therefore "price takers", i.e. they have to sell at the price set by the market. If one of the many firms were to quadruple its output, it would have negligible effect on the whole industry's supply curve.

  If a firm raised its price above equilibrium, then it would sell zero because of perfect information (see below). If a firm cut its price below equilibrium then it would pointlessly be cutting its revenue from sales, as it can sell everything it produces at the market equilibrium price.

- **A large number of buyers** - There are so many different buyers of the product that the actions of one individual buyer cannot affect the market, enough to affect the price. The number of sellers is so large that no supplier offers more than a small percentage of the total. Any change in a single firm's output, therefore, does not affect the market enough to affect the price.

- **Homogeneous products** - Consumers must believe that each supplier's product is identical to those of other suppliers, and they are therefore perfect substitutes for one another. Not only must the goods be the same, they must appear to be the same, i.e. there can be no branding, advertising or product differentiation.

- **No barriers to entry or exit** - It must be easy for firms to enter and leave an industry.

- **Perfect information** - Consumers and producers must have perfect knowledge about what prices are being charged by all firms in the market. Therefore a seller who charges fractionally more than other sellers will sell nothing.

Perfect markets Go online

Q20: Complete the following sentence.
In a perfect market there can only be .... price for the good at any moment in time.

11.10   Imperfect markets

In practice, all markets are imperfect but there are different types of imperfect markets. There are three basic types of imperfect market:

- *monopoly;*

- *oligopoly;*

- *monopolistic competition.*

The difference depends on the level of competition within the market. The level of competition in a market depends on:

- the number of firms;

- the number of consumers;

- the size of the firms;

- the level of product differentiation, i.e. the extent to which similar products are made to appear different;

- the existence of entry and exit barriers.

Imperfect markets   Go online

Select the word which correctly completes the following sentences.

Q21: Usually, the greater the number of firms the .... the level of competition.

a) greater
b) lower

....

Q22: Usually, the greater the number of consumers the .... the level of competition.

a) greater
b) lower

....

Q23: Usually the bigger the firms the .... the level of competition.

a) greater
b) lower

....

Q24: Usually, the greater the degree of product differentiation the .... the level of competition.

a) greater
b) lower

....

Q25: Usually the greater the entry and exit barriers the .... the level of competition.

a) greater
b) lower

11.10.1 Monopoly

Strictly speaking, a monopolist is a sole seller, i.e. he/she is the only person selling a particular good or service so there is only one firm in the market. However, this tells us very little as, using this definition, the seller of any branded good is a monopolist. We must therefore qualify our terms.

In a monopoly, a monopolist has the power to influence the market price by controlling the supply. Provided they can keep out potential competitors, by the existence of entry barriers, monopolists have the ability to make high profits. That is why the government has set up the Competition Commission and appointed "watchdogs" to monitor and regulate the activity of monopolists.

Pure monopolies are rare but many real world markets come close, e.g. Scottish Water, Microsoft.

Monopoly Go online

Q26: Complete the following sentence.

A monopolist, if he/she is to have any significant power, must control the supply of something with no close ....

11.10.2 The real world - a brief digression on oligopolistic markets

Note that the syllabus now excludes oligopoly so you should not be asked questions on it. However, to assist your understanding of markets, it would be sensible to fill in the "real world" between the theoretical extremes of perfect competition and monopoly. One common market type that exists is oligopoly. This exists in the energy industry, and the supermarket business, and is undoubtedly quite a common type of market.

The word oligopoly comes from the Greek word "*oligos*" which means "few". Therefore an oligopoly is a market which is dominated by a few large firms, e.g. the market for newspapers. A market dominated by two firms, e.g. the market for fast-food restaurant burgers, is called a duopoly.

The characteristics of an oligopoly are:

- Supply is concentrated in the hands of a few firms.

- Each firm is producing similar but branded products.

- Barriers to entry exist which make it difficult for new firms to enter the market.

- Interdependent decision-making. When making any decision, e.g. to change price, increase output, each firm has to take into account how its competitors are likely to react. The outcome of any decision will depend on how they do react.

- The firms tend not to compete on price as price competition often results in costly price wars. However, firms often indulge in fierce "non-price" competition, e.g. branding, advertising, after-sales service, extended warranties. Firms may even get together and informally agree to fix prices, share the market or limit output. Such collusion is illegal but difficult to prove.

Oligopoly Go online

Q27: Name some examples of non-price competition carried out by supermarkets (other than the ones mentioned above).

11.10.3 The real world - a brief digression on monopolistic competition

Monopolistic competition is also very common in the real world. One example of monopolistic competition is the clothing industry; there are many other examples.

The characteristics of an monopolistic competition are:

- a large number of firms, all acting independently;

- product differentiation. Each firm sells a slightly different product and the differentiation can be due to better design, branding, advertising, etc.;

- no significant entry barriers;

- the firms are price makers. Their control over price depends on the degree of product differentiation.

Market types Go online

In which type of market are:

Q28: hairdressers?

a) Monopoly
b) Oligopoly
c) Monopolistic competition

. . . .

Q29: restaurants?

a) Monopoly
b) Oligopoly
c) Monopolistic competition

....

Q30: Microsoft?

a) Monopoly
b) Oligopoly
c) Monopolistic competition

....

Q31: the oil industry?

a) Monopoly
b) Oligopoly
c) Monopolistic competition

....

Q32: petrol stations?

a) Monopoly
b) Oligopoly
c) Monopolistic competition

....

Q33: supermarkets?

a) Monopoly
b) Oligopoly
c) Monopolistic competition

11.11 Pricing strategies

The pricing strategy adopted by firms is largely determined by the type of market in which they are operating and the level of competition they are facing.

- In **perfect (or near perfect) markets**, each firm is so small that it cannot influence price. The price is set by the interaction of the market demand and supply curves and each firm has to accept this price. Each firm is therefore a "price taker". The price of many major commodities, e.g. oil, wheat, coffee, tin, copper, cotton, is set by the world market and individual producers must accept this price.

- In **monopoly markets**, monopolies are "price makers" and often practice "cost plus" pricing, also known as mark-up pricing. They calculate their average cost and add a mark-up (e.g.

20%) to give them a profit. The mark-up is often based on the price the market will bear, i.e.
the highest price the firms think consumers are prepared to pay.

These two market examples above are the most important in your study of this course. Below are
two other market examples that may further your understanding.

- In *oligopolistic markets*, oligopolies try to sell at cost plus, but usually sell at the price set by
the market leader. Firms which sell at a higher price than the leader run the risk of losing most
of their customers.

- In *monopolistic markets*, pricing policy depends on how successful the firms have been in
making their products appear different (product differentiation). The more different a firm's
product appears to be, the more control it has over the price. Otherwise, it will have to sell at
the price set by the market.

11.12 Summary

┌─ Summary ──

At the end of this topic you should know:

- governments often intervene in the free working of markets, because markets do
  not always allocate goods or resources in a way that is the best outcome for some
  individuals or for society as a whole;

- governments intervene to influence the price and/or quantity in the market;

- intervention can take the form of setting a minimum or maximum price, imposing
  expenditure taxes, granting subsidies or setting production quotas;

- each form of intervention affects the market differently:

  ○ minimum prices create surpluses;
  ○ maximum prices create shortages;
  ○ expenditure taxes increase the equilibrium price;
  ○ subsidies reduce the equilibrium price;
  ○ production quotas limit supply and increase the equilibrium price.

- there are basically four different types of market:

  ○ perfect;
  ○ monopoly;
  ○ oligopoly; and
  ○ monopolistic;

- this course focuses on the two theoretical extremes - perfect competition and monopoly;

- each market has different characteristics and the degree of competition in each market
  varies;

- the degree of competition is affected by the number and size of the firms, the level of
  product differentiation and the existence of entry barriers;

- the pricing policy in a market is largely determined by the degree of competition.

11.13   End of topic test

Q34: The following diagram relates to the market for bread.

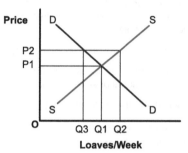

Loaves/Week

If the government imposes a minimum price of P2, what quantity of loaves would be sold per week?

a) Q3 to Q2
b) O to Q3
c) O to Q1
d) O to Q2

. . . .

Q35: The following diagram shows the demand schedule for good X.

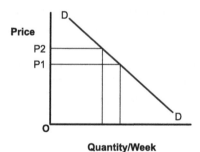

Quantity/Week

The change in the equilibrium price from P1 to P2 could have been caused by which of the following? You may choose more than one option.

a) An increase in the tax on good X.

b) An increase in the subsidy on good X.

c) A decrease in the tax on good X.

d) A decrease in the subsidy on good X.

....

Q36: A maximum price will disrupt a market if it is imposed above the equilibrium price.

a) True
b) False

....

Q37: A minimum price will *not* disrupt a market if it is placed below the equilibrium price.

a) True
b) False

....

Q38: If a tax is placed on a good, the demand for the good will fall.

a) True
b) False

....

Q39: If producers of a good are given a subsidy, the demand for the good will rise.

a) True
b) False

....

Q40: If a tax is placed on a good whose demand is perfectly price inelastic, consumers of that good will bear the full cost of the tax.

a) True
b) False

....

Q41: If a firm in a perfectly competitive market increases its price above the price set by the market, the firm will lose some of its customers.

a) True
b) False

....

Q42: If a firm in an oligopoly market reduces its price, it could lead to a price war.

a) True
b) False

....

Q43: Monopolists can charge any price they like.

a) True
b) False

. . . .

Q44: Monopolists can fix both the price and the quantity they sell.

a) True
b) False

Unit 1 Topic 12

End of unit test

End of Unit 1 test   Go online

Q1: Explain what is meant by scarcity in Economics and explain why it is the basic economic problem.
(4 marks)

....

Q2: Using a production possibility curve, explain what is meant by opportunity cost and technical efficiency.
(6 marks)

....

Q3: Give *two* reasons why consumers buy more of a product when its price falls.
(4 marks)

....

Q4: Give *one* reason why consumers might buy more of a product when its price rises.
(2 marks)

....

Q5: Explain, using a formula, what is meant by price elasticity of demand.
(2 marks)

....

Q6: Explain the relationship between price elasticity of demand and total revenue.
(4 marks)

....

Q7: Define the terms marginal cost and average total cost.
(2 marks)

....

Q8: Draw a diagram to show the relationship between marginal cost and average total cost.
(3 marks)

....

Q9: Explain, using a diagram, what is meant by the market clearing price.
(4 marks)

....

Q10: Explain how an exceptionally good strawberry harvest will affect the price of fresh cream.
(3 marks)

....

Q11: "In the short run, as long as a firm is covering its variable costs, it will not shut down."
Explain the above statement.
(4 marks)

....

Q12: Describe *two* differences between a perfect market and a monopoly.
(2 marks)

Unit 2: Economic Activity

Unit 2 Topic 1

Government finance

Contents

Prerequisites

The topic builds on and expands the concepts of taxation and government spending studied at National 5 Economics. However, prior knowledge of these concepts, although useful, is not essential.

Learning objective

By the end of this topic you should be able to:

- list the main sources and types of government revenue;

- distinguish between direct and indirect taxation;

- explain what is meant by progressive and regressive taxation;

- describe the change in balance between direct and indirect taxation in the UK in recent years;

- describe the effects of changes in taxation on individuals and firms;

- identify the main types of government expenditure;

- justify the reasons for government expenditure;

- explain the role of the budget in the UK economy;

- explain the significance of a budget being balanced, in deficit and in surplus.

1.1   Reasons for taxation

The UK has a mixed economy. This means that alongside the 'private sector' of free enterprise, there is a government administered 'public sector'.

The public sector needs to be financed. This money comes from taxation, government borrowing and charges for some services.

The public sector is needed because:

* public goods would not exist, e.g. street lighting;

* merit goods would be under-provided, e.g. education;

* without government intervention and regulation, demerit goods, e.g. cigarettes, would be over-provided;

* some sections of society need assistance with the provision of basic needs;

* it provides a method of making income distribution fairer.

Adam Smith, the famous economist, set out four criteria for good taxation which he called the four canons of taxation:

* *Equity* - Taxes should be charged according the ability to pay.

* *Efficiency* - Taxes should be relatively inexpensive to collect.

* *Certainty* - The taxpayer should know how much tax he or she is to pay.

* *Convenience* - Taxes should be paid when suitable to the taxpayer.

1.2   Direct and indirect taxation

The vast majority of UK Government Revenue comes from taxation. There are two different types of taxation - direct and indirect.

Direct taxes are taxes on income and wealth. They are levied by the Inland Revenue.

The following are direct taxes levied in the UK:

* *Income Tax* - Tax on wages and salaries;

* *National Insurance (NI) contributions* - Contribution from wages and salaries;

* *Corporation Tax* - Tax on company profits;

* *Council Tax* - Tax paid depends on the value of domestic property owned;

* *Business rates* - Tax paid by companies on property owned;

* *Capital Gains Tax (CGT)* - Tax levied on the increase in value of assets owned, e.g. interest earned on money in the bank;

- **Inheritance Tax** - Tax levied on a deceased person's estate;

- **Stamp duties** - Tax levied on the change of ownership of houses and land.

Indirect taxes are taxes on spending usually paid indirectly to the seller but end up being collected by HM Revenue and Customs.

The following are indirect taxes levied in the UK:

- **Value Added Tax (VAT)** - Tax levied on a wide range of goods and services bought in the UK;

- **Customs duties** - Taxes on imports;

- **Excise duties** - Taxes on petrol, alcohol and tobacco;

- **Petroleum Revenue Tax (PRT)** - Tax on revenues of oil companies in UK;

- **Motor vehicle duties** - Tax paid to use motor vehicles on UK roads.

Other sources of income

In terms of other revenues apart from taxation, charges are made for some services. If you go to a council-owned swimming pool there may be an entry charge. Central government charges include prescription charges (not in Scotland) and police fines.

Sources of revenue

The following table shows the sources of UK government revenue in 2013 (in £ billion).

Type of revenue	Amount (in £bn)
Income Tax	155
Corporation Tax	39
VAT	103
Excise duties	47
Business rates	27
National Insurance	107
Council Tax	27
Other revenues	107
Borrowing	108
Total	**720**

UK government tax revenue (2013)
Source: The Guardian website - http://bit.ly/1x2XGlo

Government revenue Go online

Q1: Which three taxes were the greatest sources of revenue?

....

Q2: What percentage of government revenue in 2013 came from borrowing?

....

Q3: What percentage of government revenue in 2013 came from Income Tax and National Insurance combined?

....

Q4: What percentage of government revenue in 2013 came from VAT and excise duties combined?

....

Q5: Give two examples of other government revenue.

....

Q6: Why might the government need to borrow money?

1.3 Progressive and regressive taxation

A **progressive tax** tax is one which takes account of a person's ability to pay. A progressive tax takes a larger percentage of income as income rises. Most direct taxes in the UK are progressive.

A **regressive tax** takes no account of a person's ability to pay. Lower income earners pay a higher percentage of their income in tax, e.g. through VAT and excise duties, than higher income groups. Most indirect taxes are regressive. An extreme example of a regressive tax was the Community Charge, or "Poll Tax", introduced in the 1980s. This was a flat-rate per capita tax where a worker on a £10,000 yearly income paid exactly the same as a millionaire, so it was extremely regressive.

The example in the table below shows why vehicle licence duty is a regressive tax.

	Person 1	**Person 2**
Earnings	£100,000 per year	£20,000 per year
Cars owned	2	1
Tax to be paid	£200	£100
% of Income tax paid	0.2	0.5

Comparison of vehicle licence duty on people with different incomes

1.4   Effect of taxation on individuals and firms

There have been several significant changes to UK taxation in recent years. These changes have effects on individuals and firms.

Recent governments have started to restructure the balance of taxation away from direct to indirect. The tax bands were simplified and income tax rates were reduced especially at the top end of the salary scale. The top rate has been cut from 83% to 40% and the basic rate for all taxpayers cut from 33% to 20%. The share of income tax of all government revenue has fallen from 45% to 25%.

Cuts in taxes on business, e.g. lower corporation tax and business rates, have allowed firms to keep more of their profits and so encourage investment. This has also has the effect of encouraging inward foreign direct investment and stimulating economic growth.

Income tax has been recouped from the extension of VAT to cover more goods and services and excise duties on alcohol and tobacco have been increased by more than inflation. VAT was 8% in the 1970s, but is currently 20%. As direct taxes tend to be progressive, this shift has disadvantaged those on lower incomes.

Shift from direct to indirect taxation

The reasons why the UK Government has decided to cut taxes on business and shift from direct to indirect taxation are:

* *Cutting rates of income tax may increase tax revenues* - High rates of tax encourage high earners to avoid payment. They try to exploit the tax through loopholes. Lower rates may discourage this avoidance.

* *Incentives to earn are encouraged* - If people are able to keep more of what they earn this will encourage them to work harder and unemployed people would be encouraged to take employment. Both of these will increase tax revenues further and encourage economic growth.

* *People have more choice* - Consumers of all income levels can reduce their tax burden by choosing not to buy those products on which duty is charged, e.g. cigarettes and alcohol. This will lead to a healthier population and a cleaner environment.

Some economists criticise this policy because:

* *Tax revenues may not increase* - Higher take home pay may make people decide that they need not work as long. They may take more leisure time so there is no increase in tax revenues.

* *Higher demand in the economy may lead to inflation* - Higher take-home pay may lead to spending rising faster than output and so prices will creep upwards. Higher price tickets because of VAT and other tax increases will also cause inflation.

* *The distribution of income and wealth will be more uneven* - Income tax is progressive and so cuts will favour most those on higher incomes. Indirect taxes are regressive and so increases will increase the burden on lower income groups.

Effect of taxation on individuals and firms Go online

Q7: Has the UK tax structure become more progressive or regressive in recent years? Justify your answer.

....

Q8: The UK Government's only source of revenue is tax.

a) True
b) False

....

Q9: The rate of income tax has fallen in recent years.

a) True
b) False

....

Q10: VAT is a progressive tax.

a) True
b) False

....

Q11: The UK tax system in more regressive than 20 years ago.

a) True
b) False

....

Q12: Direct taxes are taxes on income and wealth.

a) True
b) False

1.5 Reasons for government spending

In order for the UK government to play its role in the UK economy it must spend money. This is known as public spending and is the money spent by central and local government.

There are three types of public spending:

1. **Capital spending** - This is spending on capital, e.g. buildings, machinery and infrastructure.
2. **Current spending** - This covers day to day running costs of central and local government, e.g. teachers' wages, repairs and medicines.
3. ***Transfer payments*** - These are payments to individuals or firms for which there is no

economic benefit given in return, e.g. pensions, Jobseeker's Allowance and Child Benefit. It is money transferred from earners to non-earners.

The vast majority of UK Government spending is on public and merit goods.

Public goods are those goods which benefit everyone in society, e.g. defence and law and order. Non-payers cannot be excluded from the benefits of public goods. This makes it impossible to make a profit from their provision. The private sector cannot provide it via the price mechanism. The government provides public goods and raises the required money through taxation.

Merit goods are those goods which would be under-consumed if left to the private sector to produce. The price of private provision would be too high for many so some of the population could not afford them or would not spend the money on them. The UK economy benefits from a well-educated and healthy population. Therefore the government provides these services. State education and the National Health Service are examples of the government funding merit goods.

Public and merit goods   Go online

Q13: For each expenditure given, decide if it is classed as **public** or **merit** goods:

a) dustbin collections;

b) a lighthouse;

c) a new council house scheme;

d) traffic lights;

e) a state pension;

f) an aircraft carrier.

Government spending   Go online

Q14: The main areas of government spending in 2013 are shown in the table below. All figures are in £billion. Allocate the following missing numbers correctly:

- 220
- 137
- 97
- 51
- 40

Area of government spending	Amount (in £bn)
Defence	
Education	
Transport	21
Public Order and Safety	31
Health	
Industry, Agriculture and Employment	16
Housing and Environment	23
Debt Interest	
Personal Social Services	31
Social Protection	
Other	53

In the following questions, decide which area, or areas, of UK government spending would be affected. The answers include an explanation in each case.

The areas of government spending to choose from are:

- education;
- health;
- defence;
- law and order;
- social protection.

Q15: An increase in the rate of unemployment in the UK.

....

Q16: The UK becomes an ageing population.

....

Q17: Plans to increase terrorism in the UK are uncovered by MI5.

....

Q18: More and more parents are sending their children into private education.

....

Q19: Government announces large pay rises for policemen and women.

1.6 Budget deficits and surpluses

There is an obvious link between government revenue and spending. The UK government must plan what it wants to spend and how it is going to raise the revenue to finance this expenditure.

This plan is usually done once a year and is presented to the UK Parliament as **the Budget**.

There are *three* types of budget (see the following table).

Balanced budget This is a budget when planned government revenue will be equal to planned government spending.	
Surplus budget This is a budget when planned government revenue will be greater than planned government spending.	
Deficit budget This is a budget when planned government revenue will be less than planned government spending.	

A budget deficit will boost the circular flow of income (discussed in Topic 5 of this unit), generate economic growth and reduce unemployment. A budget surplus will slow down inflation by reducing demand in the economy. The multiplier effect (discussed in Topic 5 of this unit) will further enhance the initial action of government.

If spending of government is greater than revenue then it must borrow. This called the **Public Sector Net Cash Requirement (PSNCR)** and is necessary if there is a deficit budget. It is financed by selling bonds, bills and securities to financial institutions. If the government is running a surplus budget the PSNCR may be negative and the government is able to repay some of its debt.

The *National Debt* is the total amount of accumulated debt of the government. If there is a deficit budget and a PSNCR then National Debt will increase.

Public Sector Net Cash Requirement (PSNCR)   Go online

Q20: Complete the table by entering the correct figures.

Government Revenue (in £bn)	Government Spending (in £bn)	PSNCR (in £bn)
10	12	2
15	14	
20	20	
	40	5
13		-3
	60	-12

1.7   Summary

Summary

You should now know that:

- the main sources of government revenue are direct taxes, indirect taxes, charges for some services, and borrowing;
- direct taxes are on income and wealth;
- indirect taxes are on consumption and are paid initially to the seller who returns them to government;
- progressive taxes require that those on high incomes pay a higher percentage of their income in tax;
- regressive taxes require that those on low incomes pay a higher percentage of their income in tax;
- there has been a movement away from direct taxes towards the raising of more from indirect taxes, which tend to be regressive, and this shift has disadvantaged those on lower incomes;
- taxation affects the ability of an individual to purchase goods and services, and may act as a disincentive to work;
- firms will see tax as an added cost, which may reduce sales when passed on to the consumer in higher prices;
- the three largest areas for government spending are:
  - social protection;
  - health;
  - education;
- government spending is used to:
  - provide public goods;
  - make up for the under-provision of merit goods by the market economy;
  - provide basic needs for those in poverty;
- the budget is used to achieve government aims;
- the three types of budget are:
  - balanced budget, when planned government revenue will be equal to planned government spending;
  - surplus budget, when planned government revenue will be greater than planned government spending;
  - deficit budget, when planned government revenue will be less than planned government spending.

1.8   End of topic test

End of Topic 1 test   Go online

Q21: When income tax has several rates, e.g. 20%, 30%, 40%, 50%, increasing as income levels rise, then this tax could be described as:

a) direct and progressive.
b) direct and regressive.
c) indirect and progressive.
d) indirect and regressive.

....

Q22: One example of current spending by government would be:

a) widening a motorway.
b) reducing VAT rates.
c) paying teachers' salaries.
d) building a bridge.

....

Q23: One example of a transfer payment would be:

a) doctors' salaries.
b) old age pensions.
c) payments made to firms building a hospital.
d) income tax refunds.

....

Q24: A budget deficit occurs when:

a) exports exceed imports.
b) imports exceed exports.
c) government revenue exceeds government spending.
d) government spending exceeds government revenue.

....

Q25: Taxes can be used to:

a) raise revenue.
b) discourage consumption of a demerit good.
c) both of the above.
d) neither of the above.

....

Q26: Look at the table below showing UK government tax revenue data (*source: The Guardian website*).

Type of revenue	Amount (in £bn)
Income Tax	155
Corporation Tax	39
VAT	103
Excise duties	47
Business rates	27
National Insurance	107
Council Tax	27
Other revenues	107
Borrowing	108
Total	**720**

Which of these taxes satisfy Adam Smith's four criteria?

Unit 2 Topic 2

Government aims - inflation

Contents

Prerequisites

The topic builds on and expands the concept of inflation studied at National 5 Economics. However, prior knowledge of this concept, although useful, is not essential.

Learning objective

By the end of this topic you should be able to:

- describe the main economic aims of government;
- define inflation;
- explain how the rate of inflation is measured;
- list and describe the factors which can cause inflation;
- explain the difference between real and money terms;
- explain the effects of inflation on individuals, firms, government and the economy;
- describe recent trends in inflation and the reasons for these trends.

2.1 Prior knowledge

Test your prior knowledge   Go online

Q1: What is meant by "the cost of living"?

....

Q2: How do you measure standard of living?

2.2 Government macroeconomic objectives

Macroeconomic objectives are concerned with the performance of the economy as a whole.

The UK Government has four macroeconomic objectives:

1. *A low and stable rate of inflation* - Inflation is defined as a period of generally rising prices. It can also be described as a period when the value (or purchasing power) of money falls.

   The UK Government has a target for inflation of 2% per annum (CPI). The Bank of England's Monetary Policy Committee meets monthly to adjust interest rates to try and ensure this target is met.

   For governments of all political complexions, the aim of keeping these increases to a minimum is seen as a main economic objective.

2. *A high level of employment* - There used to be a simple definition of full employment as 2-3% unemployment. However this used a "claimant count" approach to measurement. If the "labour force survey" measurement method was applied then a higher percentage would represent full employment. It may be easier to describe it as a situation where the number of unemployed is equal to the number of vacancies.

   The UK Government sometimes describes the aim as a high level of employment.

3. *A sustainable rate of economic growth* - Governments aim to achieve steady and sustained levels of non-inflationary growth. Economic growth is normally achieved by annual increases in real national income. It simply means an increase in the annual output of goods and services in an economy.

   Any increase in real national income must also be divided by the population to calculate whether people have a higher standard of living. However, for the average citizen to be "better off", the distribution of this increased national income must not be skewed towards the wealthy owners of capital.

   When economic growth results in an increase in real national income per capita, then standards of living are rising.

4. *A balance in trade over the long term* - Trade is dealt with in Unit 3 of this course.

2.3 Inflation

Inflation is defined as a period of generally rising prices. It does not mean that all prices are rising and some may be actually falling.

The **rate of inflation** is the percentage increase in the general level of prices over a period of time (usually a year). The image below shows the percentage change in the rate of inflation in the UK between 2000 and 2014.

Percentage change in RPI and CPI in the UK between 2000 and 2014
Source: BBC website - http://www.bbc.co.uk/news/10612209

It is the job of the Government to measure inflation and it does this by measuring price changes in different groups of goods and services and then publishes a number of price indices:

- Retail Price Index (RPI);

- RPIX - RPI without mortgage interest payments;

- Consumer Price Index (CPI) - RPI without housing costs and Council Tax.

Changes in the price of a basket of about 600 goods are taken to represent the average inflation rate, because the items in the basket are typical of the items purchased by the average consumer. These goods do not all have equal weighting in the inflation calculation. The price of electricity will have a much heavier influence than the price of hamsters! (Yes, hamsters were in the index to represent spending on small pets.)

It must be noted that a fall in the rate of inflation does not mean a fall in prices. It means that prices are still rising but by a smaller percentage (at a lower rate). This can be confusing when questions show a graph with a falling line. As long as the line is above 0%, price rises are still taking place.

Price of leather   Go online

Q3: Why would the price of leather put up the price of leather suites?

2.4   The harmful effects of inflation

Effect on the individual

Some of the harmful effects of inflation on the individual are:

- Workers can lose their jobs if inflation in the UK makes goods and services produced here more expensive compared to other countries. Demand for these goods would fall, so less workers would be required to make them.

- Inflation reduces the real income of those whose incomes are fixed or which do not rise as fast as the rate of inflation. Their standard of living falls. This can include those on state pensions, unemployment benefit or members of trade unions with little collective bargaining power.

- It reduces the value of money. More money is necessary to buy the same amount of goods and services.

- It reduces the real value of interest rates. If inflation is 4% and interest rates 5% then savings are only earning 1% in real terms. The real interest rate is 1%. This may discourage savers but encourage borrowing as in real terms the cost of borrowing is decreased.

Effect on firms in the UK

Some of the harmful effects of inflation on firms in the UK are:

- UK firms will be less competitive with foreign competition both here and abroad which can lead to falling sales and profits which, in turn, can reduce investment.

- Firms' costs of production rise, e.g. raw materials, so firms are less profitable.

- Higher prices of products may result in a fall in sales which make firms less profitable.

- It increases uncertainty about future costs and prices. Firms may cancel proposed expansion plans if they do not know what it is going to cost them.

Effect on the economy

Some of the harmful effects of inflation on the economy are:

- The balance of payments may deteriorate. Inflation makes our goods and services dearer and so less competitive. This will encourage UK consumers to buy more imports and our exports will be less price-competitive abroad.

- Fewer exports and more imports lead to rising unemployment, placing a bigger strain on public spending as more people require state benefits and fewer are contributing through income tax.

- As investment is discouraged, it can only have an adverse effect on economic growth in the UK. Firms won't replace plant or fund expansion of premises.

- Inflation can cause further inflation! Workers ask for wage increases to maintain their real income and firms pass this on as higher prices. This is called a wage-price spiral.

- The gap between rich and poor widens as those on **fixed incomes** face falls in their real incomes. Private pensions do not necessarily increase with inflation. It is also possible that benefits and state pensions will fall behind price rises.

2.5   The positive aspects of inflation

A general and persistent rise in prices, as we have seen, has many harmful effects on consumers, firms and the economy.

However, some Economists think that there are some positive aspects of inflation, such as:

- borrowers gain because **real interest rates** are lower;

- some firms will increase their income from sales as some consumers will not be put off by higher prices;

- the government will take in more tax revenue from higher prices, i.e. VAT, and higher wages, i.e. income tax.

2.6   The causes of inflation

Economists are divided on what are the main causes on inflation.

There are two main schools of thought: **Keynesianism** and **Monetarism**.

Keynesians believe that there are three possible causes of inflation:

1. **Demand pull inflation** - This occurs when prices rise because total spending in the economy (aggregate demand) is greater than the output of the economy at that time. Output cannot increase in the short term and this excess demand by consumers pulls prices upwards.

2. **Cost push inflation** - If costs of production increase faster than productivity then unit costs increase. Producers, in order to maintain profit levels, will pass this on to the consumer in the form of higher prices.

3. *Wage/price spiral* - Because of inflation, workers ask for wage increases to maintain their real income. This puts up the costs of production of the firm and so the firm puts up prices. Other workers then ask for wage rises and so costs rise again and prices rise further.

Monetarism is the belief that increases in the supply of money which are greater than output lead to increases in price levels.

This belief is based on the **quantity theory of money**, which is expressed in the equation *MV = PQ*.

M	represents the supply of money
V	represents the velocity of circulation, i.e. number of purchases made in a certain period
P	represents the price level
Q	represents the quantity of output per period, i.e. the amount of goods and services produced

Monetarists assume that velocity of circulation is stable, i.e. we make the same number of shopping trips each year. This means that price levels will rise if any increase in the money supply is not matched by the same increase in output.

If we have a supply of money of £10m and a velocity of 5, then at an output of £25m price levels must be 2. The equation values would be:

10 x 5 = **2** x 25

If the money supply had to rise to 15, the new equation values would be:

15 x 5 = **3** x 25

Price levels had to rise because of the rise in the money supply.

Prices/wages spiral   Go online

Q4:   What is a prices/wages spiral?

2.6.1   Money supply

The money supply is the supply of money available to an economy. In a modern economy money consists of:

- coins and notes in circulation;
- bank deposits.

British pound symbol
(image courtesy of http://efffective.com/)

Bank deposits are entries in bank accounts which are created when a customer deposits money or when a bank gives a loan. Bank deposits can be spent using Switch, direct debit and transfers between accounts.

There are two major causes of increases in the money supply:

1. ***Bank lending*** - Banks aim to maximise profits and lending is very profitable. Any loan a bank gives ends up in a bank account and increases the supply of money in an economy.

2. ***Government borrowing*** - Government spending is sometimes more than they take in from taxation and they have to borrow from banks. This also increases the supply of money in the economy.

In summary, monetarists believe that excessive bank lending is the main cause of inflation. They believe that demand-pull and cost-push inflation are both symptoms rather than causes of inflation since they are caused by excessive increases in the supply of money.

Demand-pull inflation, according to monetarists, results from excessive borrowing by consumers which increases the demand in the economy. Cost-push pressures lead to firms borrowing from banks and they pass on their borrowing costs in higher prices.

Money supply	Go online

Q5: What is meant by the supply of money in an economy?

2.7 The inflation record in the UK in recent years

During the last ten years (up to 2014, when this was written) inflation in the UK has remained relatively low and steady. It has remained between approximately 1.5% and 4%.

This has been regarded as an economic success when you consider that the UK had rates of 20% during the 1970s. Inflation continued to be a significant problem for the UK economy into the 1980s.

However, the low inflation experienced during the period of the coalition government has not lifted standards of living because wage increases have generally been lower than price increases. Whilst this has meant higher levels of employment, it has lead to a sizeable drop in standards of living for many in work for several years up to 2013.

There have been various reasons for this inflation record. Some of them are to do with government economic policies. These policies are outlined in this topic and will be explained fully later in Topic 3.

There are several reasons for the relatively low UK inflation in recent years:

- good fiscal prudence on the part of the UK Government with control of public spending and public sector pay awards;

- appropriate and careful use of interest rates to control aggregate demand where necessary;

- a strong pound keeping the price of imports low;

- strong competition from the "tiger economies" of South Eastern Asia making sure we keep our prices steady to remain competitive;

- a rise in labour productivity keeping costs low;

- relatively steady (and falling in 2015) world oil prices which keep costs of production in many industries steady too;

- the absence of any prices/wages spiral leading to realistic pay awards in both the public and private sectors;

- globalisation delivers cheaper clothing and manufactures mainly from Asia;

- trade unions find it harder to engage in successful industrial action on wages;

- business costs are reduced by increasing use of zero-hour and temporary contracts;

- raw material (commodity) prices have eased as world demand slowed following the banking crisis;

- since the banking crisis, low UK demand has held back inflation.

UK inflation figures

You should research the UK inflation figures for the last ten years online so that you have the most up-to-date information. The BBC website is a useful resource for tracking the latest inflation figures.

Inflation record   Go online

Q6:   Why has inflation remained low and steady in the UK in recent years?

2.8   Calculating a price index

The government uses a price index to calculate the average price increase in the goods and services bought by typical households in the UK. The seven steps in the calculation process are outlined below.

Step	Description
1	A starting point or base year is chosen from which price changes are measured. All items are given a base index of 100.
2	Spending patterns are used to identify a basket of goods and services bought by typical households in the UK. This is not a bag of shopping but includes things like electricity, garden furniture, travel, car insurance, as well as food and clothing.
3	Each item in the basket is **weighted** according the amount of spending on it. Why? What would have the bigger effect on a consumer's cost of living: • a big increase in the price of a packet of salt; or • a small increase in the price of a litre of petrol? The answer is a small increase in the price of petrol - because a bigger proportion of most families' income is spent on petrol.
4	The percentage change in the price of every item in the basket is calculated and expressed as an index of the **base year**. The example below shows the change in price of a pint of milk. <table><tr><td colspan="2">Year 1 (base year)</td><td colspan="2">Year 2</td></tr><tr><td>Price</td><td>Index</td><td>Price</td><td>Index</td></tr><tr><td>40p</td><td>100</td><td>44p</td><td>110</td></tr></table> The change is 4p. The original price was 40p. 4/40 x 100 = 10% There was a 10% increase in the price of milk, so 10 is added to the base year index giving the new index for milk in Year 2 as 110.
5	The new price index would be multiplied by its weight.
6	This procedure would be repeated for each item in the basket.
7	The weighted indices are totalled and divided by the the total weights. We then deduct the base year value of 100. The result is the average change in the cost of living, i.e. the rate of inflation.

2.8.1 Calculating a price index - example

Step 1

We have decided our base year to be Year 1. We shall assume a small basket rather than the 460 items included in the RPI but the procedure is identical.

Step 2

Price index weight	Go online

Q7:   Arrange these five items bought in a typical household in order of weight on the price index (1 being highest, 5 lowest):

1. Clothing;
2. Food;
3. Gardening products;
4. Hair products;
5. Newspapers.

Step 3

Each item is thus given an appropriate weight:

Food	50
Clothing	30
Hair products	10
Newspapers	7
Gardening products	3

Step 4

Percentage change	Go online

Q8:   Calculate the percentage change in price for each item in the sample. Express your answer as an index of the base year.

	Year 1 (base)		Year 2	
	Price	Index	Price	Index
Food	£120	100	£132	----
Clothing	£50	100	£51	----
Hair products	£20	100	£25	----
Newspapers	£10	100	£10	----
Gardening products	£5	100	£4	----

Steps 5 and 6

We multiply the new index by its weight for all the samples.

	Index weight	Weighted index
Food	110 x 50	5500
Clothing	102 x 30	3060
Hair products	125 x 10	1250
Newspapers	100 x 7	700
Gardening products	80 x 3	240

Step 7

Total all the weighted indices to get 10750. Divide this by the total weights of 100 to get 107.5 (the figure comes in very useful later in the topic). Deduct the base year value of 100 and get an accurate rate of inflation of *7.5%* even though gardening products fell in price.

2.9   The Consumer Price Index (CPI)

The government's preferred measure of inflation is the Consumer Price Index (CPI). It also maintains the calculation of the retail price indexes as these have a longer history and allow historic comparisons.

The CPI is closer to the method used in other EU countries and so makes comparison of inflation rates more meaningful. This is the same as the RPIX but with all housing costs removed, e.g. council tax.

Selection of goods for CPI

You could research the current selection of goods. It is updated every year to reflect gradual changes in spending patterns.

Once a year there are newspaper articles describing the changes made to the consumer price index. Leg waxing made it into the basket a few years ago.

Newspaper article　　　　　　　　　　　　　　　　Go online

Read the newspaper article on inflation then answer the questions which follow.

"MORTGAGE RISES SEND INFLATION TO A NEW HIGH

The rising cost of living was confirmed by official figures yesterday showing that household inflation is soaring. The Retail Price Index (RPI) rose to 4.1 per cent last month from 3.8 per cent in July, the office of National Statistics said. Experts fear that rising oil prices in the United States could push up inflation even further.

The ONS said that the RPI rise was largely as a result of mortgage lenders passing on the July quarter-point increase in interest rates to borrowers. High food costs were another factor. People on fixed incomes are expected to see real incomes fall."

Q9: Why would dearer mortgages and food have such a significant impact on inflation?
....

Q10: Apart from the RPI name *two* other methods used to calculate inflation.
....

Q11: How do they differ from the RPI?
....

Q12: What groups in society are likely to be on fixed incomes?
....

Q13: Why could rising oil prices in the US put up inflation in the UK?

2.10　Real and nominal values

The following words in quotes are examples of statements on government spending that you might hear from two political parties.

1. "We are spending £10 billion per year on the health service. That's more than you did."

2. "That's not correct. You are spending less than we did five years ago."

It is impossible to say which statement is correct. More money might be being spent, i.e. nominal spending is higher, but if prices are higher then fewer beds and medicines might be being bought, i.e. *real* spending is lower. We need to know what has happened to prices during that time.

We must convert money values to **real values** to adjust figures to take account of inflation. Using the previous example, in *2.8 Calculating a price index*, let us assume the previous government spent £8 billion on the health service per year but prices rose by 25% over the five year period they were out of power.

More money is being spent in nominal terms but what about real spending? See the formula used below.

$$\text{Money value} \quad \times \quad \frac{\text{Base year index}}{\text{Current year index}}$$

$$\text{£10 bn} \quad \times \quad \frac{100}{125}$$

$$= \quad \text{£8 bn}$$

In real terms spending on the NHS had neither gone up or down. It had stayed the same. The same amount of products and labour had been purchased for the health service.

Government spending statements   Go online

Q14: Prices went up this year so I must be worse off in real terms.

a) True
b) False

....

Q15: My wages went up this year so I must be better off in money terms.

a) True
b) False

....

Q16: If prices go up faster than my wages I am worse off in real terms.

a) True
b) False

....

Q17: A wage increase must be at least in line with inflation to maintain real income.

a) True
b) False

2.11   Summary exercise

Inflation - summary   Go online

Q18: Complete the following sentences by selecting a word from the list below:

- more;
- less;
- the inflation rate;
- reducing;
- real;
- fixed;
- variable;
- nominal.

1. Inflation has the effect of _____ the purchasing power of money.
2. Real interest rates are _____ interest rates less _____ .
3. Inflation in the UK makes our exports _____ price competitive.
4. People on _____ incomes face a drop in _____ income because of inflation.
5. Inflation in the UK makes our imports _____ price competitive.

2.12   Summary

Summary

You should now know:

- inflation is a general and persistent increase in prices;
- inflation is measured using the Consumer Price Index;
- there are factors that cause inflation;
- there are effects of inflation on individuals, firms and the economy;
- current trends for inflation in the UK.

2.13   End of topic test

End of Topic 2 test   Go online

Q19: What is the UK target for inflation (CPI)?

a) 0%
b) 1%
c) 2%
d) 3%

....

Q20: CPI stands for Consumer Price .... ?

a) Inflation
b) Investment
c) Interest
d) Index

....

Q21: If the rate of inflation is falling can you be certain that:

a) prices on average are falling.
b) prices on average are rising more slowly.
c) Both of the above.
d) None of the above.

....

Q22: Inflation is generally seen as good news for:

a) borrowers.
b) savers.
c) exporters.
d) pensioners.

....

Q23: Which of the following add to cost push inflation?

a) Pay rises that are less than productivity gains.
b) Reductions in income tax.
c) Pay rises that are greater than productivity gains.
d) Increases in income tax.

....

Q24: Explain how inflation is measured.

(4 marks)

....

Q25: Why has UK inflation been fairly low in recent years?

(4 marks)

Unit 2 Topic 3

Government aims - unemployment

Contents

Prerequisites

The topic builds on and expands the concepts of unemployment and economic growth studied at National 5 Economics. However, prior knowledge of these concepts, although useful, is not essential.

Learning objective

By the end of this topic you should be able to:

- define unemployment in terms of unused resources;

- describe how unemployment is measured;

- list and explain the types and causes of unemployment;

- explain the effects of unemployment on individuals, firms, government and the economy;

- describe and explain recent trends in unemployment;

- define economic growth and explain how output can be increased;

- explain the meaning of standard of living.

3.1   Definition of unemployment

Economists define **unemployment** as "the under- or non-use of a factor of production". In this topic we will learn about the unemployment of one factor of production - labour. Losing a job can be the most distressing economic events in a person's lifetime.

Definition of unemployment   Go online

Q1:   What is an economic resource?

....

Q2:   Name the four factors of production.

3.2   Measurement of unemployment

Not everyone without a job is unemployed. An unemployed person is anyone who is able, available and willing to work but cannot find a job.

The **working population** of a country is all those self employed, in work, able to and seeking work. The unemployed are included in the working population.

The **dependent population** includes all those *not* in the working population.

Groups in society   Go online

Q3:   Decide whether these groups in society are part of the working or dependent population. Put the each group in the correct column - either 'Working population' or 'Dependent population':

1. student;
2. soldier;
3. child under school age;
4. bank employee;
5. househusband / housewife;
6. unemployed job seeker;
7. café owner;
8. pensioner.

Working population	Dependent population

3.2.1 The rate of unemployment

Another method of expressing unemployment is to calculate what proportion of the working population is out of work, the **rate of unemployment**.

The formula to do this is:

$$\frac{\text{Total number unemployed}}{\text{Total working population}} \times 100$$

If one million people were unemployed and the total working population was 25 million, for example, this would equate to:

$$\frac{1,000,000}{25,000,000} \times 100 = 4\%$$

Four percent, or four out of every hundred workers in the country, would be unemployed. This figure would also be seasonally adjusted.

Rate of unemployment   Go online

Calculate the percentage out of work in the following situations.

Q4: Working population: 22 million; total out of work: 1.1 million

....

Q5: Working population: 200 million; total out of work: 5 million

....

Q6: Working population: 60 million; total out of work: 4 million (give your answer to two decimal places)

....

Q7: Working population: 100 million; total out of work: 15 million

....

> **Q8:**   Working population: 3 million; total out of work: 300 thousand

3.2.2   Unemployment figures

Unemployment figures in the UK are taken from the **Labour Force Survey** and the **Claimant Count**.

The Labour Force Survey questions a large sample of households and uses this sample to work out the level of unemployment in the UK as a whole. It is quarterly, i.e. the figures are produced every three months.

The Labour Force Survey asks questions which seek to establish whether individuals without jobs are actively seeking work at present. It allows comparisons with other countries, such as European Union member states, because they also use this method. It gives a substantially higher figure for unemployment than the Claimant Count method (see below).

Many people who seek work do not register for Job Seekers Allowance. Claiming benefit might involve being sent to jobs that they would not consider. They may need a job that fits around childcare needs and they may be in a position where the benefit is not essential to them. For example a spouse may be working in the household.

The Claimant Count obtains the readily available figures for those claiming Job Seekers Allowance. The graph below shows the claimant count from 1971 to the present day.

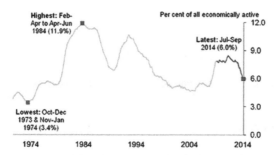

Claimant Count from January 1971 to October 2014, seasonally adjusted
(Source: Office for National Statistics website - http://bit.ly/1sYckNh)

The Claimant Count excludes those who are not claiming benefit, yet would take a job that suited them. The figures are available monthly. The Claimant Count measurement gives a much lower total than the Labour Force Survey.

3.3   Causes of unemployment

There are many complicated and varied reasons why people lose their jobs; the main reasons are outlined below.

Cyclical, general or mass unemployment is associated with a general and significant fall in aggregate demand in an economy. The demand for labour is derived from the demand for what that labour produces. A fall in demand means that less employees and needed to satisfy this demand and firms respond by reducing their labour force.

Market economies driven by the profit motive are inclined to over-exuberance in periods of growth. The psychology of high profits for business, and consumer confidence, drives forward excessive demand. This causes an overheating, inflationary economy - an unsustainable boom with full employment supply unable to keep up with burgeoning demand.

As governments seek to restrain the inflationary boom by raising interest rates, the economy slows and may even go into recession. These business cycles are typical, although Gordon Brown (former Chancellor of the Exchequer) did rashly claim that Britain would "never return to the old boom and bust" (Budget statement, 21 March 2007 - http://bit.ly/1BzJ44H).

Cyclical unemployment will affect many industries and sectors in an economy and is the most difficult type of unemployment to reduce.

Structural unemployment is associated with a long-term decline in demand in a particular industry. For example a fall in demand for UK ships will mean unemployment in the UK shipbuilding industry.

There are two main reasons for structural unemployment:

* New technology and more modern plant and machinery may mean that fewer workers will be required to produce the products. This is sometimes referred to as **technological unemployment**.

* Falling demand in an industry because they are no longer required or consumers prefer the products of another country. The produce of other countries may be more price competitive or produced to a higher standard.

Frictional unemployment is associated with barriers that prevent the unemployed smoothly filling available vacancies. An example of frictional unemployment would be the time it takes for a school leaver to match up with an appropriate job vacancy. This may be caused by:

* a lack of knowledge about job opportunities;

* disincentives to work, i.e. welfare benefits that discourage seeking employment or a tax system that does not reward employment sufficiently enough.

Seasonal unemployment is associated with industries where demand for labour changes at certain times of the year. Industries most affected are agriculture, tourism, retailing and construction.

Causes of unemployment   Go online

Q9: What type of unemployment usually affects only one industry?

....

Q10: What type of unemployment is the most serious?

....

Q11: Geographical immobility of labour prevents workers from moving from one .... to another.

....

Q12: If you were replaced by a computer at work this would be an example of what type of unemployment?

....

Q13: A lack of skill to fill a particular vacancy is an example of what type of immobility of labour?

3.4   Effects of rising unemployment

The table below shows the negative and positive effects of rising unemployment on the individual, on business and on the economy and government.

	Negative	Positive
Effects on the individual	• Reduced income • Reliance on state benefits • Debt accruing due to major commitments, e.g. mortgage, loans • Loss of relevant skills and motivation to work • Reduced status in community and social exclusion due to low income • Increased stress leading to health and relationship problems	
Effects on business	• Fall in demand for goods and services • Fall in revenue • Fall in profits • Possible reduction in labour force	• Bigger supply of available labour • Less pressure to pay higher wages • Less risk of industrial action
Effects on the economy and government	• Loss of output and falling GDP • Unemployment causing reduced demand leading to more unemployment • Less money taken in income tax, VAT and corporation tax • More government spending on benefits and training courses • Less money available for education and other public services • Increased crime and civil disorder more likely	

In terms of effects on the individual, a person losing their job will face several problems because they are no longer contributing their labour to society and being rewarded for that.

In terms of effects on business, as well as the negative effects, there can be some positive, short-term effects.

In terms of the effects on the economy and government, rising unemployment has both economic and social effects. The economic effect is that resources will be required to reduce these effects, e.g. more police required, while social effects include increased crime and the increased likelihood of civil disorder. During the latest recession there has been no link to increased crime rates and crime has been falling, so the evidence on this link is historic and rather inconclusive.

Effects of rising unemployment   Go online

Q14: How does rising unemployment affect government finances?

3.5   Trends in unemployment

The latest data for unemployment trends is available from the ONS (Office for National Statistics) website. However a much more accessible source is the BBC website which can be easily searched for the economy tracker. This will give you the up-to-date figures and trends.

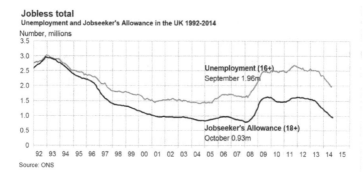

Unemployment and Jobseeker's Allowance in the UK from 1992 to 2014
(Source: BBC website - http://www.bbc.co.uk/news/10604117 (based on ONS figures))

The reasons for the fall and increase in unemployment are outlined next.

3.5.1   Reasons for the fall in unemployment

The trend from 1993 was the result of an unbroken period of economic growth. Gordon Brown (Chancellor of the Exchequer from 1997 to 2007) announced the "end of boom and bust" but, alas, this did not turn out to be correct. This decade of economic growth was achieved without the inflationary concerns that had previously dogged an expanding UK economy. As a result, interest rates did not have to be increased to slow down demand.

Unemployment fell due to low inflation and economic growth

Growth (reducing unemployment) with low inflation was achieved because:

- this was a period when manufacturing moved to low wage economies with a reduction in the costs of production. An example of this was cheaper clothing from Asia (as featured by the brand Primark, among others). The UK focused more on expanding service industries;

- the influence of trade unions in pushing for higher wages had been greatly reduced by the laws, introduced in the 1980s, limiting their power in industrial disputes. This held back wage-cost inflation as did competition from low wage economies abroad;

- membership of trade unions fell substantially and the negotiating position of many workers became weak. An example of the outcome of this weak position is zero-hour contracts;

- globalisation delivered new synergies from the rapid expansion of international trade and the ensuing cost reductions and productivity gains;

- increased entrepreneurial activity, the encouragement of start-up businesses, increased willingness of banks to lend and possibly led to the privatisation of state-run companies;

- of changes to the tax system to incentivise work and enterprise;

- of increased public spending on health and education. The government's initiative to build schools and hospitals in partnership with the private sector, e.g. the private finance initiative (PFI), meant that the demand for labour increased (with a multiplier effect through the economy);

- rising living standards and property prices creating a "feel good" factor and consumer confidence grew. Homeowners were becoming wealthier and were confident to spend their income seeing their house as a good investment;

- credit was easily obtained to re-fuel demand.

However, the pressures on employment did not go away in the UK and economists point to reasons of:

- strong competition from overseas producers, e.g. China and India. Firms in the UK could not match the prices of other countries and so lost orders and markets and had to reduce labour forces as a result;

- continued development in technology. Firms continued to innovate and find labour-saving methods of production which reduce the competitiveness of labour;

- the strong pound. This made British exports abroad more expensive and foreign imports cheaper here reducing output and the demand for labour;

- rising world oil prices. This raised costs of production so firms cut back on output and so require less labour.

Measures taken to increase employment   Go online

Q15: Suggest three measures taken by the government to increase employment.

3.5.2   Reasons for the increase in unemployment

Recklessly, banks were expanding rapidly and now allowing credit to those who were most likely to default. A culture of bonuses and commission for bank employees encouraged this reckless behaviour. So-called 'NINJA' loans to those with **no** income, **no** job, and **no** assets were allowing poorer Americans to buy property in the housing boom. This unsustainable bubble in property values was about to burst.

Unemployment increased due to the effects of unrecoverable debts

As more and more mortgages were defaulted on, the unrecoverable debts increased. What started in the USA quickly spread as the risky loans had been packaged together and sold on to other multi-national banks. Eventually "as the penny dropped", banks were declining to lend to each other for fear that the other banks themselves were about to collapse. This was the "credit crunch". Banks relied on other banks for cash to support the smooth operation of the banking system. In the UK, Northern Rock was the first bank to be refused working capital by the markets and it run out of funds. Reports suggested that the cash terminals of major banks were hours from drying up, when the government (taxpayer) stepped in to assume the liabilities and nationalise several major banks.

Recession followed and it was a long drawn-out recession in the UK. Unemployment rose because:

- consumers in Europe and the USA were also in recession which reduced exports;
- many workers accepted pay cuts rather than lose their jobs, but this reduced demand;
- public sector pay was frozen, resulting in falls in real incomes and reduced demand;
- public sector workforces were reduced to reduce public spending;
- credit was much harder to obtain and the number of mortgages granted fell;
- the construction sector was reduced and it is labour-intensive;
- consumer confidence fell as asset values (house prices) tumbled;
- reverse multiplier effects followed on, with further falls in demand;

- government policy focused on reducing borrowing as the main aim, thus taking more money out of the circular flow and further slowing any recovery.

Trends in unemployment   Go online

Decide if the following statements are True or False.

Q16: Rising interest rates are likely to result in job losses.

a) True
b) False

....

Q17: Rising property prices can create a "feel good" factor.

a) True
b) False

....

Q18: Higher real incomes are likely to create jobs in an economy.

a) True
b) False

....

Q19: A weaker pound could create more job vacancies in the UK.

a) True
b) False

....

Q20: Students in full time education are included in the working population.

a) True
b) False

3.6 Economic growth

Economic growth is defined as an increase in real national income. That means national income will have increased after the price rises due to inflation have been factored out of the figure. It can also be described as an increase in the output of goods and services by the UK economy. National income is dealt with in CfE Higher Economics Unit 2 Topic 5.

Economic growth

Rising national income per head makes it probable that standards of living will improve. Crucially this depends on how the gain is distributed throughout the population, and on the balance of political power between the owners of capital and those who supply their labour. An improving standard of living is just an accounting style calculation, and it says relatively little about the wider quality of life in a community. Economists have recently sought to measure "happiness" as improving standards of living in the prosperous West have not resulted in a happier population.

The production possibility frontier (the limit to output) can be moved outwards in the future by:

- new technology and the efficiencies it brings;
- net immigration (although the increase in output will now be shared among a greater population);
- the discovery of new resources.

Standards of living   Go online

Q21: To effectively measure changes in "standards of living" the calculation will need to include:

    1. price levels;

    2. population;

    3. income distribution.

a) 1 and 2 only
b) 2 and 3 only
c) 1 and 3 only
d) 1, 2 and 3

3.7   Summary

Summary

At the end of this topic you should know:

- how unemployment is defined and measured; the causes and types of unemployment;
- the effects of unemployment on individuals, firms and the economy;
- current trends for unemployment in the UK;
- the definition of economic growth and its impact on standards of living;
- the means of increasing output.

3.8   End of topic test

End of Topic 3 test   Go online

Q22: Cyclical unemployment is an outcome of:

a) recession.
b) imports.
c) exports.
d) technology.

....

Q23: The working population includes:

a) the employed and self-employed.
b) the unemployed.
c) both of the above.
d) neither of the above.

....

Q24: The rate of unemployment as measured by the "labour force survey" indicates:

a) the number of people registered for Jobseeker's Allowance.
b) the percentage of the total population (registered or unregistered) that are seeking work.
c) the number of people (registered or unregistered) who are unemployed.
d) the percentage of the working population (registered or unregistered) who are unemployed.

....

Q25: Real national income per head is an effective measure of:

a) average standards of living.
b) levels of poverty.
c) levels of happiness.
d) average money incomes.

....

Q26: Which of the following will reduce UK unemployment?

a) A strong pound.
b) Rapid technological progress.
c) Low wages overseas.
d) Increases in consumer spending.

....

Q27: Describe how unemployment can affect an individual.

(4 marks)

....

Q28: Describe what is meant by sustainable economic growth.

(4 marks)

. . . .

Q29: What is not measured by the standard of living, but may affect your quality of life?

(4 marks)

Unit 2 Topic 4

Government policy

Contents

Prerequisites

The topic builds on and expands on the aspects of government policy studied in National 5 Economics. However, prior knowledge of these concepts, although useful, is not essential.

Learning objective

By the end of this topic you should be able to:

- explain fiscal policy and how it is used to reach government objectives;

- explain monetary policy and how it is used to reach government objectives;

- explain the role of supply-side polices;

- explain the difficulties in achieving all the government aims at the same time.

4.1   Introduction

We shall be looking at three important branches of government policy. These are:

- fiscal policy;
- monetary policy;
- supply-side policy.

The government uses these policies to influence the nation's economy towards their main economic aims which are:

- an inflation rate target of 2% (CPI);
- a high level of employment;
- a sustainable rate of economic growth;
- a balanced trade position.

Test your prior knowledge   Go online

Q1: Explain the term 'public spending'.

....

Q2: How is public spending financed?

4.2   Fiscal policy

Fiscal policy is the government using changes in public spending and/or taxation to alter the level of aggregate demand in order to influence the performance of the economy.

Any policy which increases aggregate demand is called *expansionary* and any one that reduces it is called *contractionary*.

Chancellor of the Exchequer's Budget Box
(Gladstone's Red Box (http://bit.ly/1xUmnlv) from The National Archives (http://bit.ly/11BEU xt), via Wikimedia Commons)

The fiscal policy for the financial year is set out in the Budget. Fiscal policy is sometimes called budgetary policy. The Chancellor of the Exchequer uses fiscal policy to achieve its macroeconomic targets of low inflation, low unemployment, economic growth and a balanced international trade position.

4.2.1   Fiscal policy and macroeconomic objectives

The government's macroeconomic objectives in terms of fiscal policy are:

1. *An inflation rate target of 2% (CPI).*

    If inflation is rising caused by aggregate demand being too high then the government could lower aggregate demand by:

    - Cutting its capital and current spending which has the effect of decreasing aggregate demand;
    - Increasing taxation which will cut consumer spending and investment and also lower aggregate demand, easing inflationary pressures in the economy.

2. *A high level of employment.*

    If there is high unemployment caused by low aggregate demand then the government could increase demand by:

    - Spending more, e.g. capital spending on new hospitals and roads, or current spending, e.g. employing more nurses and teachers. These measures would inject extra spending into the economy and would raise aggregate demand;
    - Reducing taxation, e.g. reducing corporation tax. This allows firms to keep more of their profits which they could use for investment. This would stimulate aggregate demand. They could reduce income tax, allowing individuals more of their income to spend, which would also increase aggregate demand.

3. *A sustainable rate of economic growth.*

    Policies to stimulate economic growth are broadly those which lower unemployment. In both cases, rising output is required. This can be achieved by stimulating demand, or by lowering costs on the supply side.

    The government can stimulate the output of goods and services in the economy by increasing aggregate demand by:

    - Spending government money on capital investment in the economy, e.g. high speed rail;
    - Tax cuts, to encourage consumers, which in turn leads to producers making more goods.
    - Incentives to business to research and innovate and invest more.

4. *A balanced trade position.*

    Policies that reduce imports are similar to those that reduce inflation. On the demand side, the requirement is for the brakes to be put on an overheating (inflationary) economy. Supply measures can also help UK firms to compete.

    The government can use fiscal policy to improve the UK's International Trade position by:

    - Increasing income tax to cut consumers buying power and so decrease the demand for imports;
    - Spending money to lower business costs, such as by improving roads.

Changing importance of fiscal policy

The famous economist Keynes advocated the use of fiscal policy as far back as the 1930s and it was the main economic weapon of UK Government until the 1980s when **monetary policy** came to the fore. Increased home ownership and credit buying have made monetary policy more effective, by giving interest rates a greater impact on consumer spending.

The inability of government to control unemployment and inflation during the 1970s questioned the effectiveness of fiscal policy. In recent years, successive Chancellors of the Exchequer have attempted to be fiscally prudent and follow the Golden Rule (see definition below).

Key point

Golden Rule of fiscal policy

In the long run government borrowing should only be allowed to finance capital expenditure such as new hospital and schools which will benefit present and future generations and so will be paid for by present future generations.

Current spending such as teachers' salaries, medicines should be paid for now, not by borrowing, but by taxing this generation.

4.2.2   Problems with fiscal policy

A problem with fiscal policy is that it can have conflicting objectives:

- a fiscal policy used to meet one objective could actually result in another objective not being met;

- a fiscal policy which raises aggregate demand in order to increase employment might cause inflation if aggregate demand rose faster than output, or it might cause an increase in the demand for imports;

- a fiscal policy aimed at reducing aggregate demand to reduce inflation might cause unemployment to rise and growth to slow down.

Demand will change by more than the initial government action would suggest. Remembering the multiplier effect, changes in demand caused by changes in tax or public spending will be difficult to forecast.

If the government initially throws a rock in the economic pond by cutting income tax (for example) then the multiplier effect are the resulting ripples outwards that gradually reduce. The initial first wave effect is enhanced as the initial government policy cycles around the circular flow of income again and again.

Fiscal policy Go online

Q3: Decide which statements below refer to the following descriptions and put them into the correct row in the table:

- New state schools and hospitals (there are many others);
- The multiplier;
- Low inflation, high employment, sustained economic growth and a balanced trade position;
- Capital spending;
- Cutting income tax and increased government spending;
- Use of public spending and taxation to alter aggregate demand;
- Teachers' wages and medicines for NHS (there are many others);
- Raising corporation tax and cutting government spending;
- This present generation of taxpayers.

Statement	Description
Contradictory fiscal measures	
Examples of current spending by government	
A definition of fiscal policy	
Examples of capital spending by government	
Macroeconomic objectives of government	
Who the Golden Rule says should pay for current spending by government	
Expansionary fiscal measures	
Concept of aggregate demand increasing by more than the amount of government injection	
Type of government spending that can justify government borrowing	

4.3   Monetary policy

Monetary policy is the use of interest rates and the supply of money (now referred to as "quantitative easing") as a means of achieving the macroeconomic objectives of government.

Monetarists believe that if the money supply grows faster than output the inflation will result. It is their view that the control of the money supply is vital for controlling inflation and if control of inflation is achieved the other macroeconomic objectives will be easier to meet.

The Bank of England building in Threadneedle Street, London

This control of the money supply is aimed at:

*   controlling banks' ability to lend (the supply of money);

    This is when the Bank of England actively takes measures to control lending by the high street banks. This would include banks being restricted to lending a certain proportion of their deposits.

*   controlling borrowing from banks (the demand for money);

    If the Bank of England changes interest rates this will influence the demand for loans by firms and households.

*   controlling government borrowing from banks.

    Government can reduce its demand for loans by reducing the Public Sector Net Cash Requirement (PSNCR).

    ○   Any policy which lowers interest rates and increases lending is known as *expansionary monetary policy*.

    ○   Any policy which raises interest rates and decreases lending is known as *contractionary monetary policy*.

The Monetary Policy Committee

In 1997 the Labour Government gave the Bank of England independence in setting the interest rate required to achieve and maintain the underlying rate of inflation. This removed the political influence over setting interest rates.

These new arrangements mean that the Monetary Policy Committee of the Bank meets and sets interest rates every month. This committee of economists with Government representatives monitors various indicators of inflation, e.g. house prices and wage awards, then takes the necessary steps to keep inflation at its target. If the inflation target is missed then it is the responsibility of the Monetary Policy Committee.

Economic policy   Go online

Q4:   Why has monetary policy become the most important economic policy in recent years?

4.3.1   Monetary policy and macroeconomic objectives

The government's macroeconomic objectives in terms of monetary policy are:

1. ***An inflation rate target of 2% (CPI).***

   If prices are rising due to increasing aggregate demand the Bank of England could:

   - raise interest rates and decrease bank lending which will discourage consumers and firms from borrowing and spending money, encourage saving which will lower aggregate demand and ease inflationary pressure;
   - raise interest rates to strengthen the exchange value of sterling making imports cheaper, easing inflation further.

2. ***A high level of employment.***

   If there is increasing unemployment due to falling aggregate demand then the Bank of England could:

   - lower interest rates and increase bank lending which will encourage consumers and firms to spend money and discourage saving, which will raise aggregate demand and create jobs;
   - lower interest rates will also weaken the exchange value of sterling making UK exports more competitive and so create jobs;
   - use quantitative easing which increases the liquidity of banks by buying back assets (government bonds) from them. This gives banks more cash (increases their liquidity). Banks are then able to lend more, and to lower interest rates to encourage the take-up of their cash. It is an electronic equivalent of printing more money.

3. ***A sustainable rate of economic growth.***

   If the Bank of England wanted to boost demand in the economy and stimulate output it could:

   - lower interest rates and increase bank lending which will encourage demand and investment so increases output in the economy. Quantitative easing would also encourage economic growth;
   - lower interest rates which makes exports cheaper and so will encourage output of export industries to go up.

---

4. *A balanced trade position.*

If the Chancellor is concerned about an increasing trade deficit he could:

- raise interest rates and decrease Bank lending. This will encourage saving and decrease aggregate demand in the economy which includes imports;
- raise interest rates to strengthen the exchange value of sterling making imports dearer and exports cheaper, to help cure the trade deficit.

Monetary policy   Go online

Q5:   Decide which statements below refer to the following descriptions and put them into the correct row in the table:

- Low and steady inflation;
- Lower interest rates;
- Raise interest rates;
- The Monetary Policy Committee of the Bank of England;
- The manipulation of interest rates and the money supply achieve macroeconomic objectives;

Statement	Description
A definition of monetary policy	
Responsible for setting interest rates	
An expansionary monetary policy	
A contractionary monetary policy	
What macroeconomic objectives monetarists regard as the most significant	

4.3.2   Conflict of objectives

It can be seen from above that it is difficult to meet all objectives simultaneously. Policies to encourage growth and employment may result in higher prices and a bigger demand for imports.

Monetary policy has divergent aims

Despite this, it is possible to have non-inflationary, sustainable economic growth, with the divergent aims largely achieved. Equally, it is also possible to have "stagflation". This is high inflation with low growth and high unemployment and would be the worst of economic outcomes.

4.4 Supply-side policies

Supply-side policies are mainly microeconomic measures designed to improve competition in product markets, i.e. where goods and services are bought and sold, and those that aim to improve flexibility in the labour markets.

Supply-side policies are designed to increase competition

The main thrust of supply-side policies is to increase competition in the belief that competition between producers increases their efficiency and improves incentives.

These policies include:

- **Privatisation** - This was the main policy on the product market side in the 1980s and 90s. The privatisation of various large former nationalised industries was designed to break up state monopolies and encourage competition in industries like power generation.

- **Deregulation** - This involved the government reducing its control and regulation of certain areas in the private sector, e.g. transport and telecommunications. These industries had been protected from competition by government restricting new producers into the market place. The aim of this policy was to open up these markets to greater competition leading to greater cost efficiency and wider choice for consumers.

The UK Government has signed up to trade agreements made by the World Trade Organisation. The UK is also a member of the European single market. These trade agreements result in more competition in British product markets.

A reduction in corporation tax encourages capital investment resulting in greater efficiency.

> **Q6:** What is meant by the term "deregulation"?

4.4.1   The labour market and supply-side policies

A perfect labour market is one that can quickly clear surpluses or shortages of labour. It is also referred to as a flexible labour market.

An imperfect or inflexible labour market is one where the market is slow to adjust. It is difficult for employers to recruit workers when demand is rising and difficult to shed labour or reduce wage rates when demand is falling.

Supply-side polices are designed to improve the quality and availability of labour. This results in an increase in the potential productivity of the economy.

Trade union reforms

Much of the legal protection enjoyed by trade unions has been removed. This has made it far more difficult for trade unions to take industrial action, e.g. postal ballots before strikes, maximum of six pickets, no secondary action. The result has been a more flexible labour market and an enormous reduction in industrial disputes.

However, workers appear to have fallen behind in their share of the national income. Real wages are now flexible downwards and workers may not get their share of any economic growth which instead goes to the owners of other factors of production, e.g. capital, land, enterprise. In many occupations zero-hours contracts or casual labour has returned and workers have little job security and find their hours and wages changing week by week.

Increased spending on education and training

Recent UK Governments have increased spending on education as a percentage of GDP. More young people are going into higher education. This will result in a better educated workforce capable of working in highly technological or "knowledge" based industries. This will also encourage foreign firms to locate in the UK.

Firms are given subsidies and tax relief to invest in training for their workers. The Government has launched schemes designed to make the unemployed more employable and reformed the benefits system to encourage the long term unemployed to seek employment.

Improved incentives to work

Improved incentives to work include:

- **Reducing income tax** - Lower rates of income tax increase incentives for people to enter the labour market or move to a better paid job if available.

- **Adopting a "make work pay" policy** - The gap between unemployment benefit and the lowest rates of pay has been widened and the eligibility for Job Seekers Allowance has been tightened to encourage people to go back into the labour market.

- **The introduction of the minimum wage** - This has encouraged the unemployed into jobs because the rates of pay are higher than they were previously.

The labour market and supply-side policies   Go online

Q7: What is the difference between product and labour markets?

....

Q8: Why does reducing rates of income tax increase the supply of labour?

Complete the following sentences by filling in the missing word.

Q9: The introduction of the .... wage will encourage workers to take jobs they previously would not have taken.

....

Q10: The .... of various large state run industries was designed to encourage competition.

....

Q11: A .... labour market is one that can quickly clear surpluses or shortages.

....

Q12: .... rates of corporation tax will allow firms to keep more of their profits and also encourage higher levels of capital ....

---

222 UNIT 2. ECONOMIC ACTIVITY

4.5 Summary

At the end of this topic you should know:

- fiscal policy is the adjusting of taxation and/or public spending;
- monetary policy is the manipulation of interest rates and the money supply;
- supply-side policies concentrate of the output of goods and services;
- the difficulties of achieving all the government aims at the same time.

4.6   End of topic test

End of Topic 4 test   Go online

The Chancellor and his colleagues at the Treasury have been working at great speed to achieve their macroeconomic objectives. They have used a mixture of fiscal, monetary and supply-side policies to try and reach these objectives.

Q13: A fiscal policy to reduce inflation would be:

a) increasing income tax rates.
b) increasing interest rates.
c) reducing trade union influence.
d) increasing government spending.

. . . .

Q14: A monetary policy to increase economic growth would be:

a) cuts in income tax rates.
b) quantitative easing.
c) higher interest rates.
d) cuts in corporation tax.

. . . .

Q15: Which of the following are examples of supply-side policies?

1. Quantitative easing.
2. Laws to restrict trade union power.
3. Spending on education and training.

a) 1 and 2 only
b) 1 and 3 only
c) 2 and 3 only
d) All of the above.

. . . .

Q16: If the first priority was to reduce unemployment, which of the following policies could work?

a) Increasing value added tax.
b) Decreasing income tax.
c) Increasing interest rates.
d) Decreasing government spending.

. . . .

Q17: Which of the following are true of the Monetary Policy Committee?

1. It has a target of zero inflation.
2. It meets every month.
3. It sets interest rates.
4. It is independent of government.

a) 1 and 2 only
b) 1, 2 and 3 only
c) 2, 3 and 4 only
d) All of the above

....

Q18: What are the UK Government's four macroeconomic objectives?
(6 marks)

....

Q19: Briefly describe what is meant by fiscal policy.
(3 marks)

....

Q20: Briefly describe what is meant by monetary policy.
(3 marks)

....

Q21: What are supply-side policies?
(3 marks)

....

Q22: Suggest suitable fiscal and monetary measures that could be used to bring inflation under control.
(5 marks)

Unit 2 Topic 5

National income

Contents

Prerequisites

The topic builds on and expands on the aspects of national income studied in National 5 Economics. However, prior knowledge of these concepts, although useful, is not essential. You should also have completed Unit 1 and Topics 1, 2, 3 and 4 of this unit.

Learning objective

By the end of this topic you should be able to:

- explain the term national income;
- describe the circular flow of income;
- explain the meaning of injections and withdrawals;
- explain the effect of these on output and employment;
- distinguish between GDP, GNP and national income;
- explain the difference between nominal and real national income;
- describe equilibrium national income;
- describe and explain how the multiplier process works;
- calculate the multiplier and its effect on national income;
- describe what national income statistics are used for;
- describe the limitations in using national income statistics.

5.1 Prior knowledge

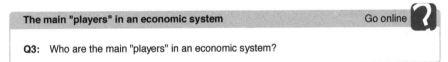

Test your prior knowledge   Go online

Q1: What is meant by economic growth?

....

Q2: How is it measured?

5.2 National income

National income is the total value of goods and services produced in an economy over a one year period. It measures the rate of economic growth, when compared with the previous year.

National income per head offers the more meaningful comparison as the higher national income may have to be shared among more citizens. Price changes further complicate the data and should be allowed for. The most useful figure then becomes real national income per head.

It is also worth considering whether the distribution of income is skewed. In that case, the majority of the population may have less than average incomes because a small number of high income individuals have acquired a disproportionate share of the national income.

The main "players" in an economic system   Go online

Q3: Who are the main "players" in an economic system?

5.3 The circular flow of income

In its most basic form, an economy consists of firms (producers) and households (consumers).

Households own the factors of production:

- **Land** - all natural resources;
- **Labour** - all human resources;
- **Capital** - all man-made resources;
- **Enterprise** - the ability to organise land, labour, capital and enterprise.

Households provide these factors to firms in return for the goods and services these firms produce using these factors.

The following simple flow diagram shows the *real flow of national income*:

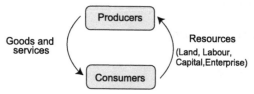

Real flow of national income

Factors of production   Go online

Identify the factors of production in each of the examples below.

Q4:   A launch of a new product

a) Land
b) Labour
c) Capital
d) Enterprise

. . . .

Q5:   A field of sheep

a) Land
b) Labour
c) Capital
d) Enterprise

. . . .

Q6:   A bottling plant

a) Land
b) Labour
c) Capital
d) Enterprise

. . . .

Q7:   A traffic warden

a) Land
b) Labour
c) Capital
d) Enterprise

5.4   Money flow of national income

Money also flows between households (consumers) and firms (producers).

All households contain consumers. In return for providing factors of productions to firms these households receive monetary rewards:

- in return for providing land they receive rent;

- in return for providing labour they receive wages;

- in return for providing capital they receive interest;

- in return for providing enterprise they receive profit.

This money is then spent by the households back to the firms in return for the goods and services consumed.

The diagram below shows the *money flow of national income*.

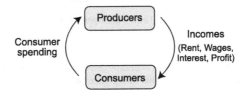

Money flow of national income

The *circular flow of national income* diagram, below, combines the real and money flows:

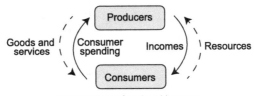

Circular flow of national income

Imagine you take a pound coin and buy a cup of coffee in your local Moonstar Coffee Shop. The pound coin goes into the till. It becomes income for the firm. The firm might use this money as rent their premises or wages for its workers. In any case it ends up as income in somebody's wallet and it will be spent again and the circular flow continues.

Flow of national income   Go online

Q8:   Complete the paragraph below by choosing from the following words:

- continues;
- expenditure;
- consumers;
- resources;
- income;
- output of firms.

Households contain .... Households own .... which they provide to firms in return for .... These are spent on buying the .... This then becomes income of firms which is then passed on to households and the process ....

5.5   Injections, withdrawals and equilibrium

Although a useful model, the circular flow of income as described above is not complete.

Injections

Consumers are not the only spenders in an economy. **Investment** by firms, government spending and exports are all **injections** into the circular flow of income. This is money going into firms but was not earned by domestic consumers.

Injections have the effect of raising income and **consumption**. This requires a bigger output of goods and services and a bigger demand for the factors of production which make them.

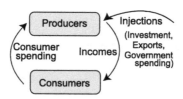

Injections into the circular flow of national income

These injections have the effect of increasing the circular flow of income:

- **Investment** is the term given to the spending by firms on capital, e.g. new plant or an extension to their factory. The main factor which determines the level of investment is interest rates. This is because firms usually need to borrow money to invest.

- **Exports** is the term given to the value of goods and services demanded by firms and individuals overseas. The main factors which determine the level of exports is the price and quality of UK goods and services.

- **Government spending** is the value of expenditure by the state in the economy. This is spending by central and local government. It includes public sector salaries and the building of NHS hospitals and is mainly determined by the policy of Government at that time.

Withdrawals

A **leakage** is a withdrawal of funds from the circular flow. It is money which households have earned but does not return to firms in the form of consumer spending.

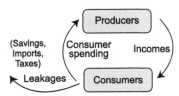

Leakages from the circular flow of national income

Savings, imports and taxation are all leakages:

- **Savings** is the term given to the amount of money a consumer does not spend from his income. The main determinants of savings are income and interest rates. At very low levels of income, consumption is greater than income and borrowing occurs. This is referred to as **dis-saving**.

  - The proportion of total income saved is known as the **average propensity to save (APS)**. If someone earns £500 a week and a saves £50 their APS is 0.1.

  - The proportion of total income spent is known as the **average propensity to consume (APC)**. If someone earns £500 a week and saves £50, spending £450, their APC is 0.9.

- **Imports** is the term given to the amount spent by resident firms and individuals of a country on goods and services produced overseas. The main determinants are income levels and the price and quality of goods produced.

- **Taxation** is the amount of revenue collected by central and local governments from consumers. This is mainly determined by the size of incomes and level of spending in the economy.

Equilibrium

Imagine national income like a balloon. If an injection occurs more air goes into the balloon and it gets bigger. If a leakage occurs less air is in the balloon and it gets smaller.

Equilibrium level of national income occurs when total injections into an economy are equal to the total leakages from an economy and total spending in the economy is equal to total income. This is a theoretical position which would rarely be achieved.

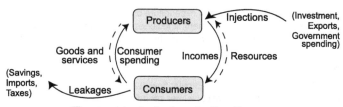

The complete circular flow of national income

Circular flow of national income   Go online

Decide what would be likely to happen to the circular flow of income of the UK in the following situations.

Q9:   An increase in tax rates in UK.

a) Increase
b) Decrease
c) No effect

....

Q10: Japanese cars fall in price.

a) Increase
b) Decrease
c) No effect

....

Q11: UK Government extends two motorways.

a) Increase
b) Decrease
c) No effect

....

Q12: Interest rates in UK fall.

a) Increase
b) Decrease
c) No effect

....

Q13: ADSA and TOSCO build four new stores each.

a) Increase
b) Decrease
c) No effect

....

Q14: UK government issue attractive saving bonds.

a) Increase
b) Decrease
c) No effect

....

Q15: UK government plans to raise public spending by £10 million and to finance it through increased taxation.

a) Increase
b) Decrease
c) No effect

5.6 Effects of national income on employment and output

An increase in real national income is the same as an increase in real national output. The incomes of the factors of production result from the increased output produced by them.

If more goods and services are being produced, this implies that more factors of production are being used. An increase in employment should result. However, if economic growth is less than 2% per annum, then it is possible that new technologies and efficiency gains may mean that no new employees are needed.

Economic growth of at least 2% per annum may be required just to maintain employment.

Q16: What might be the cause of an increase in output per worker?

....

Q17: An increase in output is not the same as an increase in productivity. What is the difference?

5.7 Real and nominal national income

Real national income is when national income has been adjusted to take account of **inflation**. It is measured at constant prices. An increase in real national income means that a real increase in output has been achieved. An increase in real national income means that there has been an increase in the volume of goods and services produced.

Real national income - Scotopia   Go online

Q18: The Chancellor of a fictional country called Scotopia has made a statement about his country's national income in the national press: *"You have never had it so good. We have experienced rising real national income in each of the past three years."*
Which of the following statements *must* be true?

a) Prices have not risen Scotopia during the last three years.
b) Everybody in Scotopia has become better off during the last three years.
c) Prices have risen slower than wages in Scotopia during the last three years.
d) All sectors of industry in Scotopia increased their output during the last three years.
e) A bigger volume of goods and services has been produced in Scotopia during each of the last three years.

Nominal national income does not take account of any changes in prices over a period of time. It is calculated using the prices at that time, i.e. current prices. Nominal national income can therefore be misleading as inflation might disguise the real value of output achieved.

To convert nominal national income to real national income we must know how price levels have changed, i.e. the rate of inflation. Inflation is measured using **price indices**.

The formula to convert nominal national income to real national income is:

$$\text{Real national income} = \frac{\text{Nominal national income}}{1} \times \frac{\text{Price index of base year}}{\text{Price index of current year}}$$

Example : Rise in real national income

In an economy nominal national income rose from £10,000 million in year one to £12,000 million in year 2. Prices rose by 5% during that year. We add 5 on to the base of 100.

Did real national income rise? We must use the formula to find out.

$$\text{Real national income} = \frac{\text{Nominal national income}}{1} \times \frac{\text{Price index of base year}}{\text{Price index of current year}}$$

$$\text{Real national income} = \frac{12,000}{1} \times \frac{100}{105}$$

$$\text{Real national income} = £11,429$$

From the above calculations, we see that national income rose by £1,429 million

---

Real national income Go online

Q19: Calculate the real national income for the following countries, when inflation is removed from the nominal income, and complete the table. The real national income for Country A has been included as an example - £40,000 x 100/119 = **£33,613** (note that the base year is always 100).

	Nominal national income (£ million)	Inflation rate (%)	Real national income (£ million)
Country A	40000	19	33613
Country B	80000	5	
Country C	100000	17	

Real and nominal national income Go online

Q20: Complete the sentences below by choosing from the following words:

- 0%;
- 5%;
- population;
- unemployment.

1. Using estimates of real national income to compare economic welfare internationally can be misleading because of disparities between nations in ....

2. During a year real and nominal national income of the UK both rose by 5%. Inflation must have been ....

5.8 The multiplier

Any injection into the circular flow of income will increase that circular flow of national income. John Maynard Keynes developed this idea further, suggesting that any injection into the circular flow will increase national income by more than the amount of the injection. Keynes suggested that an increase in investment of £10 billion will increase national income by more than £10 billion.

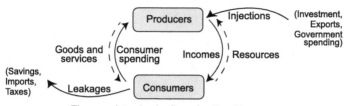

The complete circular flow of national income

Looking at the circular flow diagram above, we can see that this investment in this new factory will end up as an increase in incomes for all the workers involved in planning and building the factory. Incomes will rise by £10 bn but this extra income will also be spent and consumption would rise by £10 bn.

This spending will also end up as extra income and this in turn will also be spent. The total increase in national income will be many times the initial £10 bn.

Not all of this extra £10 bn income will be passed on to firms in the UK as extra spending. The size of the leakages will determine:

- how much income is passed on to firms during each round of spending and so the increase in national income in total;

- the size of the multiplier effect.

National income increase   Go online

Q21: Will national income increase to infinity?

5.8.1   Marginal propensity to save (MPS)

A household can do only do two things with any extra income: spend it or save it. At this stage let us only assume one leakage - saving.

This size of the multiplier will depend on the proportion of any extra income that is saved. This known as the **marginal propensity to save** (MPS).

If an extra £100 is earned and £20 is saved then the marginal propensity to save is 0.2.

That is:

- Change in saving: Change in income = 20:100 = 0.2

Marginal propensity to save (MPS)   Go online

Calculate the MPS in the following situations.

Q22: Increase in income £100; increase in saving £10.
....

Q23: Increase in income £500; increase in saving £25.
....

Q24: Increase in income £1000; increase in saving £250.
....

Q25: Increase in income £300; increase in saving £60.

5.8.2 Marginal propensity to consume (MPC)

As we already have stated any income not saved is spent. The proportion of any extra income spent is known as the **marginal propensity to consume** (MPC). In the previous example it was 0.8.

It is calculated by:

- Change in spending: Change in income = 80:100 = 0.8

Marginal propensity to consume (MPC)   Go online

Calculate the MPC in the following situations.

Q26: Increase in income £10; increase in consumption £9.
....

Q27: Increase in income £500; increase in consumption £400.
....

Q28: Increase in income £40; increase in consumption £32.
....

Q29: Increase in income £200; increase in consumption £100.

5.8.3 Calculating the multiplier

We can use any one of two similar formulae, below, to calculate the multiplier using the previous example where mps = 0.2 and mpc = 0.8 (**mps** is marginal propensity to save and **mpc** is marginal propensity to consume).

Either

$$\frac{1}{\text{mps}} = \frac{1}{0.2} = 5$$

or

$$\frac{1}{1 - \text{mpc}} = \frac{1}{1 - 0.8} = 5$$

This means that any injection into the circular flow will increase national income by five times that amount.

Example : Factory investment

Using the same figures for mps and mpc as above, calculate the national income with the original investment in a new factory of £10 bn.

This injection of £10 bn will be successively spent as households pass on their increases in income till national income increases by £10 bn × 5 = £50 bn. National income will then be £50 billion.

We can check our answer the long way. Remember 0.8 of extra income is being spent.

The next round of spending will be £8 bn × 0.8 and this will become income. If we keep doing this the total increase in income will be £50 bn.

Calculating the multiplier   Go online

Q30: If the mps is 0.1 (and, therefore, the mpc is 0.9) what would be the extra income if total national income were £1 billion and there was an initial injection of £20 million?

5.9   National income statistics

National income is the total value of goods and services produced in an economy over a one year period.

Other useful statistics are calculated when determining national income:

- *Gross domestic product (GDP)*

    This is the value of goods and services produced in an economy by business within a country.

- *Gross national product (GNP)*

    This uses GDP as a starting point but adds the value of output from resources owned abroad and takes away the value of output by foreign owned resources within that economy.

    For example the UK GNP figure would be calculated by using the UK GDP figure and adding the value of output produced abroad by UK owned resources minus the value of output produced in the UK by foreign owned resources. This figure is known as *net property income from abroad* and can be a positive or negative figure.

- *Net national product (NNP)*

  This uses GNP as a staring point but takes away the loss in the value of capital goods within that economy during the year. This loss in value is known as **depreciation**. Net national product (NNP) is national income.

A fictional country called Scotopia has the following national income statistics (see table below).

Gross domestic product (GDP)	£20 billion
Add/subtract net property income from abroad	+ £3 billion
Gross national product (GNP)	£23 billion
Subtract capital consumption	£6 billion
National income (NNP)	£17 billion

The economy of Pictopia Go online

Q31: The following table contains the national income statistics for the fictional country of Pictopia.

Complete the table by choosing the correct economic term from the following:

- Gross domestic product (GDP);
- Net property income from abroad;
- Gross national product (GNP);
- Capital consumption.

....	£15 billion
Add/subtract	+ £5 billion
....	£20 billion
Subtract	£4 billion
National income (NNP)	£16 billion

National income statistics Go online

Q32: GDP includes overseas output of goods and services.

a) True
b) False

....

Q33: NNP is GNP less depreciation.

a) True
b) False

....

Q34: NNP is national income.

a) True
b) False

....

Q35: GNP is always higher than GDP.

a) True
b) False

....

Q36: GNP always higher than NNP.

a) True
b) False

5.9.1   The uses of national income statistics

National income statistics are used in various ways:

- *They are a measure of a country's economic performance.* If a country's national income is growing then it can be assumed that earnings and profits and output are all rising and average living standards are rising.

- *They can be used to compare the economic performance of different countries.* If the UK national income is bigger than that of France then the output of goods and services in the UK is larger. The comparison of rates of economic growth in national income figures give evidence on which economy is performing best.

- *They can identify countries that require assistance from the international community.* If the national income of countries is known, it would be possible to recognise those countries with low national income and high populations. These countries would likely be those that require greatest international assistance.

- *They can be used to measure contributions from various countries.* Contributions to international organisations such as the World Bank or the European Union are proportionate to the size of economies.

- *They can pinpoint weaknesses in certain sectors and industries in an economy.* If a country has a diminishing manufacturing sector this would be revealed by the breakdown of national income statistics and appropriate action taken.

- *These statistics can help future government planning in an economy.* If certain regions show a falling output the government might take measures to attract industry to that area through grants, etc. They can also be used to judge the effectiveness of macroeconomic polices, which may then be adjusted.

To only use national income to compare the economic welfare of different countries can be misleading for various reasons:

- The size of population might be totally different so the spread of wealth might be less even. Economists may divide national income by the population to give national income earned on average by each member of the population or per capita. This is slightly more significant but still does not show the evenness of distribution of wealth in a country.

- National income statistics do not show working hours or conditions.

- Price level differences between countries are not always taken into account.

- National income statistics do not reveal what is being produced, e.g. hospital beds or bullets. Quality of life is not calculated.

- Social costs of production are not being taken into account, e.g. pollution levels and crime.

- Quality and choice in goods and services produced are not taken into account.

- In some cultures people produce much more goods and services for themselves which do not register in the figures..

In northern Europe people require to earn enough to buy winter clothing and central heating, but perhaps you can be as prosperous in southern Italy without these items and without the income to buy them!

Chancellors' disagreement Go online

Q37: At a recent gathering of economists the Chancellor of the Exchequers of India and the Republic of Ireland had a disagreement. The Indian Chancellor said because the national income of India was many times bigger than that of the Republic of Ireland it was a much better off country.

Compose a reply that the Irish Chancellor could make disagreeing with that statement.

5.10   Summary

Summary

You should now know that:

- National income is the value of goods and services produced in a country over a one year period;

- The circular flow of income describes how money is moved between households and firms;

- There are three injections and three withdrawals from the circular flow;

- Increases in national income (output) will occur alongside positive effects on employment;

- There are subtle differences in the measures of national income such as GDP and GNP;

- Real national income allows for the price changes that can be the cause of movements in nominal national income;

- Equilibrium national income is the term for a theoretical position where injections equal withdrawals;

- The multiplier adds to the initial economic impact of an injection (or reduced withdrawal);

- The multiplier can be calculated as 1 divided by the marginal propensity to save;

- National income statistics have many uses, but it is important to remember they also have limitations.

5.11   End of topic test

End of Topic 5 test   Go online

Q38: If extra government spending of £100m is made, and the marginal propensity to consume is 0.9, then by how much will total spending finally increase?

a) £10m
b) £90m
c) £900m
d) £1,000m

....

Q39: One example of a leakage from the circular flow is:

a) the excise duty paid on tobacco.
b) the export of cars overseas.
c) the interest paid on a car loan.
d) government spending on the NHS.

....

Q40: One example of an injection into the circular flow is:

a) the UK purchase of a Mercedes built in Germany.
b) the sale overseas of a Mini built in the UK.
c) an increase in prices caused by an increase in VAT.
d) a cutback in the level of government spending.

....

Q41: National Income shows:

a) the distribution of incomes.
b) the standard of living.
c) the quality of life.
d) the level of happiness.

....

Q42: Comparing the economic performance of countries is difficult because of:

a) fluctuating exchange rates.
b) different lifestyles and needs.
c) Both of the above.
d) Neither of the above.

....

Q43: "The calculation of UK national income is a slow, complex and expensive process."

Explain what is meant by UK national income and describe some of the problems involved in calculating it.

(8 marks)

....

Q44: Discuss the uses to which UK national income statistics can be put.
(8 marks)

....

Q45: Describe some of the limitations to be considered when using national income statistics.
(8 marks)

....

Q46: What is meant by the circular flow of income in an economy?
(9 marks)

....

Q47: Explain what is meant by:

a) The average propensity to consume. *(3 marks)*
b) The marginal propensity to consume. *(3 marks)*

....

Q48: Explain how an increase in investment would affect the equilibrium level of national income.
(10 marks)

Unit 2 Topic 6

Place of Scotland in the UK economy

Contents

Prerequisites

The topic builds on and expands on the aspects of the Scottish economy studied in National 5 Economics. However, prior knowledge of these aspects, although useful, is not essential. You should also have completed unit 1 and topics 1, 2, 3, 4 and 5 of this unit.

Learning objective

By the end of this topic you should be able to:

- describe the main features of the Scottish economy;

- explain the economic powers that have been devolved;

- describe the impact of UK economic policies on Scotland.

6.1   The main features of the Scottish economy

The structure of the Scottish economy is illustrated in the pie chart below. All statistics in this section are taken from Scottish Government statistics from 2013. The most recent statistics can be found on the Scottish Government website - http://www.gov.scot/Topics/Statistics/Browse/Economy.

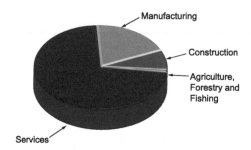

Structure of the Scottish economy

The Scottish economy comprises of the following sectors:

* Services (72.3%);

* Manufacturing (19.1%);

* Construction (7.8%);

* Agriculture, Forestry and Fishing (0.8%).

6.1.1   Scottish exports

The geographical breakdown of Scottish exports is shown in the image below.

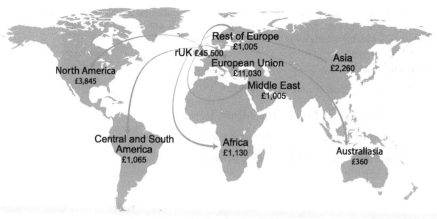

Map of the world showing Scottish exports

(World map blank without borders (http://bit.ly/1FtP8BP) by Crates (http://bit.ly/1IvaCug) is licensed under CC BY SA 4.0 (http://bit.ly/145LRHf))

The figures for Scottish exports, taken from the above map, are shown in the table below.

Area	Amount exported (in £millions)
RUK (Rest of the UK)	45,500
European Union	11,030
North America	3,845
Asia	2,260
Rest of Europe	2,115
Africa	1,130
Central and South America	1,065
Middle East	1,005
Australasia	360
Other	1,105

Geographical breakdown of Scottish exports

Scottish exports   Go online

Q1: What are Scotland's three most important export markets?

6.1.2 Structure of the economy by employment

From July to September 2014 employment rose by 22,000 to reach 2,605,000. Scotland has the highest employment rate of the four countries of the UK at 73.5% (England 72.9%). When compared against the 34 members of the OECD, Scotland ranks 14th for employment rate.

The structure of the Scottish economy by employment is shown in the image below.

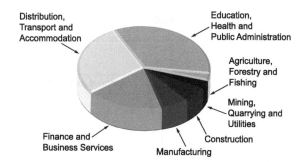

Distribution, Transport and Accommodation

Education, Health and Public Administration

Agriculture, Forestry and Fishing

Mining, Quarrying and Utilities

Finance and Business Services

Construction

Manufacturing

Structure of the Scottish economy by employment

In percentage terms, the structure of the economy by employment is shown in the table below.

Industry	Percentage
Education, Health and Public Administration	34%
Distribution, Transport and Accommodation	28%
Finance and Business Services	19%
Manufacturing	7%
Construction	6%
Mining, Quarrying and Utilities	3%
Agriculture, Forestry and Fishing	3%

Structure of the Scottish economy by employment

6.1.3   Unemployment in Scotland

The labour force survey shows that unemployment fell by 10,000 to 164,000 in the period July to September 2014. This puts the rate of unemployment at 5.9%, fractionally better than the UK average of 6%.

In October 2014 the number of people out of work and claiming Jobseeker's Allowance was 89,900. The claimant count rate is now 3.3% of the working population.

Unemployment statistics   Go online

Check the latest Scottish unemployment statistics at http://www.scotland.gov.uk/Topics/Stati stics/Browse/Labour-Market.

Comparing Scotland's unemployment to the rest of the UK   Go online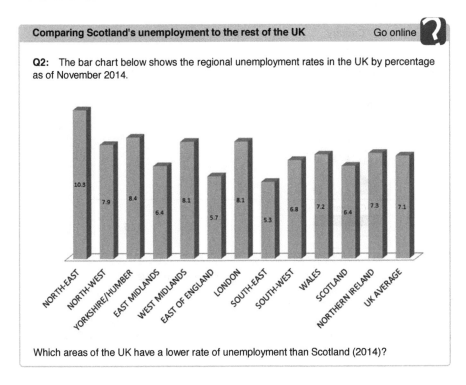

Q2:   The bar chart below shows the regional unemployment rates in the UK by percentage as of November 2014.

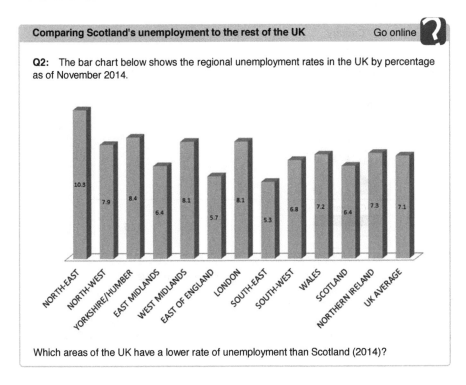

Which areas of the UK have a lower rate of unemployment than Scotland (2014)?

6.1.4   Scotland's largest international export markets

Scotland's largest international export markets are shown in the table below (figures from 2012 - source: *Scottish Government website - http://bit.ly/2s9vcjQ*).

Country	Amount (in £bn)
USA	3.6
Netherlands	2.7
France	2.2
Germany	1.5

Scotland's largest international export markets

6.1.5   North Sea oil: facts and figures

The following facts and figures relate to North Sea oil (The future estimates below are a matter of political debate, and are in any case predictions. You may be able to find updates of these figures, but always take regard of their source.):

- 40bn barrels extracted;

- 24bn barrels could remain;

- 30-40 years of production remaining;

- £57bn tax revenue predicted by Scottish Government by 2018;

- 38% fall in oil revenue predicted by Office for Budget Responsibility by 2017-18.

Oil rig in the Cromarty Firth
(Oil Rig and Life Boat at Invergordon Cromarty Firth Ross-shire Scotland (http://bit.ly/17p9ywz)
by Dave Conner (http://bit.ly/1APkObK) is licensed under CC BY 2.0 (http://bit.ly/17p9Wu
W))

The industry employs 450,000 people across the UK and in 2012-13 the industry paid £6.5 billion in taxes to the UK government. North Sea oil supplied 67% of the UK's oil demand in 2012 and 53% of the country's gas requirements and is a major boost to the country's economy.

If oil revenues are included in GDP figures, Scotland is shown to generate more per head of population than the UK as a whole. Since a peak in 1999, production has steadily declined.

6.1.6 Relative living standards

The GDP per person for the UK and Scotland is shown in the table below.

Country	Including oil and gas revenues	Excluding oil and gas revenues
UK	£22,336	£20,873
Scotland	£26,424	£20,571

GDP per person for the UK and Scotland

6.1.7   Scotch whisky exports

In 2013 the value of whisky exports was £4.3 billion. This is an increase of more than 80% since 2003. By volume of sales the top five markets are listed in the table below.

Top five markets by sales	Country
1	France
2	USA
3	Spain
4	Singapore
5	Germany

Top five export markets for Scotch whisky

6.1.8   Total tax revenue

In 2011-12, Scotland generated 9.9% of UK tax receipts with 8.4% of the population.

Total Scottish tax revenue (onshore and offshore) was £56.9 billion. (Again, It could be viewed that off-shore oil and gas are intrinsically UK owned and that these tax figures are produced solely to support the argument for independence. We take no view on that, but if oil and gas taxation were to be regionalised, it would indeed add somewhat to the taxation paid by the Scottish section.)

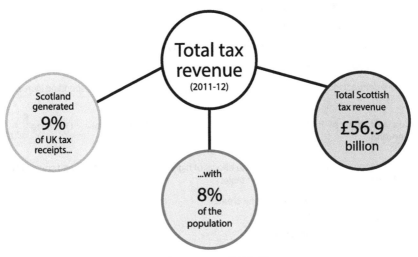

Total tax revenue (2011-12)

6.2   Devolution powers - income tax

Some changes to the devolved Scottish powers may be made following the report of the Smith Commission in January 2015. It would be useful to research the final outcomes resulting from the Smith report when it is acted upon. Be aware that there will be some adjustments to the devolved powers outlined below which you must note.

One of the Scottish Parliament's **devolution** powers is to vary the basic rate of income tax by three pence in the pound. This power has never been used.

It would be politically difficult for a party to gain power by offering a higher rate of income tax even if public services were to improve. It may just not happen under devolution.

There are many examples of thriving economies with higher tax rates than the UK. The prosperous economies of Scandinavian countries are examples. However, the "contemporary wisdom" in the UK has favoured lower income tax in recent decades. There has been little appetite even from left of centre political parties to advocate higher income tax.

Possible effects of higher income tax in Scotland include:

- less inequality and social division from the resulting redistribution of income;

- some higher income individuals moving their tax location across the border;

- improving public services;

- discouraging small businesses and entrepreneurs from taking risks, if returns are reduced;

- leading to more public sector employment and they would spend their incomes in private businesses generating a multiplier effect;

- acting as a disincentive to work;

- improving transport infrastructure which gives gains to private business;

- reducing consumer spending (disposable incomes down) with negative multiplier effect;

- more contracts for private firms in construction and engineering as public spending increases.

Pros and cons of higher income tax accompanied by higher public spending   Go online

Q3:   Choose which of the listed possible effects of higher income tax are pros and cons, and put them into the correct column in the table:

- Construction and engineering jobs created;

- Disincentive to work;

- Improved transport infrastructure;

- Less inequality;

- More public sector jobs;

- Moving location south of the border;

- Reduced disposable incomes.

Pros	Cons

6.3   Other devolution powers

The Scottish legal system remains separate. The Scottish Parliament also has devolved power in the following areas:

- agriculture;

- forestry and fishing;

- education;

- environment;

- fire service;

- health;

- housing;

- justice;

- policing and courts;

- local government;

- some areas of transport.

The Scottish Parliament can also legislate on tourism, economic development, planning, natural and built heritage, sport and the arts, as well as statistics, public registers and records.

Westminster (London) retains powers over foreign policy, defence, immigration, trade and industry, and UK economic policy.

Devolved and reserved powers   Go online

Q4: Choose which of the following powers are devolved and which are reserved, and put them into the correct column in the table:

- Housing;
- Justice;
- Local government;
- Immigration;
- Social security;
- Environment;
- Education;
- Employment;
- Health;
- Fishing;
- Fire service;
- Nuclear energy.

Devolved powers	Reserved powers

6.4 Impact of UK economic policies on Scotland

For the greater part, the impact of UK economic policies in Scotland will be the same as the impact on the rest of the UK. Decisions over fiscal, monetary and supply-side policies will impact on Scotland in a broadly similar way to the impact on the rest of the UK. Here, we highlight some potential differences in the Scottish and UK impact. It is our contention here that the differences are more "north-south" than "Scotland-England", and therefore the following points will also relate to much of the UK beyond the south-east.

The UK economy could be divided into two sections:

- Section 1 is the south-east of England.

- Section 2 comprises the rest of the UK, including Scotland.

National policies which reflect the influence of London and the south-east can have a detrimental effect on the rest of the UK.

Increasing interest rates in reaction to booming house prices in London.

In 2014, house price inflation in London stands at 17%. In Scotland, it is merely 4%. In parts of the north of England, house prices are recovering more slowly than in Scotland.

As a response to an unsustainable bubble in London prices, interest rates are likely to be raised by the Bank of England at an earlier point or by a greater amount than would otherwise be the case. An overheating economy in the south-east has to be calmed down before the rest of the UK has experienced significant economic growth.

Monetary policy in the UK is skewed by the need to cap the surge in house prices in the south-east. This will have negative economic consequences, slowing down the recovery elsewhere in the UK.

Reductions in public sector employment

A higher proportion of employment is in the public sector in Scotland. This is also true of the north-east of England. Reductions in public sector employment have hit hardest in areas such as the north-east of England. Scotland's devolved administration has enough control over budgeting to mitigate the worst effects on employment of this UK economic policy.

National spending decisions

Major budget decisions such as the cost of replacing the Trident nuclear deterrent are taken by the UK government. Such decisions have varied impact on Scotland. In the example of nuclear weapons, some jobs are generated when the weapons and infrastructure are located near Glasgow.

However, there is an opportunity cost for the UK economy because these vast resources could have been spent in many other ways. The weapons will be imported from the USA, and funds will leave the UK circular flow of income. National spending decisions show the continuing major influence of UK economic policy decisions on Scotland.

If the decision to build a fast rail line north from London is taken, then this will involve enormous costs with very limited benefits to Scotland. Generally, infrastructure in the south-east of England is extremely expensive. Diseconomies of scale, e.g. congestion, arise from the concentration of business in the south-east and attempts to overcome these problems are very expensive.

6.5   Summary

Summary

You should now know:

- the main features of the Scottish economy;

- the major exports of Scotland;

- the devolved powers of the Scottish government, including the ability to vary income tax;

- the impact that UK economic policies have on Scotland.

6.6   End of topic test

End of Topic 6 test   Go online

Q5:   Of the following, which is the most important sector of the Scottish economy?

a) Services
b) Manufacturing
c) Construction
d) Agriculture, forestry and fisheries

. . . .

Q6:   Where do most of Scotland's exports go?

a) Asia
b) European Union
c) North America
d) Rest of the UK

. . . .

Q7:   Devolved powers do *not* include:

a) Education
b) Health
c) Local government
d) Social security

. . . .

Q8:   Which of the following is the greatest source of employment in Scotland?

a) Manufacturing
b) Education, health and public administration
c) Distribution, transport and accommodation
d) Finance and business services

. . . .

Q9:   Scotland's largest international export market (by country) after the USA is:

a) France
b) Germany
c) Netherlands
d) Spain

. . . .

Q10: What could be the impact of Scotland having a lower rate of income tax than the rest
of the UK?

(5 marks)

Unit 2 Topic 7

End of unit test

End of Unit 2 test

Go online

Read the passage below and answer the questions which follow.

A paper setting out the government's intentions in the area of economic policy will be published next Tuesday. It is expected to contain a mixture of fiscal, monetary and supply side policies. The Chancellor is very aware of how his actions next week may affect the UK circular flow of income and how his decisions may lead to him meeting his four main macroeconomic objectives.

Q1: Draw a fully labelled diagram showing the circular flow of income in an economy.
(4 marks)

....

Q2: Explain the 'multiplier effect' of an injection into the circular flow.
(4 marks)

....

Q3: Describe fully the four main macroeconomic objectives of UK Governments.
(6 marks)

....

Q4: Outline the main features of:

1. Fiscal policy
2. Monetary policy
3. Supply side policies

(6 marks)

....

Q5: Describe how an early increase in interest rates to quell an overheating London economy could affect the Scottish economy.
(4 marks)

Unit 3: Global Economic Activity

Unit 3 Topic 1

Understanding global trade

Contents

Prerequisites

The topic builds on and expands the concept of trade studied in National 5 Economics. However, prior knowledge of this concept, although useful, is not essential.

Learning objective

By the end of this topic you should be able to:

- name the major UK exports;

- name the major UK imports;

- describe the reasons for global trade;

- explain the benefits of trade for consumers and companies;

- explain the advantages and disadvantages of global trade;

- explain the theory of absolute advantage;

- explain the theory of comparative advantage;

- explain trends in UK export and import patterns;

- name the UK's major trading partners;

- understand why it is more likely the UK will trade with some nations than others.

1.1   UK imports

The following information on the origin and composition of UK **imports** comes from the government's 'Pink Book'. The top 20 countries of origin of UK imports of goods in 2011 are shown below (UK imports of services are in brackets).

1.	Germany (4)	11.	Japan (5)
2.	China (23)	12.	Sweden (15)
3.	USA (1)	13.	Hong Kong (21)
4.	Netherlands (8)	14.	Switzerland (9)
5.	Norway (19)	15.	Russia (27)
6.	France (2)	16.	Poland (20)
7.	Belgium/Luxembourg (11/17*)	17.	Canada (16)
8.	Italy (6)	18.	Denmark (21)
9.	Ireland (7)	19.	India (10)
10.	Spain (3)	20.	Turkey (19)

The missing top 20 nations in the 'services' list are Australia (12), Singapore (13), Greece (14) and Portugal (18).

*Note that Belgium and Luxembourg are separated for services, but together for goods.

UK imports - EU countries   Go online

Q1:   Select those countries which are in the EU, from the top 20 nations above.

In summary, the most important sources for UK imports of goods are the European Union, the United States, China, Norway and Japan. The most important sources for UK imports of services are very similar. Note that China and Norway are significantly lower on the services list and India is fairly significant as a source of imports for services.

The higher positions of Spain, Greece, Portugal and Cyprus will reflect the importance of UK tourists to these countries.

1.1.1   UK imports (composition)

Compare the imports with the exports in the same categories in the section *1.2.1 UK exports (composition)* and you may spot the following:

- the UK is now a net importer of oil;
- far from being the nineteenth century "workshop of the world" we are now net importers of both semi-manufactured and finished goods;

- the latest figures for whisky exports can be accessed online - an article in January 2015 claimed this was the most significant sector in the category 'food and drink'. (Note that news articles are currently available from The Guardian and The Daily Telegraph websites without pay walls. The BBC is another useful source.)

The table below shows the composition of UK imports of goods in 2011 with the amount imported (shown in millions of pounds).

Trade in goods (imports)	Amount imported (in £millions)
Food, beverages and tobacco	36,069
Basic materials	11,928
Oil	49,490
Coal, gas and electricity	12,353
Semi-manufactured goods	196,494
Finished manufactured goods	187,701
Others	3,542

The table below shows the composition of UK imports of services in 2011 with the amount imported (shown in millions of pounds).

Trade in services (imports)	Amount imported (in £millions)
Transportation	19,951
Travel	31,830
Communications	4,704
Construction	1,065
Insurance	2,197
Financial	12,170
Computer and information	3,993
Royalties and license fees	6,654
Other business	30,246
Personal, cultural and recreational	640
Government	3,829

1.2   UK exports

The following information on the origin and composition of UK **exports** comes from the government's **'Pink Book'**. The top 20 countries of origin of UK exports of goods in 2011 are shown below (UK exports of services are in brackets).

1.	USA (1)	11.	India (21)
2.	Germany (2)	12.	Switzerland (6)
3.	Netherlands (3)	13.	Hong Kong (23)
4.	France (4)	14.	Russia (25)
5.	Ireland (5)	15.	United Arab Emirates (24)
6.	Belgium/Luxembourg (15/20)	16.	Canada (12)
7.	Italy (8)	17.	Japan (10)
8.	Spain (9)	18.	Australia (7)
9.	China (14)	19.	Poland (27)
10.	Sweden (13)	20.	Turkey (31)

The missing top 20 nations in the 'services' list in brackets are: Singapore (11), Denmark (16), The Channel Islands (17), Norway (18) and Saudi Arabia (19).

*Note that Belgium and Luxembourg are separated for services, but together for goods.

In summary, the most important destinations for UK exports of goods are the European Union and the United States. The most important destinations for UK exports of services are very similar.

1.2.1   UK exports (composition)

The table below shows the composition of UK exports of goods in 2011 with the amount exported (shown in millions of pounds).

Trade in goods (exports)	Amount exported (in £millions)
Food, beverages and tobacco	18,098
Basic materials	9,017
Oil	37,998
Coal, gas and electricity	4,724
Semi-manufactured goods	88,056
Finished manufactured goods	137,246
Others	3,848

The table below shows the composition of UK exports of services in 2011 with the amount exported (shown in millions of pounds).

Trade in services (exports)	Amount exported (in £millions)
Transportation	23,120
Travel	21,888
Communications	6,465
Construction	1,653
Insurance	10,210
Financial	50,833
Computer and information	9,167
Royalties and license fees	8,848
Other business	56,126
Personal, cultural and recreational	2,877
Government	2,472

1.2.2   UK trade by category

The table below gives a breakdown of UK exports and imports of goods by category in 2001 and a comparison with UK exports and imports of goods in 2011 to see if we can establish trends.

For simplification only a selection of the total number of categories is used in the table below. To understand this table you will need to be aware that the year 2009 is the base year and therefore

awarded a volume index of 100 in every case. All the numbers relate to the volume (quantity) of
goods, rather than the value.

Category	Exports			Imports		
	2001	2009	2011	2001	2009	2011
Crude oil	191	100	74	83	100	108
Oil products	62	100	97	107	100	86
Motor cars	74	100	165	104	100	122
Finished manufactured goods	104	100	123	91	100	114
Food, beverages and tobacco	83	100	113	78	100	102

Trade in goods (volume) by category

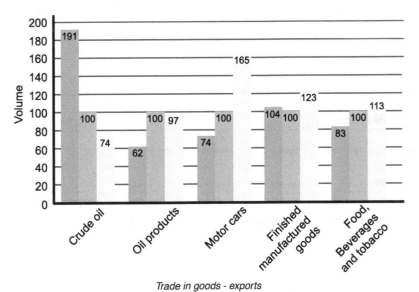

Trade in goods - exports

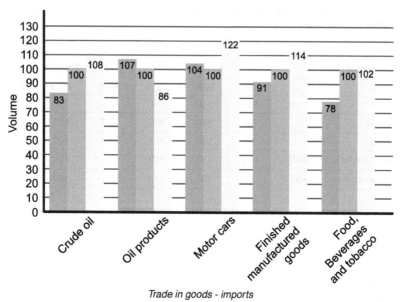

Trade in goods - imports

Analyse these figures to answer the following statements as true or false.

UK trade by category   Go online

Q2:   Exports of crude oil have reduced between 2001 and 2011.

a) True
b) False

....

Q3:   Imports of total finished manufactured goods have reduced between 2001 and 2011.

a) True
b) False

....

Q4:   Between 2009 and 2011, exports of cars grew faster than import of cars.

a) True
b) False

....

Q5: The UK's exports of food, beverages and tobacco have remained largely flat over the period 2001 to 2011.

a) True
b) False

....

Q6: Exports of total finished manufactured goods have declined over the decade.

a) True
b) False

Note that given the big changes in the value of a barrel of oil over these 10 years, that a fall in the *volume* of oil exports should not be taken to automatically mean a fall in the *value* of oil exports.

1.3 The advantages of trade

The theories of absolute and comparative advantage highlight one significant gain from trade. The world will produce more output from the same resource inputs. Other gains from trade can be categorised as gains for consumers or gains for producers.

The gains for consumers are:

- *variety* - new products from around the world;

- *choice* - greater variety of brands to select from;

- *price* - lower prices because of the increased competition;

- *quality* - competition encourages quality improvements and innovation.

The gains for producers are:

- *larger market* - opportunities for **economies of scale** increase with the greater number of customers;

- **diversification** - more than one market gives the benefits of diversification. Companies facing a recession at home will still hope to sell in export markets and vice versa;

- **multinational activity** - firms can produce at lowest cost locations, to increase efficiency and cut prices;

- *raw materials and components* - can be sourced from the cheapest locations around the world.

The advantages of trade   Go online

Q7: Giving three reasons, explain why countries engage in trade.
(6 marks)

Impact of international trade   Go online

Trade is likely to have an impact on UK consumers in the five areas in the questions below. In each case state whether trade is likely to decrease or increase.

Q8: Choice

a) Increase
b) Decrease

....

Q9: Competition

a) Increase
b) Decrease

....

Q10: Prices

a) Increase
b) Decrease

....

Q11: Quality

a) Increase
b) Decrease

....

Q12: Standard of living

a) Increase
b) Decrease

1.4   The disadvantages of trade

The disadvantages of trade are:

- workers (especially less-skilled workers) may lose their jobs to lower-wage economies as firms move production overseas;

- local firms may go out of business in the face of efficient competition from low-cost locations. The resulting unemployment may be concentrated in one region. Workers will need to be flexible and retrain, or move to a new location;

- the movement of goods around the planet will add to pollution;

- reliance on imports for some products may impinge on national security. For example, a dependence on imported armaments may be a weakness in time of conflict.

1.5   Global specialisation

The gains from international trade are vast. The rapid expansion of world output and the accompanying increase in standards of living stem in part from the growth of international trade. Specialisation by countries is a similar concept to specialisation by workers. The economies of scale associated with all forms of specialisation are a powerful engine of economic growth.

Globalisation is the term coined for the rapid expansion of trade in the last few decades. It refers to the increasingly inter-connected world economy. Developments such as the internet and modern communications have been factors. They have assisted the move to internationally recognised brands, and the standardisation of products. It also stems from technological developments such as "containerisation" which reduces the cost of transport. Multi-national firms have moved their production facilities to new locations as they seek ever lower costs of production.

Trade creates synergies. A synergy describes a situation where the sum is greater than the parts. The gains from trade outnumber any disadvantages. Politicians recognise the gains from trade and devote much energy to creating free trade areas such as the European Union. Trade increases economic growth and the resulting rise in **standards of living** assists politicians in their re-election.

Globalisation	Go online

Q13: Complete the paragraph below by inserting the correct words from the following list:

- brand;
- containerisation;
- internet;
- locations;
- specialisation;
- synergies;
- trade;
- workers.

Globalisation describes the rapid expansion of international .... Some developments that have contributed are the reduction in the costs of transporting goods through the development of .... and the increasing ease of modern communications using the .... These developments have led to multi-national firms reducing costs by finding new .... for production plants and the increasing prevalence of internationally recognised .... names.

1.6   Absolute advantage

The **theory of absolute advantage** shows that trade has the potential to increase the efficiency with which the world's scarce resources are used. By increasing efficiency, trade can increase world output from the same amount of inputs. Any increase in world output contributes to reducing poverty on the planet, providing the benefits are distributed in a way that reaches the poorest.

To create our example of absolute advantage we must simplify the world's complex trading patterns. Assume that:

- there are only two nations;
- and there are only two products.

To make the example straightforward, we need to select two very diverse countries: Australia and Belize. We also need to select two diverse products as the only two products in our world: aircraft and bananas.

The selection of two countries and products with the initials *a* and *b* will assist you in remembering this example is about ***ab***solute advantage.

Now we need to compare two positions, before trade and after trade, to find out if trade has benefits.

Before-trade output

Firstly, before trade, when both nations have to produce both goods for themselves. We assume that both countries have 100 units of factors of production. They have to produce both items so they each will use 50 factors to produce bananas and 50 factors to produce aircraft.

Australia is efficient at producing aircraft, but less so at producing bananas. In Australia, one factor of production will produce one aircraft. However, they find producing bananas more difficult and five factors of production are required for every ton of bananas.

Meantime, in Belize, bananas grow on trees and only one factor of production is needed to produce one ton of bananas. Producing aircraft in Belize would be expensive and difficult so it requires two factors of production to produce an aircraft.

The factors of production required for one unit of each output in each country are summarised in the efficiency table below. This shows the efficiency of each country at producing each product.

Country	Aircraft	Bananas
Australia	1	5
Belize	2	1

Efficiency table

We can use this table to work out how many of each product will be produced if no trade is taking place. Countries (with 100 factors each) use 50 factors for the production of each product.

Country	Aircraft	Bananas (tons)
Australia	50	10*
Belize	25	50
Total output (before trade)	75	60

Before-trade output

To ensure you understand how the figures above were calculated, have a close look at one of the figures. Our example* can be Australia producing 10 tons of bananas.

This is worked out as follows: Australia has 100 factor inputs, but because there is no trade and it also needs aircraft, we only allocate 50 (half) of the factor inputs to producing bananas. As Australia (see the efficiency table above) needs 5 factor inputs to produce 1 ton of bananas, then with its 50 factors it can only produce 10 tons of bananas. The other figures above are calculated in a similar way with reference to the efficiency table.

Finally, by adding the figures together we can see that total output before trade is 75 aircraft and 60 tons of bananas.

After-trade output

Next we allow trade between these nations. The inefficient producers are undercut by imports. It is no longer profitable for Australia to grow bananas or for Belize to make aircraft. If these products are produced in inefficient locations then the opportunity cost is high. Both countries specialise in what they are best at. All 100 factors are devoted to one product. The after-trade output follows:

Country	Aircraft	Bananas (tons)
Australia	100	0
Belize	0	100
Total output (after trade)	100	100

After-trade output

By specialising and trading, total output has risen by 25 aircraft (100 after trade less 75 before trade) and 40 tons of bananas (100 after less 60 before).

There was no increase in factor inputs. Factors of production (scarce resources) have merely been more efficiently used.

Transport costs

We have ignored transport costs - pretending they don't exist. The gains from international trade are so big that even after resources are used transporting products around the globe, there is still a gain. There are plentiful examples of how transport costs can be overcome. Fresh flowers flown in from Kenya to the UK and wine from New Zealand are two such examples. Clear evidence that even in the face of transportation costs from halfway round the globe, trade prospers and products can remain competitive.

Before-trade and after-trade output (absolute advantage)   Go online

The table below shows the output of two nations before trade. They must divide their factors of production equally between the manufacture of two goods.

Country	Cars	Vegetables
Urbania	50	20
Ruritania	40	60

Q14: What is the before-trade world output of cars?

....

Q15: What is the before-trade world output of vegetables?

....

Q16: What will be the after-trade world output of cars?

....

Q17: What will be the after-trade world output of vegetables?

....

Q18: Has world output increased as a result of trade?

a) Yes
b) No

1.7   Comparative advantage

The **theory of comparative advantage** refers to this situation - one nation has an efficiency advantage in making both products. We will test what happens if the advanced nation specialises in the product that it has the greatest efficiency advantage producing. This means we have to compare the efficiency advantages to find out which product the advanced nation has the greatest comparative advantage making.

To create our example we must again make assumptions to simplify the world's complex trading patterns. We therefore assume that:

- there are only two nations;
- there are only two products;
- transport costs are negligible;
- our inputs are homogeneous factors of production;
- these factors are flexible in changing use as required.

We need to select two goods to produce as the only two products in our world: cars and oranges. The choice of products beginning with *c* and *o* will help you associate this example with *co*mparative advantage.

Our two countries can be the USA and Mexico. We can realistically view the USA as the more advanced economy in this example.

Now we need to compare two positions, before trade and after trade, to find out if trade is still beneficial to both countries.

Before-trade output

Firstly, before trade, when both nations have to produce both goods for themselves. We assume that both countries have 100 units of factors of production. Because they have to produce both products, they each will use 50 factors to produce cars and 50 factors to produce oranges.

The USA has an absolute advantage in producing **both** cars and oranges. This can be shown in the efficiency table below, showing factors of production required for one unit of each output in each country.

Country	Cars	Oranges
USA	1	2
Mexico	2	5

Efficiency table

We can use this table to work out how many of each product will be produced if no trade is taking place. Countries (with 100 factors each) then have to use 50 factors for the production of each product.

Country	Cars	Oranges (tons)
USA	50	25*
Mexico	25	10
Total output (before trade)	75	35

Before-trade output

To ensure you understand how the figures above were calculated, have a close look at one of the figures. Our example* can be the USA producing 25 tons of oranges.

This is worked out as follows: the USA has 100 factor inputs, but because there is no trade and it needs to produce both cars and oranges, we only allocate half (50) of the factor inputs to producing oranges. As the USA (see the efficiency table above) needs two factor inputs to produce one ton of oranges, then with its 50 factors it can produces 25 tons of oranges. The other figures above are calculated in a similar way with reference to the efficiency table.

Finally, by adding the figures together we can see that total output before trade is 75 cars and 35 tons of oranges.

Logically you may at first glance expect there to be no gain for the USA from trading with a less efficient nation. As we will shortly see, the theory of comparative advantage proves that trade will still lead to a more effective use of scarce resource inputs. Even when one nation is more efficient in making both products it will allow an increase in total world output from the same quantity of inputs.

After-trade output (temporary)

Next we allow trade between these nations. First we have to recognise that the USA is two times as efficient at producing cars as Mexico. The USA produces 50 cars with 50 inputs of factors of production. In the case of oranges the USA is 2.5 times as efficient. It produces 25 tons of oranges with 50 inputs whereas Mexico produces 10 tons with 50 inputs. Look again at the efficiency table above to confirm this.

As a temporary step on the way to proving comparative advantage, we need to allow the USA to produce only that product in which it has the greatest comparative advantage. In this example that will be oranges. This is because it is 2.5 times as efficient at producing oranges and only 2 times as efficient at producing cars. Therefore Mexico has the least comparative disadvantage in producing cars. The after-trade output will temporarily look like this:

Country	Cars	Oranges (tons)
USA	0	50
Mexico	50	0
Total output	50	50

After-trade output (temporary)

You will notice that so far we are unable to confirm that world output has increased. We have more oranges and fewer cars.

After-trade output (amended)

One adjustment must be made to confirm that world output can increase. We allow the efficient nation to produce just enough cars to take us back to the original before-trade world output of 75 cars. We reduce their oranges production appropriately to reflect that some factors have been diverted back into car production.

Now with the USA making up the shortfall in cars, we obtain the following amended after-trade output.

Country	Cars	Oranges (tons)
USA	25	37.5
Mexico	50	0
Total output after trade	75	37.5

After-trade output (amended)

Now we have proved that world output has increased. We have the same number of cars and more oranges than we had before trade. Therefore the theory of comparative advantage proves that even when trade occurs between advanced economies and less efficient economies, it is effective in raising world output and improving the use of scarce resources.

Before-trade and after-trade output (comparative advantage)   Go online

This table shows the output of two nations before trade. They must divide their factors of production equally between the manufacture of two goods. Answer the questions that follow the table.

Country	Cars	Vegetables
Urbania	50	40
Ruritania	10	20

Q19: Both nations will benefit from specialisation and trade.

a) True
b) False

....

Q20: Ruritania has a comparative advantage in producing cars.

a) True
b) False

....

Q21: Urbania enjoys an absolute advantage in producing both cars and vegetables.

a) True
b) False

....

Q22: This is an example that can illustrate the theory of comparative advantage.

a) True
b) False

....

Q23: After trade, Ruritania will specialise in producing vegetables.

a) True
b) False

David Ricardo   Go online

The original explanation of comparative advantage (1817) is attributed to David Ricardo, the classical economist, in his book 'On the Principles of Political Economy and Taxation'. His example used Portugal and England, with the two products of cloth and wine.

Use the internet to find and read the original example from 200 years ago.

1.8   Trends in UK imports and exports

Let us now compare UK exports of goods in 2006 with UK exports of goods in 2012 to see if we can establish trends. To simplify we will select only five nations: United States, Germany, China, India and Japan. Germany's inclusion, the one example selected from the EU, is as a representative of the overall significance of EU nations.

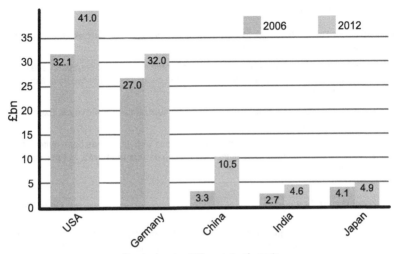

Graph showing UK exports of goods

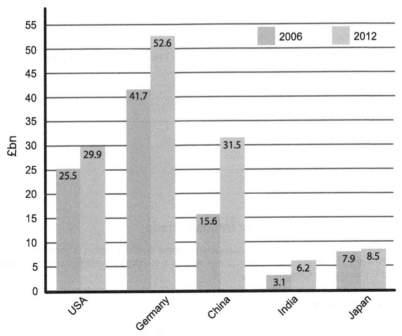

Graph showing UK imports of goods

Analysing the figures in the above graphs it is possible to come to the following conclusions about the geographic trends of UK trade:

- Despite closer links with the EU, the USA remains a major trading partner. In 2012 we had a surplus with the USA in trade in goods;

- Germany is another very significant trading partner, and it can be inferred that trade with other EU nations has also grown substantially. In the case of Germany we have a continuing deficit in trade in goods;

- The value of imports of goods from China has risen substantially in six years. Exports to China are also growing;

- Trade in goods with India is growing, but trade in goods with Japan has been quite flat over the decade. Japan remains a more significant trading partner than India, but perhaps not for much longer.

Trade surplus or deficit   Go online

Q24: Looking at the 2012 figures in the above five-nation graphs. Work out where the UK has a trade surplus in goods (exports more than imports) and where the UK has a trade deficit in goods (imports more than it exports).

Complete the table below, indicating whether the country has a trade surplus or deficit by entering Yes in the correct column.

Trade in goods (2006)	Trade surplus	Trade deficit
USA		
Germany		
China		
India		
Japan		

1.9   Patterns and reasons for trends in trade

When analysing the trade of the UK, the application of some everyday logic is a good way to start. Even without any specialised knowledge of Economics there is a good chance that you would select the correct options in the following activity.

Patterns and reasons for trends in trade   Go online

Select from the following pairs of statements the ones that you believe to be true.

Q25: It is easiest and cheapest to trade with .... nations.

a) neighbouring
b) distant

....

Q26: We can expect to sell more exports to nations with .... prosperous consumers.

a) less
b) more

....

Q27: We are likely to sell more exports to nations with .... populations.

a) large
b) small

....

Q28: We are .... likely to trade with fellow members of a free trade area.

a) more
b) less

The factors making large-scale trade with another nation probable are:

- **Geographic closeness** - transport costs have to be added to any product that is traded, and these will be less if the distance involved is less. This will allow traded products to sell at competitive prices in nearby export markets.

  If you are to sell goods successfully in a distant market, you will need to be very efficient producers so that even after long-distance transport costs, your goods are still price-competitive. Distant markets may be distant in a socio-cultural way as well as geographically and consumers may have very different tastes and expectations;

- **Prosperous consumers** - the higher the standard of living of the consumers, the more they will buy of all products (including your **exports**). Internationally traded goods are often luxury goods. For example, if you hope to sell cars in a foreign country, then high-income consumers are needed;

- **Large population** - the greater the number of potential consumers of your exports, the more likely you are to find a large market for your exports. The **European Union** has over 500 million consumers making it a very significant for UK trade. Similarly the United States is a very large and prosperous market for UK goods;

- **Free trade** - as yet you have not had free trade explained to you, but it sounds like a positive term and it is. Trade is more likely to occur if no obstacles such as taxes are put in the way. The European Union is a free trade area of 28 countries (in 2014) and over 500 million consumers.

Trading nations   Go online

Look at the data in the table below then consider how the following four nations "tick the boxes" for our factors making large-scale trade probable.

Nation	Near UK	Rich	Populated	EU member
Ireland	√	√	x	√
Japan	x	√	√	x
Germany	√	√	√	√
Morocco	x	x	x	x

Q29: Which of the above four nations would you expect the UK to export *most* to?

a) Ireland
b) Japan
c) Germany
d) Morocco

....

Q30: Which of the above four nations would you expect the UK to export *least* to?

a) Ireland
b) Japan
c) Germany
d) Morocco

From this approach you can see that Germany will be an important market for the UK's exports. It offers over 80 million affluent consumers just across the North Sea and has no trade barriers to UK goods.

Morocco is clearly unlikely to import much from the UK. Between them in importance will lie Japan and Ireland. We would have to guess if Japan's 127 million consumers compared to Ireland's 4.3 million will compensate for Japan's distance and non-membership of the EU.

Trading nations - Japan and Ireland   Go online

Q31: Considering only Japan and Ireland, which would you expect the UK to export more to?

a) Ireland
b) Japan

A little bit of research on the internet will check if our predictions are correct. On the internet it is possible to access the UK's trade figures in the UK Government's Pink Book. This provides the following data, in the graph below, for 2012.

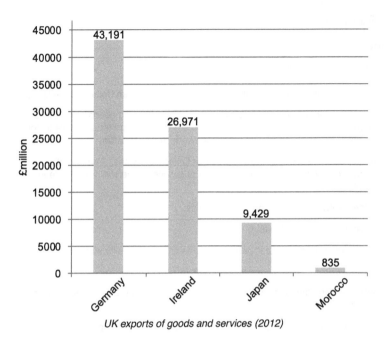

UK exports of goods and services (2012)

The results show the importance of nearness and membership of a free trade area. Ireland has significance for our exports out of proportion to its small population.

1.10   Summary

Summary

You should now know that:

- the UK's most significant trading partners are the European Union and the USA;

- our major exports of goods include finished manufactured goods, semi-manufactured goods, crude oil and oil products, and food, beverages and tobacco. We import more goods in the same categories and have a trade in goods deficit;

- in services, the UK is a major exporter of financial services. Transportation and travel feature highly in the value of UK imported services. The UK has a trade in services surplus;

- trade involves specialisation among nations;

- trade increases world output;

- trade increases competition resulting in greater variety, quality and innovation;

- increased competition also reduces prices;

- increased standards of living result as falling prices allow consumers to buy more with their incomes;

- trade will cause some workers to lose their jobs to foreign competition;

- trade with emerging economies such as China is increasing;

- trade with the EU and the USA remains of great significance;

- trade patterns reflect the geographic closeness, prosperity and population of partner nations, along with the absence/level of trade barriers.

1.11 End of topic test

End of Topic 1 test   Go online

Q32: Describe the main trends in UK trade.

(12 marks)

....

Q33: Which of the following nations specialises in financial services because of an educated workforce?

a) Canada
b) China
c) Israel
d) Italy
e) United Kingdom
f) Zambia

....

Q34: Which of the following nations specialises in wine production because of a suitable climate and soil?

a) Canada
b) China
c) Israel
d) Italy
e) United Kingdom
f) Zambia

....

Q35: Which of the following nations specialises in basic manufactured goods because of low labour costs?

a) Canada
b) China
c) Israel
d) Italy
e) United Kingdom
f) Zambia

....

Q36: Which of the following nations specialises in wheat production on abundant land?

a) Canada
b) China
c) Israel
d) Italy
e) United Kingdom
f) Zambia

. . . .

Q37: Which of the following nations specialises in oranges because of climate?

a) Canada
b) China
c) Israel
d) Italy
e) United Kingdom
f) Zambia

. . . .

Q38: Which of the following nations specialises in copper production by mining a natural resource?

a) Canada
b) China
c) Israel
d) Italy
e) United Kingdom
f) Zambia

. . . .

Q39: Complete the paragraph below by inserting the correct words from the following list:

- bananas;
- choice;
- competition;
- living;
- prices;
- quality;
- standard.

As a result of trade, consumers will have more .... , for example, ... , that cannot be easily grown in the UK. Companies will face increased .... and as a result will have to increase .... and reduce .... to stay in business. This will mean that consumers will have a higher .... of ....

. . . .

Q40: Explain the theories of absolute and comparative advantage. *(SQA 2007)*

(8 marks)

Unit 3 Topic 2

Multinationals

Contents

Prerequisites

This topic assumes no previous knowledge and is intended to be accessible for those studying Economics for the first time. However, if you have already completed National 5 Grade Economics you will be familiar with some of the concepts outlined.

Learning objective

By the end of this topic you should be able to:

- define the term 'multinational' and name an example;

- explain the factors that affect the location of a multinational;

- describe the effects of a multinational on the home and host countries.

2.1   Defining multinational

A **multinational** is a company that is based in one country, but also has production or service facilities in other countries. It should not be confused with companies that merely export from their home base.

Most of the world's largest companies are multinationals, for example Ford, Nestle and BP. You can probably name some other examples off the top of your head.

The countries in which BP operates	Go online

Q1:   Go on to the BP website and compile a list of all the countries in which it operates.

2.2   Location factors

The location factors for multinationals, outlined below, are not very different from the location factors for any firm:

- **Costs of production** - Minimising costs of production is vital. To reduce costs, companies find locations where wages are lower and/or raw materials are cheaper. Transport and distribution costs to major markets cannot be overlooked and will come into the final decision.

  An additional factor may be the existence of tariffs or other trade barriers between nations, which could greatly restrict the choice of location.

- **Infrastructure** - This is a broad term which we can divide into three components:

  - *Transport* - Are the road, rail, sea and air links sufficient to allow the firm to operate efficiently and without unpredictable delays in getting goods to the market?

  - *Technology* - Does the country have access to the latest information and communications systems and will these systems function adequately?

  - *Institutional* - Is there a framework of business and contract law that facilitates business?

- **Markets** - This is a major factor.   Developing local markets is often crucial to success, and multinationals may withdraw from markets where they cannot reach a suitable level of customer demand and are consequently unable to deliver the economies of scale that lead to profit.

- **Risk** - There are political and economic risks to consider. What are the chances of a violent revolution? Will the exchange rate of the currency move against you? Could there be an epidemic or a natural disaster such as a flood?

Location factors   Go online

Select the correct location factor group for the following location factors.

Q2: Good harbour facilities

a) Cost factors
b) Infrastructure concerns
c) Risk factors

....

Q3: Hyperinflation

a) Cost factors
b) Infrastructure concerns
c) Risk factors

....

Q4: Mobile phone communications

a) Cost factors
b) Infrastructure concerns
c) Risk factors

....

Q5: Raw materials are cheaper

a) Cost factors
b) Infrastructure concerns
c) Risk factors

....

Q6: Rebels in the hills

a) Cost factors
b) Infrastructure concerns
c) Risk factors

....

Q7: Wages are lower

a) Cost factors
b) Infrastructure concerns
c) Risk factors

2.3   The effects on the host country

Some of the effects on the host country in which a multinational operates include:

- creating employment, and this has a positive multiplier effect on the economy;
- training of workers;
- largely repatriating profits to the home nation, so profits are not always reinvested locally. This money leaves the host's circular flow as a leakage;
- improving standards by offering better working conditions than local firms;
- undercutting local firms' prices which may put them out of business;
- introducing modern technology and management methods;
- potentially causing pollution and long-term environmental damage;
- increasing exports, improving the balance of payments, and injecting money into the country's circular flow;
- delivering only low-skilled jobs, retaining top jobs in management and research at the home base;
- potentially may be footloose with little loyalty, and move on in a few years to a cheaper location;
- exploiting workers by taking advantage of weak labour laws.

The effects on the host country

Go online

Q8: Separate the following effects on the host country into the positive or negative column in the table below:

- creates employment;
- improves working conditions;
- increases exports;
- introduces modern technology;
- may cause pollution;
- may switch location;
- only provides low skill jobs;
- profits often repatriated;
- trains workers;
- undercuts local firms' prices.

Positive	Negative

2.4 The effects on the home country

Some of the effects on the home country in which a multinational operates include:

- jobs being lost overseas, with a negative multiplier effect;
- **deindustrialisation**, and loss of skills in the workforce;
- profits are often repatriated and contribute to investment in the home country;
- home-based firms continue to compete on world markets and survive (or even thrive);
- fewer exports and negative impact on balance of trade.

The effects on the home country   Go online

Q9: Separate the following effects on the home country into the positive or negative column in the table below:

- deindustrialisation;
- fewer exports;
- jobs are lost overseas;
- profits repatriated;
- survival of home-based firm.

Positive	Negative

2.5   Summary

Summary

You should now be able to:

- define the term 'multinational';
- describe location factors that multinationals must consider;
- describe effects on the home country;
- describe effects on the host country.

2.6 End of topic test

End of Topic 2 test   Go online

Q10: One example of a UK-based multinational would be:

a) Ford
b) Tata
c) Nestle
d) First Group

....

Q11: A multinational company must:

a) export goods or services.
b) produce in more than one country.
c) Both of the above.
d) Neither of the above.

....

Q12: One negative outcome for the host country of a multinational is:

a) the repatriation of profits.
b) the creation of low skilled jobs.
c) the introduction of modern technology.
d) increasing exports.

....

Q13: One positive outcome for the home country of a multinational is:

a) deindustrialisation.
b) the repatriation of profits.
c) the creation of low skilled jobs.
d) increasing exports.

....

Q14: One risk factor for multinationals to consider is:

a) training required for workers.
b) poor communications.
c) political instability.
d) poor transport infrastructure.

....

Q15: Describe the factors that a multinational firm must consider before taking the decision to locate overseas.
(6 marks)

Unit 3 Topic 3

Exchange rates

Contents

Prerequisites

This topic assumes no previous knowledge and is intended to be accessible for those studying Economics for the first time. However, if you have already completed National 5 Grade Economics you will be familiar with some of the concepts outlined.

Learning objective

By the end of this topic you should be able to:

- define the meaning of the term "exchange rate" and name several world currencies;

- explain why a currency is demanded or supplied;

- understand the effect of high and low exchange rates on individuals, firms and the current account;

- compare the advantages and disadvantages of fixed and floating exchange rates;

- describe the trends in the value of the £ over the last decade.

3.1   Exchange rates

An **exchange rate** is the rate at which one currency can be converted into another. It is the value of one currency priced in a different currency.

Here are some exchange rates for currencies equal to 1 British pound sterling at the time this item was composed:

- 1.29 **Euros**;

- 1.52 US Dollars;

- 177.62 Japanese Yen;

- 1.55 Swiss Francs;

- 3.49 Turkish Lira;

- 94.36 Indian Rupees;

- 5.53 Polish Zloty;

- 9.40 Chinese Yuan.

An exchange rate is determined by market conditions. The market is called the foreign exchange market, sometimes abbreviated to **FOREX**. In this market, demand and supply interact to create the market price for a currency.

The fundamental reason why a currency has to be changed into another currency is to enable international transactions. However, the currency transactions required for trade to take place are now dwarfed by other market activity. Speculators buy and sell currencies as they see an opportunity to profit. Central banks, such as The Bank of England, intervene in foreign currency markets to influence the market price and enact a government's foreign exchange policy. Multi-national companies attempt to profit (or at least not lose) by their trading activity on the currency markets.

Current exchange rates   Go online

Research the current exchange rates for the eight currencies above.

There are many sites which will do this for you. One possibility is to go to the BBC website and follow the trail: news > business > market data > currencies. Another possibility is using a search engine. For example, using Google search for the term 'exchange rate pound' displays a currency converter at the top of the search results. A drop down menu of currencies allows you to compare the current value of the pound sterling with all the world's currencies.

Present your answers in a table using Word or Excel if possible. You can then look back in a week's time to see what the changes are. The actual exchange rates will vary from minute to minute, so there is no definitive solution to this activity, but you should compare and discuss your answers with a classmate.

3.2   The demand for sterling

The demand for sterling comes from the purchase of UK exports by foreign consumers and companies. The consumers pay in local currency and are unaware of their involvement, but somewhere down the supply chain an importer will need to convert the local cash into pounds because the UK producer expects to be paid in pounds. The foreign currency is presented (supplied) by the importer's bank to the foreign exchange market and pounds are demanded.

It follows that export success helps to drive the value of a country's currency upwards, because it increases demand for that currency. Apart from purchases of UK goods and services by foreign consumers and companies, foreign firms will need to obtain pounds if they are investing in the UK.

When the demand for pounds is higher than the supply, then the exchange rate of the pound will rise. This effect can be illustrated on the demand diagram below.

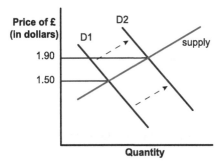

The market for currency: increasing demand for pounds

In the above diagram the demand for pounds increases from D1 to D2, shown by a rightwards movement of the demand line. The value of the pound increases and one pound is now able to buy $1.90 compared to $1.50 previously.

'**Hot money**' flows are placed in pounds whenever attractive interest rates are available in the UK. 'Hot money' describes liquid funds that can be switched to another currency at short notice. Increases in UK interest rates can lead to an increased demand for pounds, because of the improved returns available in UK banks. Therefore, increases in UK interest rates relative to the interest rates available elsewhere, will increase demand for pounds and take the value of the pound upwards.

Professionals operating in markets make money when they predict the next move by a market. Often when a change in interest rates happens, the market experts have already altered the currency value in the preceding days. The currency makes little further move and the markets are said to have discounted the interest rate change in advance. Expectations impact on the market as well as actual events.

Demand for currency   Go online

Select the option *increase* or *decrease* in the questions below to indicate whether or not the following scenarios would cause the demand for the pound to increase or decrease (other things being equal).

Q1: Expectation that the Bank of England is about to raise interest rates.

a) Increase
b) Decrease

....

Q2: The European Central Bank puts up the euro interest rate.

a) Increase
b) Decrease

....

Q3: Record levels of foreign investment in the UK.

a) Increase
b) Decrease

....

Q4: The US Federal Reserve puts down its dollar interest rate.

a) Increase
b) Decrease

3.3   The supply of sterling

As an effective student you should know that the reasons that cause an increase in the supply of a currency are largely the reverse of the factors listed as causing the demand for a currency.

UK consumers and companies purchasing imports will supply pounds to the foreign exchange market for conversion into the currency they require. UK companies investing overseas will do the same. Speculators can become involved in selling currencies and the Bank of England may also supply pounds to the market if it prefers the pound not to rise in value. Hot money can leave the UK as quickly as it arrives with one phone call or a tap on a computer.

When the supply of pounds is greater than demand then the exchange rate of the pound will fall. This effect can be illustrated on the supply diagram below.

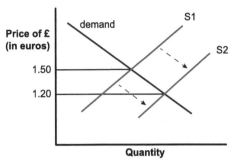

Quantity

The market for currency: increasing supply of pounds

In the above diagram the supply of pounds increases from S1 to S2, shown by a rightwards movement of the supply line. The value of the pound decreases and it is now able to buy euro1.20 compared to euro1.50 previously.

The supply of currency   Go online

Select the appropriate words from the alternatives offered to reverse the section on demand for sterling. In the following three questions your aim is to make up correct sentences about the **supply** of pounds (sterling).

Q5: The *(demand for/supply of)* sterling comes from the purchase of UK *(exports/imports)* by *(foreign/UK)* consumers and companies.

....

Q6: It follows that *(import penetration/export success)* helps to drive the value of a country's currency *(downwards/upwards)*, because it increases *(demand for/supply of)* that currency.

....

Q7: 'Hot money' flows are *(placed in/taken out)* of pounds whenever attractive interest rates are available *(in the UK/outside the UK)*. *(Increases/Decreases)* in UK interest rates can lead to an *(increased demand for/increased supply of)* pounds, because of the *(diminished/improved)* returns available in UK banks.

3.4   The effect of a rising exchange rate on the economy

Exchange rates cause changes in other economic variables. We will now look closely at the effect a changing exchange rate can have on the levels of exports and imports, the inflation rate, economic growth and the level of employment.

When the pound increases, the price of UK exports in foreign markets will rise.

Example : Jaguar

Let us consider a Jaguar car selling for £40,000.

At first the exchange rate is £1 = euro1.25.

To allow Jaguar to receive the price of £40,000, the car will be priced at euro50,000 in the eurozone (e.g. Germany). This is arithmetic: 40,000 × 1.25 converts the pounds into euros.

Next, the exchange rate of the pound increases to £1 = euro1.50. Each pound will buy more euros than it used to, so this is described as the pound increasing in value.

To allow Jaguar to receive the price of £40,000, the car will be now priced at euro60,000 in the eurozone (e.g. Germany). To convert the pounds into euros we now multiply £40,000 × 1.5.

Therefore, we can conclude that a rise in the value of the pound is bad news for UK exporters such as Jaguar. To continue receiving £40,000 and maintain the profit margin on each car they will need to increase their eurozone price by 20%, exactly the percentage that the pound has risen by against the euro in our example. Meantime makers such as BMW and Mercedes are able to hold their prices, and thus Jaguar are at a competitive disadvantage.

It is feasible that companies who have invested heavily in acquiring market share or have a franchised dealer network may choose to take a cut in profits or even make a loss in the short term rather than see market share fall and their hard work undone. They cannot adopt this position for long.

Improving productivity can also offset price rises abroad but that would be a gradual process and could not compensate for a rapid increase in an exchange rate. Unless the exchange rate rise is temporary the price competitiveness of UK exports is bound to deteriorate. The volume of UK exports will therefore decrease.

By reversing the process described above, imports into the UK become cheaper. Our example, Jaguar, will be hit again. This time it will be under pressure in its UK home market because BMW and Mercedes will be able to reduce their price in pounds. The volume of UK imports will increase when the exchange rate of the pound rises.

The effect of a rising exchange rate on the economy	Go online

Q8: Assume a Mercedes car costs euro90,000 and the exchange rate is £1 = euro1.25. Calculate the selling price in pounds in the UK required to return euro90,000 to Germany.

. . . .

Q9: Assume the exchange rate changes. The pound strengthens and £1 will now buy euro1.50. Calculate the selling price in pounds in the UK now required to return euro90,000 to Germany.

We can conclude that Mercedes can cut their price in the UK to £60,000 or increase their profit on each car sold in the UK by a further £12,000. Possibly they will do a bit of both - cutting price by a portion and increasing profits. This shows how dramatic changes in profits and price competitiveness can be when exchange rates move.

3.5 The effect of a rising exchange rate on inflation, economic growth and employment

The effect of a rising exchange rate on inflation

The previous section established that importers are able to reduce their prices when the exchange rate rises. In the example, BMWs and Mercedes were going to be cheaper in the UK. Imports are items we buy and therefore feature in the consumer price index (CPI) which is the measure of inflation. If some items in the CPI are reduced in price then the index will rise more slowly so inflation slows down.

The effects on UK companies may include:

- seeking new ways to reduce costs or accept a profit cut to remain competitive. They may also reduce prices. Therefore, at least for internationally traded goods, a rising exchange rate will cut inflation;

- having to lay off workers if their sales reduce. This will reduce demand in the economy, and again slow down inflation;

- UK producers using components and raw materials from abroad. As the cost of these reduces, UK companies may pass these savings on to customers by reducing their prices.

The effect of a rising exchange rate on economic growth and employment

UK exporters are going to struggle to remain competitive abroad. In home markets, imports are going to have a competitive edge. These are conditions that will lead to many UK firms cutting costs to survive. They will look at all their operations and assess. The conclusions they are likely to come to will involve closing less efficient plants and looking to reduce labour costs through redundancies. Words like "restructuring", "rationalisation", "downsizing" and "delayering" will occur frequently in the business pages. The weakest UK firms and those slow to adjust will go out of business.

Other effects may include:

- jobs will be lost, economic growth will slow down and there is the possibility of recession. The danger then is that recession drags down even efficient firms as a negative multiplier effect takes hold on the general economy;

- on a more positive note, the slowdown may not go as far as recession and during the process UK productivity will rise under the competitive pressures and a leaner, more efficient UK economy will emerge;

- when the least efficient go out of business, average productivity in the economy can be expected to improve as only the most efficient survive.

The effect of a rising exchange rate on inflation, economic growth and   Go online
employment

Q10: A rising exchange rate makes our exports more *(expensive/cheaper)*, and our imports *(expensive/cheaper)*. This *(increases/decreases)* unemployment because UK goods are *(less/more)* price competitive in world markets. With less output economic growth *(increases/decreases)*, and combined with a *(negative/positive)* multiplier effect, there is a danger of *(inflation/recession)*.

3.6 The effect of a falling exchange rate on individuals, firms and the current account

A falling exchange rate logically works in the opposite way to a rising exchange rate. As a student, you have a shortcut to completing your understanding of the effects of changing exchange rates.

If you have followed the reasoning in the previous sections on rising exchange rates, it should not be difficult to work out the effects of a falling exchange rate. Let us fill in some missing words to check your understanding.

The effect of a falling exchange rate   Go online

Q11: Complete the paragraph by choosing the correct words from the following list:

- employment;
- exports;
- growth;
- imports;
- inflation;
- more;
- raise.

A falling exchange rate for the pound will make our .... cheaper and our .... more expensive. This will make UK exporters .... price competitive. In home markets foreign firms will be under pressure to .... prices. As a result UK firms may increase output thus increasing economic .... This will create more .... in the UK. However the cost of imports will make .... higher.

To summarise the effects of a falling exchange rate:

- Inflation will tend to rise because of the rising costs of imported goods and services, and the rising price of imported raw materials and components. If rising inflation encourages expectations of future inflation then trade unions will demand higher wage rises and inflation in the UK economy could become built-in and difficult to reduce.
- UK exporters will enjoy a price advantage in foreign markets. In the home market, it will be

harder for imports to remain competitive. Both of these outcomes of a falling exchange rate will increase sales by UK firms and hence UK output. Faster economic growth will lead to higher employment.

3.7 Fixed exchange rates

An **exchange rate that is fixed** will be set by a central bank at a level which it intends will be maintained. This will involve agreements with other central banks so that an appropriate level can be agreed for each exchange rate in a fixed system. Historically the best example was the gold standard. Each country's currency was exchangeable at the central bank for a fixed weight of gold. In effect this fixed the relative values of currencies. Britain abandoned the gold standard in 1931.

More recently in the run-up to the creation of the Euro currency, there was a period when the currencies lining up to convert to the euro sought to maintain their values against each other. This process of "convergence" was similar to a fixed exchange rate system as central banks sought to maintain approximate levels within the European Exchange Rate Mechanism (ERM) and to narrow down the fluctuations between these currencies. There were several realignments along the way, so "fixed" is better thought of as "flexible". When these currencies were finally traded in for euros, this was in a sense a permanent fix of these exchange rates. Fixed so firmly that they vanished and became one.

The advantages of fixed exchange rates

Fixed exchange rates could be claimed to have the following benefits:

- Speculators, for long periods, accept these exchange rates in the knowledge that concerted action from central banks will maintain them making successful speculation difficult.

- Stability is created for business in international markets, encouraging trade and foreign investment as there is certainty that unpredictable currency movements will not impact on profits.

- The soft option for governments of devaluing a currency to recover price competitiveness is not easily available. Rather, they must address underlying economic problems such as inflation or low productivity.

The disadvantages of fixed exchange rates

Speculators over time will notice the divergence of different economies. They will appreciate that the prevailing fixed exchange rates are historic. Some economies will advance rapidly with export-led economic growth and increasing productivity. The relative position of other economies will decline. A shift sooner or later will have to occur in the fixed exchange rates.

Speculators (who always understand economics) will see the opportunity of a one-way bet. As there is only one possible direction for an exchange rate in a fast advancing economy to go, they will begin buying this currency (and selling currencies of countries with the least positive economic outlook). If they are wrong it will probably just be in the timing, and meanwhile they can always extract their money from the foreign exchange market at no loss. This is a bet you can win without much risk: a one-way bet.

Stability in currency markets as a generator of international trade can easily be over-rated. Markets have developed, such as the futures market, where companies can fix the currency value for their trade. Speculators then take the risk of any ups and downs in the currency, and the company knows exactly what it will receive from its foreign transaction. Note that speculators perform a useful function in markets when they take on risk.

On the issue of devaluing a currency being a soft option - if repeated devaluations occur that is perhaps so. However, as an alternative to stringent fiscal or monetary policies, taking the so-called soft option may be an effective escape route for a troubled economy, allowing it to avoid unemployment. Why reduce the number of economic options available to a country? **Devaluation** should be considered on its merits as a possible breathing space for an economy while issues of low productivity are addressed.

Central banks require to hold large reserves of gold and foreign currency to use for intervention in the market to defend fixed exchange rates.

Fixed exchange rates   Go online

Q12: Complete the paragraph by choosing the correct words from the following list:

- automatically;
- central;
- certainty;
- intervention;
- profitability;
- quality;
- reserves;
- speculation.

Fixed exchange rates allow firms to trade with .... that exchange rate movements will not affect the .... of international contracts. For long periods, ... will not take place because .... banks will successfully maintain the currency value.

3.8   Floating exchange rates

An exchange rate that floats freely in the foreign exchange market moves according to supply and demand. A distinction is often made between a **"clean" float** and a **"dirty" float**.

A "clean" float is where the central bank does not intervene in the market as a buyer or seller of the currency. The pound sterling is a clean floating exchange rate.

A "dirty" float describes a floating exchange rate that is managed by central bank intervention in the market. The government has a clear view on what the value of its "floating" exchange rate should be. Through its central bank it buys and sells on the market to influence the currency value.

The advantages of floating exchange rates

Floating exchange rates are claimed to have the following benefits:

* They adjust constantly to the prevailing economic conditions and thus speculators are unable to spot a misalignment of the currency that would provide an opportunity for speculation.

* If large-scale intervention by a central bank to support a currency is no longer going to take place then large reserves of gold and foreign currency are not required.

* The economic problems such as inflation or unemployment that can be exacerbated by too high or too low a currency value can be avoided.   The currency adjusts constantly and automatically to reflect prevailing economic conditions. The market mechanism of supply and demand is relied upon to set an appropriate exchange rate.

The disadvantages of floating exchange rates

Markets can over-shoot. Market sentiment is not the same as speculation. Markets are made up of traders and there will always be a psychological component to their behaviour. The prevailing conventional wisdom may temporarily lead markets in an inappropriate direction.   Belief in the benevolence of markets should be tempered.

The steady decline of a currency over time remains an option for a government that refuses to deal with supply-side productivity problems within its economy. Allowing your currency to sink slowly may be an option taken to avoid hard decisions that address fundamental economic problems with tough fiscal, monetary or supply-side policies.

Exchange rate policy such as having a higher exchange rate to reduce inflation is no longer an option. By allowing a free float, you exclude the possibility of using the exchange rate to control your economy.

Speculators will not go away. The currencies of small countries will be particularly open to bouts of speculation. The act of speculation brings about the expected outcome. If a currency is heavily sold its price will fall. The speculators bring about the very outcome they were speculating on. In early 2008 there were rumours that the Icelandic currency was witnessing just such a bout of market manipulation.

Stability of exchange rates assists international trade. The futures market allows firms to be certain as to the exchange rate they will receive even in a world of floating exchange rates. However the speculators taking on risk by trading on the futures market will expect to return an overall profit from their dealings. Therefore using the futures market must create an extra cost for companies.

Floating exchange rates   Go online

Q13: Complete the paragraph by choosing the correct words from the following list:

- automatically;
- floating;
- intervention;
- over-shoot;
- profit;
- quality;
- reserves;
- speculators.

Floating exchange rates .... adjust to prevailing economic conditions. No .... by central banks means that large .... of foreign currency are not required and .... find it difficult to spot an inappropriate exchange value to .... from when the rates reflect prevailing economic conditions.

3.9   Exchange rate systems summary

Exchange rate systems   Go online

For each question on exchange rate systems, decide if the scenario is an advantage for a fixed or a floating exchange rate.

Q14: Controlling inflation with a high exchange rate.

a) Advantage for fixed exchange rate
b) Advantage for floating exchange rate

....

Q15: Reducing the need for gold and currency reserves.

a) Advantage for fixed exchange rate
b) Advantage for floating exchange rate

....

Q16: Automatic adjustment to reflect state of economy.

a) Advantage for fixed exchange rate
b) Advantage for floating exchange rate

....

Q17: Stability and certainty that encourages trade.

a) Advantage for fixed exchange rate
b) Advantage for floating exchange rate

3.10 Trends in the pound to dollar exchange rate - a historical perspective

The exchange rate between the UK pound and the US dollar is one of the longest established in history. The table below shows a selection of the figures over the years from 1791.

Year	$s to £s	Notes
1791	4.55	Earliest available figure
1875	5.59	High point of nineteenth century
1900	4.87	End of Nineteenth Century
1934	4.93	During the Great Depression
1942	4.04	Middle of World War 2
1950	2.80	This rate was maintained until the late 1960s
1970	2.40	After devaluation of 1960s
1977	1.75	1970s low point

Trends in the pound to dollar exchange rate   Go online

Q18: From the table below of recent dollar to pound exchange rates produce a line graph for the years 1992 to 2014. This can be done on MS Excel or by hand.

Year	Rate	Year	Rate
1992	1.77	2004	1.83
1993	1.50	2005	1.82
1994	1.53	2006	1.84
1995	1.58	2007	2.00
1996	1.56	2008	1.85
1997	1.64	2009	1.57
1998	1.66	2010	1.55
1999	1.62	2011	1.60
2000	1.52	2012	1.58
2001	1.44	2013	1.56
2002	1.50	2014	1.56
2003	1.64	2015	n/a

3.11 Summary

┌─ Summary ───

At the end of this topic students should know that:

- an exchange rate is the price of one currency in terms of another currency;

- the pound is demanded when:

  o the UK's exports are purchased;

  o tourists come to the UK;

  o foreign companies invest in the UK;

  o the Bank of England supports it by buying pounds;

  o UK interest rates increase;

- the pound is supplied when:

  o UK consumers purchase imports;

  o UK tourists go abroad;

  o UK companies invest abroad;

  o the Bank of England sells pounds;

  o UK interest rates decrease;

- the exchange rate has implications for individuals, firms and the current account of the balance of payments;

- a fixed exchange rate system offers stability and certainty about returns and encourages trade and international investment. If the fixed rate begins to look untenable then speculators will profit by taking positions in advance of an inevitable devaluation or revaluation;

- a floating exchange rate in theory adjusts automatically to the prevailing economic conditions. Market sentiment can change and the adjustment process can be quite rapid;

- the volatility of currencies as shown by the pound / dollar exchange rate over time.

3.12   End of topic test

End of Topic 3 test   Go online

The UK has decided not to join the Eurozone and will continue to allow sterling to float. One reason for this is that joining the Eurozone would result in a large fall in the UK rate of interest. *(SQA 2007)*

Q19: The demand for the pound increases when:

a) exports from the UK increase.
b) UK tourists go abroad.
c) the Bank of England lowers interest rates.
d) there is expectation that the pound will devalue.

....

Q20: Other things being equal, a fall in the exchange rate of the pound should:

a) decrease employment.
b) decrease inflation.
c) increase imports.
d) increase exports.

....

Q21: Compared to floating exchange rates, fixed exchange rates have the problem that:

a) as economies grow at different rates, they become unsustainable.
b) international business contracts are more difficult to conclude.
c) Both of the above.
d) Neither of the above.

....

Q22: If the UK joined the eurozone, it would lose independent control of:

a) taxation.
b) transport infrastructure.
c) government spending.
d) interest rates.

....

Q23: The demand for a currency with speculative 'hot money' will depend on:

a) relative interest rates being high for that currency.
b) the risk of a fall in the exchange rate of that currency being low.
c) Both of the above.
d) Neither of the above.

....

Q24: Explain factors that determine the demand for sterling on the foreign exchange markets.

(8 marks)

. . . .

Q25: Discuss the advantages and disadvantages for a country of having a floating exchange rate.

(10 marks)

. . . .

Q26: Explain some of the economic problems that could result from a large fall in the UK rate of interest.

(7 marks)

Unit 3 Topic 4

The balance of payments

Contents

Prerequisites

This topic assumes no previous knowledge and is intended to be accessible for those studying Economics for the first time. However, if you have already completed National 5 Economics, you will be familiar with some of the concepts outlined.

Learning objective

By the end of this topic you should be able to:

- be able to define the terms balance of payments, current account and capital account;

- be able to explain the components of the current account of the balance of payments;

- understand the trade terms visibles and invisibles;

- be able to explain the components of the capital and financial account of the balance of payments;

- understand the reasons why the balance of payments may move into surplus or deficit;

- be familiar with trends in the balance of payments over the last 10 years, and the reasons for these trends;

- be able to explain the methods that can be used to reduce current account deficits.

4.1   Definition of the balance of payments

The economic transactions of UK residents with the rest of the world are recorded in an account called the **balance of payments**. It also shows how these transactions are funded.

Items in the balance of payments include:

- exports and imports of goods;
- exports and imports of services;
- dividends and interest paid across national boundaries (**income flows**);
- international investment flows in and out of the UK (**financial flows**);
- foreign aid and transfers to and from international organisations such as the European Union (**transfers**).

The balance of payments is a balance sheet. As an accountant will tell you, a balance sheet is supposed to balance. Every transaction that goes into a balance sheet is subject to a system called double entry accounting. The value of the item purchased is entered on one side of the accounts and how you paid for it (the same value) is entered on the other side. An accountant would say that "every debit has a credit". Therefore technically, the final figures on the balance of payments always balance. When it doesn't, an entry **'errors and omissions'** is made to force the balance.

The balance of payments is divided into two sections:

- the **current account**;
- the **capital and financial account**.

An example of the layout of the balance of payments with the main components highlighted is shown below.

1. Current account	Credits (exports in £ million)	Debits (imports in £ million)
A. Goods and services	369,691	424,128
B. Income	241,350	222,795
C. Current transfers	16,165	28,064
Total current account	**627,206**	**674,987**
2. Capital and financial accounts		
A. Capital account	3,818	2,988
B. Financial account	687,387	654,582
Total capital and financial accounts	**691,205**	**657,570**
Total (totals of current account + capital and financial account)	1,318,411	1,332,557
Net errors and omissions	14,146	
Balance	**1,332,557**	**1,332,557**

Pink Book - balance of payment figures   Go online

The latest figures for the UK's balance of payments can be researched in the UK Government's annual 'Pink Book' of balance of payments details. The Pink Book can be accessed on the internet.

Locate the balance of payments figures for the most recent available year and present them in a table as in the example above. Be prepared to read carefully through the contents list to find the correct page.

Note: There is no definitive solution to this exercise as it will depend on the year.

4.2   Definition of current account

The current account measures income flows during the year. The most significant items in this section are payments for exports and imports of both goods and services.

Non-trade items in the current account include investment income (repatriation of profits and dividends). The transfer of interest payments from money in overseas accounts is also included in the current account. You may see this summarised as IPD (interest, profits and dividends).

The term 'transfers' is used to describe:

- overseas aid;

- contributions to the budgets of international organisations (e.g. the European Union);

- money sent overseas by immigrant workers to their families.

The current account on the UK balance of payments   Go online

Watch the following YouTube video for further information about the current account - https://youtu.be/piqWu1kSSOE ('Balance of Payments The current account balance') .

4.3   Component elements of the current account

Goods are tangible objects. Goods of all sorts are termed '**visibles**' in trade talk, presumably because you possess the object and can look at it or show it to somebody else. The difference between visible exports and visible imports has a particular title. It is called the **balance of trade**.

The UK balance of trade has rarely been in the black (visible exports greater than visible imports) in recent history. Balance of trade deficits are the norm for the UK.

Services are also traded. Curiously, they are termed '**invisibles**' in trade terminology. It does seem a little strange to be counting invisibles. Services are quite difficult to describe other than by giving examples. Often they are said to be intangible, which at least has the advantage of being easily remembered if goods are tangible.

A service generates a receipt or an accounting entry. If you buy insurance for your Greek owned, Panamanian registered, oil tanker at Lloyds in London, you will pay the UK company for the insurance. They will give you an insurance document in return and ring the Lutine Bell if it sinks! As the service has been provided by a UK company and the price charged is paid into the UK, this would count as an invisible export.

The UK invisible balance has been in surplus (invisible exports exceed invisible imports) for many years.

Visible or invisible   Go online

For each item below, decide if it is a visible or invisible.

Q1: Cars

a) Visible
b) Invisible

....

Q2: Tourism

a) Visible
b) Invisible

....

Q3: Banking

a) Visible
b) Invisible

....

Q4: Bananas

a) Visible
b) Invisible

Visibles Go online

Q5: Complete the final column in the following table.

Year	Export of goods (£ billion)	Import of goods (£ billion)	Visible balance (£ billion)
2010	271	368	
2011	309	406	
2012	305	414	
2013	307	419	
2014	292	412	

. . . .

Q6: Present the figures from your table in a line graph. You may do this by hand in which case some squared paper would be a help. Alternatively if you are familiar with MS Excel and have access to it, you can prepare a chart using Excel.

Invisibles Go online

Q7: Complete the final column in the following table.

Year	Export of services (£ billion)	Import of services (£ billion)	Invisible balance (£ billion)
2010	176	116	
2011	190	118	
2012	196	121	
2013	209	130	
2014	208	123	

. . . .

Q8: Present the figures from your table in a line graph.

We can assemble the UK current account for 2013 as follows. (Note recent trade figures are subject to revisions and different sources can provide slightly different figures depending on when they obtained the details. This explains the slight variation between the revised figures below and earlier details for 2013.)

	Exports (in £ billion)	Imports (in £ billion)	Balance (in £ billion)
Goods	307	419	-112
Services	209	130	79
Net income and current transfers			-39
Current account balance			-72

Pink Book - trade figures   Go online

Locate the Pink Book on UK trade figures on the internet. Find the latest figures that would update the UK current account table to the latest year available.

Note: The solution will change with every year that passes, so a definitive one cannot be given.

4.4   Surpluses and deficits

Focussing firstly on the current account section, the following can be noted. The UK has a **trade in goods deficit** - imports of goods exceed exports. The UK has a **trade in services surplus**. Combined in the current account, the total for trade in goods and services shows an overall current account deficit (imports exceed exports). This indicates that the surplus in services is smaller than the deficit in goods, thus giving an overall deficit in goods and services.

The UK imports more goods than it exports. Why does this happen? Is it important?

There are several possible reasons for this deficit:

- As a fairly densely populated island we are a net importer of food;

- Many of our natural resources (e.g. coal) have been exploited over the centuries to the extent that what is left is difficult and expensive to get at. Therefore we are a net importer of many commodities and raw materials. However, the windfall of North Sea oil does mean that trade in oil is closer to balance;

- Comparative advantage in many manufacturing industries has moved abroad where the factor inputs (e.g. labour) are cheaper. For example wages are lower in the Far East;

- Some calculations suggest the UK economy has lower productivity (efficiency) than, for example, the USA or Germany. These international comparisons are fraught with calculation problems so this cannot be relied upon;

- The value of the pound has at certain times been unhelpfully high. This makes import prices cheaper and our export prices dearer. In early 2008 the pound was high against the dollar making exporting to the USA difficult. In 2014, the pound has again risen, reflecting a recovery in the UK economy;

- There have been question marks in the past over the quality of management and the quality of design in this country, although improvement has occurred in both these areas;
- Investment in modern capital can be lower than in many other countries.

Much of the deficit in goods is made up by a surplus in services, thus reducing the size of the overall current account deficit. The UK has a comparative advantage in financial services based on the activities of the City of London. Edinburgh is also a significant financial centre. The UK attracts inflows of capital investment.

There is no special significance attached to trade in goods. Services have the same potential to generate income and employment - perhaps more.

The UK's comparative advantage in some services is related to the high level of education required, and possibly to English being the international business language. A long history of activity in financial services ensures we have the suitably qualified personnel, and the infrastructure that gives some external economies of scale for bases in London. Weak regulation of financial services and a favourable tax regime may also be factors.

When the television news speaks of a trade deficit of several billion pounds, non-economists may worry that the government has to pay this money (from taxes) to foreign countries and that in some sense we are losing out. This is incorrect. As an economics student, you will realise that the trade deficit is a private sector matter. When you bought that Sony or Volkswagen product you handed over the money to pay for it. The UK government does not have to pay again. The trade deficit does not mean that the government pays again for goods you have already bought.

Surpluses and deficits   Go online

Q9: Complete the paragraph by choosing the correct words from the following list:

- capital;
- current;
- deficit;
- financial services;
- high;
- London;
- surplus;
- wages.

The UK has a .... in trade in goods, but a smaller .... in trade in services. Taken together the overall UK .... account is in deficit. Two factors causing this are low .... overseas and a £ exchange rate that for periods can be .... Fortunately the UK enjoys net .... inflows and has a strong .... sector based around the pre-eminence of ....

4.5   Methods of reducing current account deficits

The holy grail of economic policy in this area is export-led growth of the type enjoyed by Germany. This requires a highly efficient economy, the output of which competes successfully in world markets. Supply side policies are aimed at improving the competitiveness of the UK economy.

The following can address a current account deficit:

* Fiscal policies that act to slow the economy such as increasing taxation or cutting back on government spending act to improve the balance of payments for the same reason a recession did - less aggregate demand means less demand for imports;

* Monetary policies that curtail demand such as higher interest rates work in a similar way;

* Devaluation of the pound. If the exchange rate of the pound falls then UK exporters can cut prices in foreign currency and still receive the same return in pounds. Exports are encouraged and the converse effect reduces imports;

* Increased productivity in UK firms enables our goods and services to compete better in markets at home and abroad;

* Supply-side measures can make our economy more flexible and adaptable may give us a competitive edge.

In recession, UK consumers buy less of everything, including fewer imports. Thus while many economic variables point in an adverse direction in recession at least the balance of payments should improve.

Pink Book - current account trends   Go online

Locate the Pink Book on UK trade figures on the internet. Analyse the current account trends over the last ten years.

Note: The solution will vary as years pass. The underlying trend for some years has been a trade in goods deficit that is greater than the trade in services surplus. The trend in individual sections such as oil can be interesting. Note that the UK is no longer self-sufficient in oil. You should look for other interesting trends and contemplate why they have come about.

4.6   Capital and financial account

The capital and financial account (previously known as the capital account) measures money flows that are connected to investment and savings.

The capital and financial account includes foreign direct investment. This happens when a company builds an overseas factory. It is capital investment in fixed assets, that will generate current account money flows for years ahead. An example of this is the Japanese based firm Nissan building a factory in Sunderland. It works in both directions as UK based firms also invest overseas.

'Portfolio investment' is the purchase of shares in foreign firms, and is also in the capital and financial account.

'Other investment' is the label attached to financial hot money flows and this section can be volatile. Changes in the UK's official reserves of gold and foreign currency are also recorded in this section.

| Costs and benefits of foreign direct investment | Go online |

Q10: Describe the costs and benefits of foreign direct investment for the Scottish economy. (SQA 2004)

(10 Marks)

4.7 Trends in the current account

The following is an extract from the annual reference for trade figures, 'The Pink Book 2014'. It covers trade figures up to 2013:

"The UK has recorded a current account deficit in every year since 1984. From 1984, the current account deficit increased steadily to reach a high of £24.7 billion in 1989. This is equivalent to 4.7% of Gross Domestic Product (GDP). From 1990 until 1997, the current account deficit narrowed to a low of £1.3 billion in 1997, equivalent to 0.1% of GDP.

Between 1998 and 2008, it widened sharply, peaking at £56.4 billion in 2008. The current account deficit narrowed over the following three years to reach £27.0 billion in 2011, before widening significantly in 2012 when it recorded a deficit of £61.9 billion.

In 2013, the deficit reached a record £72.4 billion, the highest recorded in cash terms. It was equivalent to 4.2% of GDP, the highest since 1989 (4.7%)."

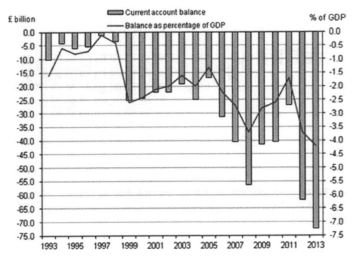

'Current account balance and balance as percentage of GDP' taken from 'The Pink Book 2014' (htt

Trends in the current account	Go online

Q11: Summarise the trends illustrated in the graph (above).

....

Q12: Research online the latest year available and print out a note of the up-to-date version of the statistics and summary shown in the graph (above).

4.8   Trends in the trade in goods and services

The trade in goods account recorded net surpluses in 1980 to 1982, largely due to the growth in exports of North Sea oil. Since then, the trade in goods account has remained in deficit. The deficit grew significantly in the late 1980s to reach a peak of £25.2 billion in 1989, before narrowing in the early 1990s to levels of around £10 billion to £14 billion.

In 1998, the deficit jumped by £9.5 billion to £22.2 billion and increased in every year since, except for 2009 and 2011. In 2013, the deficit reached £110.2 billion.

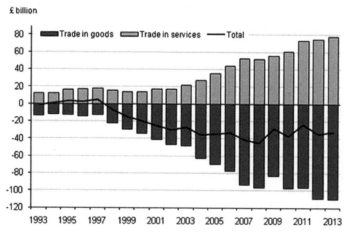

'Trade in goods and services balances' taken from 'The Pink Book 2014' (http://bit.ly/194PvEA). Licensed under Open Government Licence v3.0 (http://bit.ly/1uzupHL) via The National Archives.

Trends in the trade in goods and services   Go online

Q13: Summarise the trends illustrated in the graph (above).

4.9   Summary

Summary

At the end of this topic students should know that:

- the definition of the relevant terms:
  - balance of payments;
  - current account;
  - capital and financial account;
- the components of the balance of payments;
- visible trade (goods) and invisible trade (services) are the main parts of the current account;
- income flows from previous investments abroad are also in the current account;
- the UK has a deficit in visible trade, and a surplus in invisible trade;
- the reasons why a deficit may occur;
- fiscal, monetary and supply-side policies can all be used to reduce a balance of payments deficit;
- the latest trends in the UK balance of payments.

4.10   End of topic test

End of Topic 4 test   Go online

Q14: The current account of the balance of payments includes:

a) portfolio investment.
b) hot money flows.
c) trade in services.
d) flows to and from reserves of foreign currency.

....

Q15: The UK's trade in goods and trade in services:

a) are both in deficit.
b) are both in surplus.
c) show a deficit for goods and a surplus for services.
d) show a surplus for goods and a deficit for services.

....

Q16: Current account deficits could be improved by:

a) improving productivity.
b) devaluing the pound.
c) Both of the above.
d) Neither of the above.

....

Q17: The capital and financial account of the balance of payments includes:

a) trade in goods.
b) trade in services.
c) foreign direct investment.
d) interest, profits and dividends.

....

Q18: The categories 'trade in goods' and 'trade in services' are also generally referred to as (respectively):

a) visibles and invisibles.
b) tangibles and intangibles.
c) physicals and non-physicals.
d) exports and imports.

In 2004, the UK had a trade in goods deficit of £61 billion and a budget deficit of £37 billion. *(SQA 2006)*

Q19: Explain the difference between a trade in goods deficit and a budget deficit.
(4 marks)

....

Q20: Explain how budget deficits can lead to increased trade deficits and decreased unemployment.

(8 marks)

....

Q21: Other than budget deficits, suggest and explain two reasons for the UK's large trade in goods deficits in recent years.

(6 marks)

Unit 3 Topic 5

Understanding the impact of the global economy

Contents

Prerequisites

This topic assumes no previous knowledge and is intended to be accessible for those studying Economics for the first time. However, if you have already completed National 5 Economics you will be familiar with some of the concepts outlined.

Learning objective

By the end of this topic you should be able to:

- discuss the pros and cons of the UK joining the euro;

- explain the role of the European Central Bank;

- describe the process of enlargement and explain the advantages and disadvantages enlargement may bring the UK;

- explain the role of the common external tariff;

- describe the economic characteristics of an emerging economy;

- explain the policies that may lead to economic development;

- describe the economic characteristics of a developing country;

- discuss the merits of aid and trade to developing countries.

5.1 The European Union (EU) - introduction

The European Union was founded in 1957. Before that in 1951 the six original members formed the European Steel and Coal Community, out of which grew the European Union. For the next few decades it was generally called the 'common market' in the non-member United Kingdom. The UK joined in 1973.

The European Union is a free trade area of 28 countries and over 500 million consumers. For a long period it was called the European Economic Community (EEC), but in recognition of it developing beyond just an economic union, the middle word was dropped and it became plain EU.

We will consider four aspects of the EU. These are:

- the eurozone;
- enlargement;
- the European Central Bank;
- the common external tariff.

5.2 The eurozone

By 2015 the number of members of the euro had grown to 19. Twelve of the EU members started using the euro on 1 January 2002. These countries formed the eurozone and pooled their monetary policy.

A single currency requires only a single interest rate. The European Central Bank was created to manage a eurozone-wide monetary policy.

The eurozone Go online

Q1: From the following list of 28 EU countries put the 19 countries in the eurozone into the table below: Austria; Belgium; Bulgaria; Croatia; Cyprus; Czech Republic; Denmark; Estonia; Finland; France; Germany; Greece; Hungary; Ireland; Italy; Latvia; Lithuania; Luxembourg; Malta; Netherlands; Poland; Portugal; Romania; Slovakia; Slovenia; Spain; Sweden; United Kingdom.

Eurozone countries

5.2.1   The advantages and disadvantages of joining the euro for the UK

The advantages of joining the euro for the UK are similar to the benefits of the single currency which are that:

- it reduces the risk for UK firms that adverse exchange rate fluctuations will affect profits;

- it removes conversion costs for firms and tourists (no need to exchange currency and pay commission);

- it is expected that a European Central Bank will be firm on inflation;

- it will create **price transparency** so that consumers can easily compare prices across the EU;

- it is more likely that the UK would continue to attract foreign investment because the uncertainty of fluctuating exchange rates when exporting to the EU is removed;

- the UK's flexible labour markets should help it be successful within the eurozone.

The disadvantages of joining the euro include:

- the initial costs of changing currency are large - slot machine changes are one example.

- a need for the UK economy to become largely **convergent** with the existing eurozone. Key economic indicators such as stage of the business cycle and inflation will need to be broadly in line with the existing eurozone members. Otherwise you will be joining a currency with an inappropriate interest rate - hardly a good start!

- losing control of monetary policy. The UK will have little influence with the European Central Bank and the interest rate it sets could be out of line with UK economic needs. (It could be argued that the current UK interest rate is typically set in response to the needs of the south-east of Britain and rarely reflects the economic needs of other parts of the UK - so little difference for the Western Isles, then.)

- devaluation is removed from the UK's economic policy options, so the UK will no longer be able to stimulate its economy by devaluing its currency and increasing exports.

- the significance of interest rate changes for the UK economy is greater because of the UK's focus on house purchase, rather than rental. The UK is more sensitive to interest rate changes than other countries. This adds weight to the argument to retain control of interest rates by not joining the eurozone.

- increased regional aid within Europe will be needed to offset economic inequalities that can no longer be addressed through national currency realignments. As one of the richer nations the UK may be a net contributor of this funding.

- if some eurozone members increase their borrowings and national debt, this will lead to the single interest rate rising throughout the zone.

- the euro is essentially a fixed exchange rate arrangement, and in time may be subject to the same pressures from diverging economies that fixed rates have always been subject to. In early 2008 it was reported that, with Spain moving towards recession, there were already those arguing to leave the euro.

Joining the euro - advantages and disadvantages for the UK   Go online

Q2: Place the following advantages and disadvantages for the UK of joining the euro into the appropriate column:

- Easier for consumers to compare prices in different countries;
- No commission on changing currency;
- One interest rate set for all of eurozone;
- Exchange rate certainty for firms within eurozone;
- Devaluation of the pound no longer possible;
- Multinational investment in UK more likely.

Advantages of joining the euro	Disadvantages of joining the euro

5.3 European Central Bank (ECB)

The European Central Bank is the monetary authority for the eurozone. It performs a role in setting interest rates that is similar to the Bank of England's role as the UK's central bank.

As the central bank for the euro currency, the ECB's central aim is to maintain the purchasing power of the euro by setting an interest rate that ensures low inflation across the eurozone.

European Central Bank building in Frankfurt (http://bit.ly/1D4BjGl) by ArcCan (http://bit.ly/1Az mTie). Licensed under CC BY-SA 3.0 (http://bit.ly/18TLJ0u) via Wikimedia Commons.

5.4 EU enlargement

EU enlargement is the process of widening the EU through the admission of new members. Initially progress was slow with only nine members until 1981. The former dictatorships of Greece, Spain and Portugal then joined as democracies in the 1980s. Austria, Finland and Sweden made it fifteen. In the case of Austria and Finland, the break-up of their powerful communist neighbour the Soviet Union made it politically easier to join what had until then been a Western European club.

The waning control and influence of the Soviet Union and emergence from communism led to a wave of east European countries joining in 2004. The islands of Malta and Cyprus also joined at this time. In 2007 Rumania and Bulgaria made 27 nations of what had been 15 just over 3 years earlier. Croatia is the first member from the breakup of Yugoslavia to join (2013) and that makes 28 members.

The table summarises when countries joined the EU in ascending order of years. Note that the unification of East and West Germany in 1990 did not add an extra member.

Year	Nations joining	Total membership
1957	Belgium, France, Italy, Luxembourg, Netherlands, West Germany	6
1973	Denmark, Eire, United Kingdom	9
1981	Greece	10
1986	Portugal, Spain	12
1990	Unification of East and West Germany	12
1995	Austria, Finland, Sweden	15
2004	Cyprus, Czech Republic, Estonia, Hungary, Latvia, Lithuania, Malta, Poland, Slovakia, Slovenia	25
2007	Bulgaria, Rumania	27
2013	Croatia	28

Around the edges of the current map, below, the Balkan states formed on the break-up of Yugoslavia will shortly be looking for entry (e.g. Croatia may be followed by others such as Serbia). Turkey has long been interested, but is perhaps not as close to membership now as a few years ago. North African countries just across the Mediterranean have historic links to many European countries and are also possible members.

Switzerland retains an independent outlook and has historically sought to remain neutral. Norway voted against entry when its Scandinavian neighbours joined. It has a small population similar to Scotland and its immense oil reserves make it very prosperous outside the EU. Also, its important fishing industry does not have to abide by EU policies.

Eurozone and EU member states

5.4.1   The benefits and problems of enlargement for the UK

For the UK the process of enlargement has several benefits:

*   consumers will have a greater choice of products, as new members begin to export to the UK;

*   it increases competition. Competition drives down prices, leads to innovative behaviour by firms, and can improve the quality of products;

*   it allows labour shortages to be met with foreign workers. This addition to supply in the labour market will help to keep down wage inflation. Good news for companies and a benefit for the overall economy;

*   it provides new markets (no trade barriers) for our exports, and exporters should gain more from economies of scale as they supply a free trade **single market** of over 500 million consumers;

*   it provides opportunities for UK based firms to improve profitability by moving to the lower wage economies of the new members.

Enlargement can create problems for the UK:

- UK workers will face more competition in the labour market and their wages are less likely to rise (however, unemployment may not rise, because much of the money earned by foreign workers will be spent in the UK and thus they create jobs as well as take jobs);

- subsidies for the economic development of the new members may be expensive for richer countries such as the UK. The UK will be a net contributor to the EU budget through the **CAP** and regional aid;

- firms may move manufacturing to the new member countries to take advantage of lower costs (e.g. wages) and this will lead to some job losses in the UK.

Enlargement of the EU - benefits and problems for the UK   Go online

Q3: Place the following benefits and problems for the enlargement of the EU into the appropriate column:

- Additional EU budget costs for the UK;
- Wider markets for UK goods;
- Increased choice for UK consumers;
- Multinationals move to cheaper locations;
- Skilled workers from abroad to fill vacancies.

Benefits of enlargement for the UK	Problems of enlargement for the UK

5.5   Common Customs Tariff (CCT)

A tariff is a tax on imports. It makes imports less price competitive in the EU market. The Common Customs Tariff (CCT) is often referred to as the common external tariff. It applies to the import of goods across the external border of the EU. The tariff rates do vary according to the kind of import.

The EU claims that the tariff ensures that EU domestic producers are able to compete fairly against imports from non-EU countries. Others may regard it as a form of protectionism. It does have serious implications for the economies of developing countries by making it harder to sell in the affluent EU market.

5.6 Levels of development

There are many labels given to groups of economies at different stages of development. Some of these labels even overlap each other. A selection of labels would include: "tiger economies", "big emerging market economies" (BEMs), first world nations, industrialised nations, less economically developed countries (LEDCs) and most economically developed countries (MEDCs).

To clarify the position, only three will be used in this section, namely:

- **developing countries**;
- **emerging economies**;
- **developed countries**.

The United Nations has an index for measuring the level of development of a nation. It combines life expectancy at birth, knowledge and education, and the standard of living. Combining these three components gives the **Human Development Index (HDI)**.

Knowledge and education is mainly judged through adult literacy rates which have a two thirds weighting in that section, with the level of enrolment in the education system as the other factor.

Standard of living is measured as gross domestic product *per capita.*

The HDI top five nations in 2007 were listed as: Norway, Iceland, Australia, Luxembourg and Canada. The United Kingdom came fifteenth.

Of the countries that contributed information to allow the calculation of the index, the bottom five nations were: Chad, Mali, Burkino Faso, Sierra Leone and Niger, occupying places 174th to 178th respectively.

Human Development Index (HDI) of the countries of the world

A variety of websites contain maps showing the Human Development Index (HDI) of the countries of the world.

Use a search engine, such as Google, entering the keywords "hdi map". Note where the majority of developing countries and where the majority of less developed countries are located. Check your findings with your teacher and tutor.

Levels of development Go online

Q4: Consider the statistics in the table below.

Decide whether each country is developing, emerging or developed.

Nation	Income per person ($)	Life Expectancy (years)	Literacy Rate (%)	Developing/ Emerging/ Developed
Malawi	900	60	75	
India	4,000	68	63	
Bangladesh	2,100	71	58	
Japan	37,100	84	99	
South Africa	11,500	50	93	
Sweden	40,900	82	99	
Chad	2,500	49	35	
United Kingdom	37,300	80	99	
Brazil	12,100	73	90	

World Factbook   Go online

Go the CIA website (http://www.cia.gov) and click the "World Factbook" link. Click on some regions on the interactive map to find statistics for countries from different parts of the world, choosing different countries from those used in the previous activity (above).

In the statistics for your chosen countries, go to the 'Economy' and the 'People and society' sections and search for GDP per capita (i.e. income per person), life expectancy, and literacy rate.

Make these items into a table as in the example from the previous activity (above).

5.7   Developing countries

Developing countries can be identified by items such as average income, life expectancy and literacy rate. These are outcomes created by the weaknesses developing countries have with their resource inputs. Looking at the factors of production (resources) one by one, it will be possible to spot problems with either the quantity of each factor or the quality of it.

It is a good idea, for memorising, to organise your thoughts in a systematic way. When it comes to the problems facing less developed countries, one approach is to take the four factors of production in turn and recite quality and quantity issues they face:

1. **Natural resources** (land) will not be fertile. Either the climate or the soil type will prevent it from producing plenty. If it is fertile, then it may be prone to seasonal flooding or drought. Crop yields will either be low, or not reliable.

   Mineral deposits will be limited, or difficult to access. Those mines that do exist will be owned by multi-nationals and the workers may be poorly paid with the profits going to shareholders in developed countries.

2. *Human resources* (labour) will not be skilled. The education system will be poor and literacy rates low. As a result labour productivity will be low, and foreign investment will not be attracted. Workers may be weakened by malnutrition or disease.

Life expectancy will be low. There may be a burgeoning young population of dependents but quite a small population of working age. The number of able workers of working age will be restricted by health issues.

3. *Man-made resources* (capital) will be of poor quality. Operating at near subsistence level there will be no surplus put aside to assist with future production. Machinery will tend to be cheap and basic when it does exist. The lack of social capital and infrastructure such as roads and harbours will make the country unattractive to foreign investors.

A lack of savings will lead to a lack of funds being recycled into investment. The banking system will be poor.

4. *Entrepreneurs* (enterprise) will exist on a small scale in local markets. Any excess farm output will find its way to a market stall. The growth of enterprise is dependent on the availability of capital to invest, and partly on the education levels of the entrepreneurs.

The number of entrepreneurs and the size of companies will be restricted by the small incomes of consumers.

Developing countries   Go online

Q5: Match up the following issues for developing countries with the correct factor of production. All of these items will also potentially pose problems for entrepreneurs attempting to run a business:

- Droughts leading to crop failure;
- Few natural resources;
- Lack of modern technology;
- Little is saved;
- Low literacy rates;
- Poor health;
- Poor transport infrastructure;
- Seasonal flooding;
- Unskilled workers;
- Weak banking system.

Land	Labour	Capital

5.7.1   Longer term problems of developing countries

The problems with the four factors of production lead to longer term problems:

- **Debt** - Small incomes and little business activity mean that the tax base for the governments of less developed countries to raise income from is tiny. Governments will have budget deficits because they try to meet many demands for funds but have little income. They borrow from abroad and get into debt problems. The interest payments on their debts are an additional charge every year.

- **Political instability** - Economic weaknesses and instability lead to political problems. Corruption and bribery is endemic. Democratic governments struggle to survive and dictators with military support often take over. The little government spending that is available is siphoned of into purchasing armaments. Against this volatile backdrop, foreign investors will think long and hard before making commitments.

- **Dependence on primary products** - The economies of developing countries may have 90% of their workforce in agriculture. The main export is typically an agricultural crop, and the country's balance of trade depends on a successful harvest and world prices for that product. Sometimes a mineral is mined, but much of the profit goes overseas.

5.7.2   Developing countries - case studies

Here are statistics showing the economies of Malawi and Chad, two developing countries.

Developing country case study 1: Malawi

Age structure	0-14 years: 47%, 15-64 years: 50%, 65+ years: 3%, median age: 16.3 years
Exports	tobacco, tea, sugar, cotton, coffee, peanuts
Foreign debt	$1,556 million
GDP per capita	$900
Imports	food, petroleum products, semi-manufactures, consumer goods
Infant mortality rate	48 per thousand
Labour force by occupation	agriculture: 90%, industry and services: 10%
Life expectancy	60
Literacy rate	75%
Major infectious diseases	bacterial and protozoal diarrhoea, hepatitis A, typhoid fever, malaria, schistosomiasis
Below poverty line	53% of population

Developing country case study 2: Chad

Age structure	0-14 years: 45%, 15-64 years: 52%, 65+ years: 3%, median age: 17.2 years
Exports	oil, cattle, cotton, gum arabic
Foreign debt	$1,828 million
GDP per capita	$2,500
Imports	machinery and transport equipment, industrial goods, foodstuffs, textiles
Infant mortality rate	90 per thousand
Labour force by occupation	agriculture: 80%, industry and services: 20%
Life expectancy	49
Literacy rate	35%
Major infectious diseases	bacterial and protozoal diarrhoea, hepatitis A and E, typhoid fever, malaria, schistosomiasis
Below poverty line	80% of population

The two case studies above give a vivid account of the problems faced by developing countries. Note that, unusually for a developing country, Chad has some oil that it exports. Despite this it remains very underdeveloped.

World Factbook - Malawi and Chad   Go online

Go the World Factbook at http://www.cia.gov and check the up-to-date details for these countries for any significant progress.

Senegal   Go online

Go the World Factbook at http://www.cia.gov and check the up-to-date details for Senegal and answer the following questions .

Q6: What is the life expectancy in Senegal?

a) 41
b) 61
c) 81

....

Q7: What is the literacy rate in Senegal?

a) 50%
b) 60%
c) 70%

....

Q8: What is the GDP per capita in Senegal?

a) $1,100
b) $2,100
c) $3,100

....

Q9: What percentage of the population of Senegal lives below the poverty line?

a) 14%
b) 34%
c) 54%

....

Q10: What percentage of the labour force in Senegal work in agriculture?

a) 38%
b) 58%
c) 78%

....

Q11: What percentage of the population is aged under 15?

a) 33%
b) 43%
c) 53%

5.8   Aid versus trade

Developing countries are on a subsistence treadmill. Struggling to adequately feed and shelter their people, there is no surplus left to contribute to investment in the future. In 2007 the economy of Chad was estimated to have shrunk by 1.3% - things got worse.

There are some terms related to aid that you should be familiar with:

- **bilateral aid** given by one country to another country;

- **multilateral aid** given by an international agency such as the World Bank.

Some examples of the types of aid that may be given by developed countries are:

- emergency aid consisting of gifts of food and medicine;

- grants that, although free, may carry conditions;

- loans at commercial rates of interest;

- **'soft' loans** at low rates of interest;

- writing off past debts;

- technical assistance - such as economists seconded to their governments;

- education - financing students to attend universities in developed countries.

There are several problems associated with the methods of aid described above:

- all loans increase the debt interest, which then weighs on future government budgets;

- aid may encourage dependency rather than self-sufficiency;

- it may create problems for local businesses if they are to compete with free or subsidised products. The incentive of profit is needed by entrepreneurs;

- political corruption may stop aid reaching those in greatest need;

- bilateral aid may be **tied** to purchasing from the donor country. This may not be the best option as, for example, you might finish up with second-rate tractors;

- multilateral aid from the IMF or the World Bank usually attaches strings. Balanced budgets and free market solutions are sometimes conditions required by these organisations and in the short-run this can make the poor poorer;

- grants may be available for prestigious infrastructure projects, but will there then be any money available in future years to run and maintain the finished dams and airports.

Aid versus trade   Go online

Q12: Complete the following table by putting the correct description and problem next to the type of aid:

- Disaster relief (food and medicine);
- Economic "strings" attached (e.g. balanced budget);
- From international organisation;
- From one country to another;
- Increases debts;
- Low interest finance to assist development;
- May encourage dependency;
- Tied to buying from donor country.

Type of aid	Description	Problem
Bilateral aid		
Multilateral aid		
Emergency aid		
Soft loans		

5.8.1   The advantages of trade

Encouraging trade may be a better solution. Major economic trading areas such as the European Union have external tariffs that unfairly keep out imports from less developed countries. These less developed countries would gain from profits made by selling in developed markets. These could be re-invested and economic progress would take hold. Enterprise would be encouraged.

Jobs would be created and the tax base expanded. Foreign investment would be more likely, bringing with it technology. A positive multiplier effect would spread to other areas of the economy. The trade balance would be improved.

5.9   Emerging economies

Emerging economies are a group of nations that have rapidly growing economies but are still some way behind developed countries. In many ways the experiences of emerging economies are similar to those of the UK during its industrial revolution.

Population movements to the factories and industries of a growing urban sprawl mimic a process carried out in centuries gone by in the UK. The citizens on the move from inefficient family farms become far more productive in their now secondary or tertiary occupations. Often they will find decent accommodation in the cities beyond their means in the early years, and rather like the mill

---

workers of nineteenth century Britain, they will live in densely peopled, sub-standard housing.

These emerging economies have reached "takeoff". No longer do they go round in circles on the subsistence treadmill. A critical mass has been reached, generating saving, consumer spending and investment. Opportunities for quick-witted entrepreneurs abound. The labour is still cheap by international standards and foreign investment builds factories and pays wages, bringing with it newer technologies and big advances in productivity.

Governments now have something to tax - company profits, consumer spending and rising incomes. Judiciously used on infrastructure - roads, railways, harbours, dams, healthcare, education - these taxes when spent are a catalyst in the mix. Governments in emerging economies still tend to borrow heavily, but instead of patching up poverty and fending off crises, now it is used to fund education, transport and health care for an upwardly mobile population.

Policies leading to economic development

What enables a country to reach this virtuous circle of economic growth and rising living standards? The first steps probably depend on political stability, raising basic literacy rates and the encouragement of small business activity. The world price of a mineral or crop that they export needs to be high enough to make profits for local farmers, or to encourage inward investment. Against this background government has to plan improvements in infrastructure that will nurture the infant industrialisation - even if it has to borrow to do so.

Much can still go wrong. The world prices for major exports may fall. Natural disasters such as flood and drought may hold back progress. Even success will bring the risk of inflation for a booming economy. Workers may demand higher wages that reduce your competitive advantage.

Emerging economies	Go online

Q13: In the following sentences, when given a choice, select the correct option.

Emerging economies such as (*Brazil/Belgium*) no longer depend on (*primary/secondary*) production. They tend to have (*low/high*) levels of spending on infrastructure. Literacy rates are (*over/under*) 50% as a result of these spending levels on education. (*Low/High*) levels of foreign investment occur, encouraged by political (*stability/instability*). GDP per capita, for example, could be (*$1,000/$10,000*) per annum and standards of living are (*rising/falling*). With (*increasing/decreasing*) levels of birth control, the age structure of emerging economies shows more people in the (*dependent/working*) age categories.

5.9.1   Characteristics of emerging economies

Emerging economies do not all have an identical profile, but several of the following characteristics will be found in each one:

- political stability - it may involve a strong and charismatic leader who may or may not be democratically elected. Singapore is an excellent example with its first prime minister from independence in 1959 until 1990, Lee Kwan Yew;

- free trade and open markets - encouraging trade, entrepreneurs and foreign investment;

- high levels of foreign investment and the presence of multinationals;

- a move away from dependence on primary production such as crops or mineral resources and into areas where value is added to products - manufacturing and services;

- high levels of government debt, but it is invested effectively in developing infrastructure to support and develop the economy - education, healthcare, water and sanitation;

- high rates of economic growth. Rapidly improving technology and increasing productivity of labour drive up output;

- rising standards of living;

- birth control is often encouraged in emerging economies. In the late 1960s Singapore began a "stop at two" family planning campaign encouraging sterilisation after two children and reducing economic benefits for third and fourth children.

5.9.2   Emerging economies - case studies

Here is a selection of statistics that illustrate the economies of India and Brazil, two emerging economies.

Emerging economies case study 1: India

Age structure	0-14 years: 29%, 15-64 years: 65%, 65+ years: 6%, median age: 27 years
Exports	petroleum products, precious stones, machinery
Foreign debt	$412 billion
GDP per capita	$4,000
Imports	crude oil, gems, machinery, fertiliser, iron and steel
Infant mortality rate	43 per thousand
Labour force by occupation	agriculture: 49%, industry: 20%, services: 31%
Life expectancy	43
Literacy rate	61%
Major infectious diseases	bacterial diarrhoea, hepatitis A and E, typhoid fever, malaria, dengue fever, leptospirosis, rabies
Below poverty line	30% of population

Emerging economies case study 2: Brazil

Age structure	0-14 years: 24%, 15-64 years: 68%, 65+ years: 8%, median age: 31 years
Exports	transport equipment, iron ore, soybeans, footwear, coffee, vehicles
Foreign debt	$476 billion
GDP per capita	$12,100
Imports	machinery, electrical and transport equipment, chemical products, oil, vehicle parts, electronics
Infant mortality rate	19 per thousand
Labour force by occupation	agriculture: 16%, industry: 13%, services: 71%
Life expectancy	73
Literacy rate	89%
Major infectious diseases	none
Below poverty line	21% of population

Malaysia   Go online

This is a quick quiz on the country, Malaysia. This emerging economy has some fairly typical figures for key indicators of development. See if you can pick the appropriate answers for a typical newly industrialised country.

Hint - go back and review the two case studies.

Q14: What is the life expectancy in Malaysia?

a) 65
b) 75
c) 85

. . . .

Q15: What is the literacy rate in Malaysia?

a) 53%
b) 73%
c) 93%

. . . .

Q16: What is the GDP per capita in Malaysia?

a) $7,500
b) $17,500
c) $27,500

. . . .

Q17: What percentage of the population of Malaysia lives below the poverty line?

a) 4%
b) 14%
c) 24%

. . . .

Q18: What percentage of the labour force in Malaysia work in agriculture?

a) 11%
b) 31%
c) 51%

. . . .

Q19: What percentage of the population is aged under 15?

a) 9%
b) 19%
c) 29%

5.10   Summary

Summary

At the end of this topic students should know that:

- the euro requires eurozone members to set a single interest rate thus relinquishing national control of monetary policy. Advantages include savings in currency conversion costs and increasing price transparency;

- the European Central Bank is the monetary authority for the eurozone and sets the euro interest rate;

- enlargement to 28 countries (at the time of writing) has led to significant movements of workers from new members (e.g. Poland) to the UK. By creating a larger single market, opportunities for labour and enterprise are extended. Firms face greater competition and come under increased pressure to cut costs and lower prices which benefits consumers;

- the EU places a common external tariff on goods imported from non-EU countries;

- developing countries are the nations with the lowest incomes and are characterised by low literacy rates and low life expectancy. They are often dependent on primary production for much of their income;

- emerging economies are rapidly growing economies, diversifying into secondary and tertiary sectors. They attract investment from foreign multinationals;

- developed economies are the most advanced. Most workers are employed in the tertiary sector and standards of living are high;

- aid can provide short-term relief in emergencies. Grants and loans can be used to develop the infrastructure needed to make economic progress. Long-term progress can be encouraged by the opening up of markets such as the European Union to trade from developing countries.

5.11   End of topic test

End of topic test   Go online

Q20: If the UK joined the Eurozone, one disadvantage would be losing control of:

a) fiscal policy.
b) monetary policy.
c) Both of the above.
d) Neither of the above.

....

Q21: Which one of the following groups consists of a developing country, an emerging economy, and a developed country, in that order?

a) India, Brazil, France.
b) Malawi, India, Japan.
c) Chad, Belgium, Germany.
d) Brazil, India, Sweden.

....

Q22: Which of the following is **not** true of a typical emerging economy?

a) Growing significance of the secondary sector of their economy.
b) High levels of foreign investment.
c) Free trade with EU members.
d) Significant levels of debt to foreign countries.

....

Q23: Which of the following is true for 'bilateral aid'?

a) It is given by the World Bank.
b) It may have to be spent with the donor country.
c) It is investment from multinational companies.
d) It is the reduction of trade barriers.

....

Q24: Which one of the following groups contains an EU member, a Eurozone member, and a country **not** in the EU, in that order?

a) Spain, Ireland, Finland.
b) Sweden, Denmark, Switzerland.
c) UK, Poland, Cyprus.
d) Slovenia, Germany, Norway.

Do not use bullet points to answer the following questions, as this usually leaves answers brief and undeveloped. Think in terms of 2 to 3 mark paragraphs. Make the basic point and then add an example or develop your first comment into something more complex. Move on to make another separate relevant point in a new paragraph.

Q25: Even before EU enlargement, the majority of UK trade was within the EU. If the UK were to join the eurozone, this would further strengthen its trade links with the EU.

Suggest reasons why the majority of UK trade is with the EU. *(SQA 2005)*

(5 marks)

. . . .

Q26: What are the advantages and disadvantages for the UK of EU enlargement?

(10 marks)

. . . .

Q27: Explain the main economic costs and benefits for the UK of joining the eurozone.

(10 marks)

. . . .

Q28: Discuss how effective different types of aid are in increasing the growth rates of developing countries. *(SQA 2006)*

(12 Marks)

. . . .

Q29: Discuss the view that "what developing countries need is free and fair trade, not aid". *(SQA 2006)*

(8 marks)

Note: one approach in answering this question would be to give the positive advantages of trade, and the negative side of aid. For balance, finish by pointing out that aid may sometimes be necessary.

Unit 3 Topic 6

End of unit test

End of Unit 3 test

Go online

Q1: Match up the following nations with an appropriate description in the table below *(where there is more than one correct option, please choose the nation that is most suitable)*:

- Brazil;
- Canada;
- China;
- Japan;
- Malawi;
- Malta;
- Norway;
- USA.

Description	Nation
Major export market for UK	
Major source of UK imports	
Uses the yen as currency	
Uses the euro as currency	
Example of emerging economy	
Example of developing economy	
Example of developed economy	
European nation not in EU	

(10 marks)

For the following questions, always attempt to extend and develop any initial point that you make. Think in terms of 2-mark paragraphs and support your assertions with evidence and/or examples. Economics can be a subtle subject and answers that explain the complex points well are generally well rewarded. Avoid bullet points - they will just encourage you to keep answers too brief and you will make unsupported assertions.

The solutions consists of paragraphs with mark allocations. You do not have to include all the points in your answer to gain full marks.

Q2: Describe three trade barriers and explain the reasons governments may give to justify the imposition of trade barriers.

(10 marks)

....

Q3: Explain possible economic effects on UK firms and consumers of the sterling exchange rate being high for a period of time?

(10 marks)

. . . .

Q4: Discuss the advantages and disadvantages for the UK economy of joining the euro.

(10 marks)

. . . .

Q5: Compare and contrast the main economic characteristics of developing countries with those of emerging countries.

(10 marks)

Glossary

Absolute advantage theory

a theory that shows numerically the gains from trade that occur when each of two nations produces the good it is more efficient at making

Average cost

the cost per unit of output

Average fixed costs

calculated by dividing fixed costs by output

Average propensity to consume

the proportion of income spent

Average propensity to save

the proportion of income saved

Average variable costs

calculated by dividing variable costs by output

Balanced budget

planned expenditure equals planned income

Balance of payments

an account recording the international transactions of UK residents. It consists of the current account, and the capital and financial account

Balance of trade

visible exports minus visible imports. The balance of trade refers only to trade in goods

Bank of England

UK central bank

Base year

year inflation is measured from

Bilateral aid

aid from one country to another

The Budget

an annual statement of Government fiscal plans for the coming year

Capital and financial account

includes transactions with the European Union and foreign direct investment

Capital spending

spending on assets or repayment of loans

Ceteris paribus

the assumption that all determinants other than price are not changing

Clean (or pure) float

a floating exchange rate set entirely by the market without government intervention

Common Agricultural Policy (CAP)

an expensive system of subsidies paid to European Union farmers

Common external tariff

a tariff applying to the import of goods across the external border of the EU

Comparative advantage theory

a theory that shows numerically the gains from trade that occur when an advanced nation produces the good it has the greatest efficiency advantage in; the less advanced nation makes the good it has the least disadvantage in producing. Note that initially the advanced nation has an absolute advantage in producing both goods

Competitive demand

when the goods are close substitutes; an increase in demand for one usually results in a fall in demand for the other

The conditions of demand

the determinants of demand, other than price

Consumption

spending by households

Convergence

the need for an economy joining the single currency to match up with the economic indicators of existing eurozone members before joining

Cost push inflation

prices rising because of dearer production

Current account

includes visibles (goods) and invisibles (services)

Current spending

day-to-day spending, e.g. wages

Cyclical, general or mass unemployment

jobs lost due to a general fall in demand

Deficit budget

planned expenditure exceeds planned income

Deindustrialisation

loss of manufacturing capacity in a home country as manufacturing moves to lower cost locations abroad

Demand

the quantity of a good or service bought per unit of time at a given price

Demand pull inflation

prices rising due to excess demand

Demerit goods

the market over-provides these because producers do not have to pay the wider costs for the community. e.g. alcohol

Dependent population

everyone *not* included in the working population

Depreciation

fall in the value of capital equipment

Deregulation

reducing state control of the private sector

Devaluation

a decrease in the value of a currency on the foreign exchange market. Under a fixed exchange rate system this would be announced as a step change. The term is also valid if applied to a decline in value in a floating system

Developed countries

advanced economies with high standards of living

Developing countries

the weakest economies with the lowest standards of living

Devolution

the transfer of powers from a central to a regional authority

Direct taxes

tax on incomes

Dirty float

the government (using its central bank) intervenes in the market to manipulate the exchange rate

Diseconomies of scale

disadvantages facing very large firms that act to increase average cost in the long-run

Diversification

the term, in this topic, is applied to operating in more than one country - in diverse markets. This has the advantage that sales are unlikely to reduce in all markets at the same time

Division of labour

refers to the breaking down of complex production processes into sequences of simpler tasks which increases productivity

Economic efficiency

when the most valued goods and services are produced and no one can be made better off by transferring resources

Economies of scale

advantages (mainly cost per unit reductions) that companies benefit from as they serve larger markets

Effective demand

the desire for a good backed by the ability to get it using money

Elasticity

a measure of responsiveness

Emerging economies

economies with high rates of foreign investment and economic growth, rapid industrialisation and increasing exports of manufactured goods

Enlargement

the widening of the European Union to include new members

Equilibrium

total leakages = total injections

Equilibrium price

the price established where the demand for the good equals the supply of that good

Errors and omissions

this figure corrects any imbalance in the balance of payments. The double entry accounting system for recording international transactions means that the end figures on the balance of payments technically must always balance

Euro

the currency used by those EU members who have joined the eurozone

European Central Bank

the monetary authority for the eurozone

European Union

a free trade area of 28 countries (2014), including the UK

Eurozone

the name given to the group of EU countries that have adopted the euro as their currency

Exchange rate

the rate at which one currency can be changed for another

Exports

UK goods and services being sold outside the UK

External economies of scale

the result of the concentration of firms in one area enjoyed by the firm and its neighbours

Externalities

business costs do not reflect the wider impact on third parties, e.g. pollution. (Note it is also possible to have positive externalities)

Factor mobility

the speed and ease with which a factor can move - either from place to place (geographical mobility) or from job to job (occupational mobility)

Factors of production

the four categories into which resources are divided - land, labour, capital and enterprise

Financial flows

international investment flows in and out of the UK

Fiscal policy

the use of tax and/or public spending to reach government targets

Fixed costs

costs that remain the same in the short run, irrespective of the level of output, e.g. rent

Fixed exchange rate

an agreed fixed rate for currency exchange set by governments

Fixed incomes

incomes that don't change short term

FOREX

an abbreviation of foreign exchange, the FOREX market is the market in which one currency can be exchange for another

Free goods

goods of which there are enough to satisfy everyone's desire for them at a zero price

Frictional unemployment

jobs lost due to barriers to employment

Hot money

money that is moved quickly from one currency to another to take advantage of the best interest rates or in anticipation of making a profit from changing currency values

Human Development Index (HDI)

a system for measuring economic development by combining three factors - life expectancy, education levels and living standards

Imports

foreign goods and services being sold to the UK

Income effect

when a good falls in price and existing consumers of that good will experience a rise in their real income

Income flows

dividends and interest paid in and out of the UK

Indirect taxes

tax on spending

Inflation

a general rise in price levels

Infrastructure

a broad term usually referring to the economic framework provided by the transport and communication networks, the social facilities such as health, sanitation and education, or the legal system that enables business and government to operate effectively

Injections

inputs into the circular flow

Internal economies of scale

advantages enjoyed by large firms that reduce long-run average cost

Investment

firms spending on capital goods

Invisibles

refer to trade in services only

Joint or complementary demand

when two goods tend to be demanded together; an increase in the demand for one will tend to lead to an increase in the demand for the other

Joint supply

when two or more goods are produced together

Keynesianism

a school of thought that aggregate demand is the main determinant of price levels

The law of diminishing returns

explains that short run average cost will ultimately rise because adding more variable factors to one fixed factor eventually reduces productivity

The law of supply

the quantity of a commodity produced and offered for sale will tend to increase if its price increases and decrease if its price falls - *ceteris paribus*

Leakage

a withdrawal from the circular flow

Long-run

the period that allows all factors to be changed and no factor is fixed

Marginal cost

the addition to total costs resulting from the production of one more unit

Marginal propensity to consume

the proportion of extra income spent

Marginal propensity to save

the proportion of extra income saved

Marginal utility

the extra satisfaction a consumer gains from consuming one more of a product

Market

buyers and sellers come into contact in some way in order to agree a price and exchange a good or service

Market clearing price

the price established where there is no unsatisfied demand and no unsold supplies

Merit goods

under-provided by the market which supplies them only when they return a profit. e.g. education

Monetarism

a school of though that the money supply is the main determinant of price levels

Monetary policy

the use of interest rates and the supply of money to reach government targets

Multilateral aid

aid donated by international institutions such as the IMF or the World Bank

Multinational

a company that has production units based in foreign countries, rather than merely exporting from one base

Needs

the basic requirements for survival such as shelter

Nominal

monetary value

Opportunity cost

the sacrifice of the next best alternative choice

Optimum output

the output level where the average cost is at a minimum, i.e. the lowest point on a U-shaped average cost curve

Output

the amount of a good that a firm produces

Perfectly price elastic

the quantity demanded of a good falls to zero when its price changes

Perfectly price inelastic

the quantity demanded of a good does not change when its price changes

The Pink Book

annual statistical publication on UK trade

Price elasticity of demand (PED)

measures the extent to which the quantity demanded of a good changes when its price changes

Price indices

method of measuring inflation

Price transparency

comparisons of prices in different countries are made easier for consumers through the use of a single currency

Privatisation

selling of state-owned assets to the private sector

Productivity

the value of output obtained with one unit of input. Labour productivity would be output per worker or output per worker hour. It is a measure of efficiency

Progressive tax

a tax where the proportion of income paid in tax rises as income rises

Public goods

cannot be supplied by entrepreneurs because there is no way of excluding non-payers. e.g. lighthouses

Public Sector Net Cash Requirement (PSNCR)

the amount by which planned Government Expenditure exceeds income

Quantity theory of money

$MV = PQ$

Rate of inflation

percentage increase in prices

Rate of unemployment

the percentage of working population not in work

Real

adjusted to take account of inflation

Real interest rates

interest rate less inflation rate

Real values

adjusted to take account of inflation

Regressive tax

a tax where the proportion of income paid in tax falls as income rises

Returns

the resource inputs of land, labour, capital, and enterprise receive returns of rent, wages, interest, and profits respectively

Scarcity

the basic economic problem that arises from our limited resources being unable to fully satisfy unlimited human wants

Shortage

a temporary market position when demand exceeds supply

Short-run

the period during which at least one factor is fixed

Single market

a programme of policies adopted by the EU on 1 January 1993 which advanced beyond the mere abolition of trade barriers

Soft loans

loans given to developing or emerging economies at reduced interest rates

Specialisation

another term for division of labour

Standard of living

calculates the increased ability to purchase goods and services of the average consumer. It is used to define whether consumers are "better off" in material terms

Structural unemployment

jobs lost due to a decline in a particular industry

Substitution effect

when a good for which there are close substitutes falls in price and becomes "a better buy" than its substitutes

Supply

the quantity of a good or service that firms are willing and able to offer for sale per unit of time at a given price

Surplus budget

planned income exceeds planned expenditure

Technical efficiency

the maximum output from minimum inputs

Technological unemployment

jobs lost due to new technology

Tied aid

aid from donor countries that requires developing economies to spend the money on goods supplied by the donor country

Total costs

the total of fixed costs plus variable costs

Total utility

the total amount of satisfaction a consumer gains from consuming a good or service

Trade deficit

imports of goods (or services) exceed exports of goods (or services)

Trade surplus

exports of goods (or services) exceed imports of goods (or services)

Transfers

payments to or from international institutions

Unemployment

the non- or under-use of the factors of production

Utility

the amount of satisfaction a consumer gains from consuming a good or service at any moment in time

Variable costs

costs that vary directly with the level of output, e.g. materials

Visibles

refer to trade in goods only

Wants

humans strive to improve their standard of living with material possessions and luxuries

Weighting

a measure of proportion of income spent

Working population

all those self employed, employed or seeking employment

Answers to questions and activities for Unit 1

Topic 1: The economic problem

Economic problems (page 7)

Q1:

No.	Consumers	Producers	Governments
1	Spend or save	What to produce	Increase or decrease taxation
2	*What to buy*	*What price to charge*	*Spend more on health or Education*
3	*Pay cash or use a credit card*	*How much to spend on advertising*	*Build nuclear power plants or Wind Farms*

The reasons why our wants are unlimited (page 8)

Q2: b) False

Q3: a) True

Q4: a) True

Q5: a) True

Needs (page 9)

Q6:

TV	Car	*Clothing*
Fridge	*Food*	Computer
Shelter	Newspaper	Washing machine

Although some people might regard all of these goods as being essential, the only true needs are *food* (including water), *clothing* and *shelter*.

Q7: The usual answer is no, which implies that our wants are huge and virtually endless. Economists believe that, for a variety of reasons, people's wants are unlimited.

Factors of production (page 9)

Q8: Capital

Q9: Labour

Q10: Enterprise

Q11: Land

Q12: The combination of *unlimited* wants for goods and services but *limited* resources to make the goods and services, creates the basic economic problem.

Scarcity (page 10)

Q13: No country in the world has enough *resources* to produce enough *goods* and *services* to satisfy completely all the *wants* of its people.

Answers from page 11.

Q14: b) If a good is scarce, it must be limited in supply.

Answers from page 11.

Q15: Demand is the want for a product backed by the ability to buy it with *money*.

Q16: Although our wants are unlimited, our demand is limited by *our money / income*.

Defining the economic problem (page 11)

Q17: The basic economic problem is *scarcity*. This comes about because our *wants* for *goods* and *services* are *unlimited* but the *resources* we need to produce the *goods* and *services* are *limited*.

Q18: Consumers must choose what to *buy* because their *money / income* is limited.

Q19: Producers must choose what to *make / produce* because their *resources* are limited.

Q20: Governments must choose what *services* to provide because their *tax revenues* are limited.

Q21: Every choice is the result of *scarcity*.

Q22: b) is not

Identifying free goods (page 12)

Q23: The free goods are: *sand*, *sea* and *strawberries that were growing wild*.

Opportunity cost (page 13)

Q24: The opportunity cost to a consumer of buying a Mars bar might be *buying a Toffee Crisp* or *buying a packet of crisps*.

Q25: The opportunity cost to a farmer of buying a combine harvester might be *employing more workers* or *buying a tractor*.

Q26: The opportunity cost to the government of building a hospital might be *building a school* or *cutting the rate of income tax*.

Q27: Opportunity cost is the direct result of *scarcity* and occurs every time a *choice* is made. All economic goods therefore have opportunity costs as something has to be sacrificed to produce and/or consume them. If a good has no opportunity cost it must be *a free good*.

Q28: b) 1.5. Every 1,000 shorts results in 1,500 lost t-shirts.

Correct choice (page 15)

Q29: To make a correct choice, consumers, producers and governments must weigh up all the alternatives and then choose the one that has the *lowest* opportunity cost.

Obstacles to labour mobility (page 16)

Q30: a) Geographical

Q31: a) Geographical

Q32: b) Occupational

Q33: a) Geographical

Q34: b) Occupational

Q35: b) Occupational

Q36: a) Geographical

Answers from page 17.

Q37: The three missing words are *goods and services*.

End of Topic 1 test (page 20)

Q38: d) All of the above

Q39: d) £500

Q40: b) 2.5 cars

Q41: Economics is a *social* science. The basic economic problem arises because of the mismatch between the unlimited *wants* of people and society and the limited *resources* available. As a result *choices* must take place. This applies to all *scarce* goods, but a few *free* goods are excluded because they have no opportunity cost to produce.

The four factors of production are *land* (natural resources), *labour* (human resources), *capital* (man-made resources) and *enterprise* (the organising and risk-taking factor). When one item is selected, then there is an *opportunity* cost. This is the *second* preference that cannot now be achieved.

Topic 2: Production possibility curves

Economic and technical efficiency (page 24)

Q1: Although scarcity can never be eliminated, because resources will always be *limited* and wants will always be *unlimited*, its effects can be reduced by making full use of our *resources*.

Q2: a. Greater specialisation by workers, b. Increased mechanisation, and d. Improved education and training.

Expanding and declining industries (page 26)

Q3: a) Expanded

Q4: a) Expanded

Q5: b) Declined

Q6: b) Declined

Q7: a) Expanded

Q8: b) Declined

Consumer and capital goods (page 27)

Q9:

Consumer good	Capital good
apple	supertanker
private plane	work uniform
television	factory machine
personal computer	taxi
casual clothes	hard hat

Q10: If the car is used for business purposes, it is a capital good. If it is being used for private purposes, e.g. going to Tesco, it is a consumer good.

Q11: It is how a good is *used* that determines whether it is a consumer or capital good.

Production possibility curve (PPC) (page 28)

Q12: If the economy is producing at a point on the curve, its production must be *technically efficient*.

Q13: Nothing! - the curve measures potential output; a rise in unemployment will affect actual output but not potential output. However a fall in production is the cause of the unemployment and actual output will move inside the curve of potential output.

Q14: If an economy is currently producing at a point on the curve, the only way it can produce more capital goods is by **producing fewer consumer goods**. A PPC is simply a diagrammatic representation of **opportunity cost**.

Q15: AX consumer goods.

Q16: 0X consumer goods.

Economic growth (page 31)

Q17:

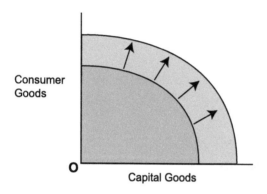

End of Topic 2 test (page 32)

Q18: d) Producing its normal output but with fewer factors.

Q19: b) It remains constant.

Q20: a) It increases.

Q21: c) C

Q22: b) If a production process is economically efficient, it must also be technically efficient.

Q23: b) MN capital goods

Topic 3: Theory of demand

Theory of supply (page 37)

Q1: The theory of supply attempts to explain *producer* behaviour.

Total and marginal utility (page 37)

Q2:

Number of packets per day	Total utility	Marginal utility
1	100	100
2	180	*80*
3	250	*70*
4	300	*50*
5	320	*20*

Plotting total and marginal utility (page 38)

Q3:

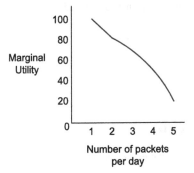

The law of diminishing marginal utility (page 38)

Q4: In money terms, the law of diminishing marginal utility states that "the more we have of a good, the less we are willing to *pay* for one more".

Rational behaviour (page 39)

Q5: A consumer spends all his money on two goods - cans of juice, which cost £1 each, and packets of crisps, which cost 50p each. He will maximise his total utility when he buys the goods in such amounts that the satisfaction he gets from the last can of juice is *twice* the satisfaction he gets from the last packet of crisps.

Effective demand (page 39)

Q6: b) No

The price of the product (page 40)

Q7: For most goods, the higher the price the *lower* the quantity demanded. When price rises some consumers will regard the good as being too expensive and so will buy *less* of it. If the price falls some people will regard it as a 'good buy' and therefore the quantity demanded of it will *rise*. Price and quantity demanded therefore are therefore *inversely* related.

The law of demand (page 40)

Q8: There is *an inverse* relationship between price and quantity demanded.

Income and substitution effect (page 42)

Q9: Nothing.

Q10: It falls.

Marginal utility curves and demand curves (page 42)

Q11: They are the same curves, i.e. a marginal utility curve *is* a demand curve.

Categorise the goods (page 44)

Q12:

Ostentatious goods	Speculative goods	Giffen goods
Rolex watch	shares	rice
fine wines	oil	bread
Rolls Royce		

End of Topic 3 test (page 45)

Q13: b) Marginal utility and price

Q14: b) John's marginal has decreased but his total utility has increased.

Q15: c) It decreases continuously.

Q16: d) By a leftwards movement up the demand curve.

Q17: c) Both of the above.

Q18: c) both his marginal and total utility increase.

Q19:

Scenario	Term
The demand for Bentley cars rises with an increase in their price.	*Article of ostentation*
More people rush to buy houses as prices begin to increase rapidly.	*Speculative buying*
As the price of rice rises, more is bought.	*Giffen good*
A cheap brand of tea sees its sales (demand) rise when it increases price	*Price assumed to indicate quality*

Topic 4: Determinants of demand

Determinants of demand (page 49)

Q1:   a) Increase

Q2:   b) Decrease

Q3:   a) Increase

Conditions of demand (page 49)

Q4:   The conditions of demand are the factors which may cause the demand for a product to change other than **price**.

Q5:   In order to isolate the effect on the demand for a good of a change in its price, we assume that all other influences, i.e. **the conditions of demand**, are not changing and we assume **ceteris paribus**.

Changes or shifts in demand (page 50)

Q6:   By a change or shift in demand we mean that demand has changed at all **prices** - resulting in a **new** demand curve. A movement along a demand curve indicates that a different **quantity** is being demanded because the **price** of the good has changed.

Changes in demand (page 50)

Q7:   The conditions of demand are the factors, other than the **price** of the good, which may cause demand to change.

Increase in demand (page 50)

Q8:

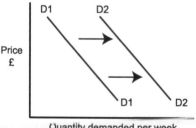

Q9:   If the demand for a good increases, the demand curve will shift *to the right*.

Causes of an increase in demand (page 51)

Q10:

Increase	Decrease
Income	Price of a complement
Fashion	
Price of a substitute	

Causes of an increase in demand (page 52)

Q11: A decrease in price will cause a movement along the demand curve, not a shift of the curve.

Q12:

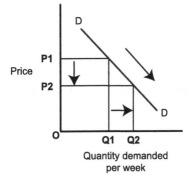

Decrease in demand (page 52)

Q13:

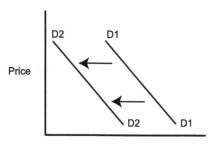

Quantity demanded per week

Q14: If the demand for a good decreases, the demand curve will shift **to the left**.

Causes of a decrease in demand (page 52)

Q15: b) a decrease

Q16: a) against

Q17: b) a decrease

Q18: a) an increase

Q19: An increase in price will cause a movement along the demand curve, not a shift of the curve.

Increased price (page 53)

Q20:

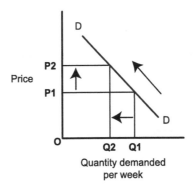

End of Topic 4 test (page 54)

Q21: c) An increase in the price of Shell Petrol.

Q22: d) Existing consumers of the good experience a rise in their real income.

Q23: d) By a leftwards movement up the demand curve.

Q24: b) Goods A and B are substitute goods.

Q25: c) A decrease in the price of fish.

Q26: c) A decrease in the price of tea. Tea can be a substitute for coffee so a fall in the price of tea will attract some customers away from coffee and the demand for coffee will shift leftwards towards the origin with less sold at every price.

Q27: d) An increase in disposable incomes. Rising incomes are associated with increased consumer spending. Answers a) and b) would result in a slide along the existing line.

Q28: c) A rainy day. Answer b) is wrong because it would affect the supply line as an increase in the costs of production. Answers a) and d) are good for ice cream sales and shift demand to the right.

Q29: b) The anniversary of Robert Burns. This is because haggis is eaten at Burns Suppers. Answer c) affects supply. Answer a) would decrease sales (leftwards). Answer d) would increase the price of the combination of haggis and turnip because it is a complementary good (leftwards shift).

Q30: All three statements are true.

Topic 5: Price elasticity of demand (PED)

Elasticity (page 59)

Q1: Elasticity is a measure of *responsiveness*.

Price elasticity of demand (PED) (page 59)

Q2: Price elasticity of demand is a measure of the extent to which the demand for a good changes when there is a change in *its price*.

Answers from page 60.

Q3: £1,800 (from £40,000 to £41,800)

Answers from page 60.

Q4: £770,000 (from £14,000,000 to £13,230,000)

PED calculations (page 61)

Q5: -0.5

Q6: 240

Q7:

1. The % change in demand must have been *greater* than the percentage change in price.
2. The % change in demand must have been *less* than the percentage change in price.
3. The % change in demand must have been *equal to* the percentage change in price.

Price elasticity (page 61)

Q8: If price elasticity of demand is greater than one, demand is *price elastic*.

Q9: If price elasticity of demand is less than one, demand is *price inelastic*.

Q10: If price elasticity of demand is equal to one, demand is *unitary price elastic*.

PED effects on the demand curve (page 62)

Q11: Curve X is price inelastic and curve Y is price elastic.

Q12: Zero (PED = 0/price = 0)

Q13: Infinity (PED = demand/0 = ∞)

Q14:

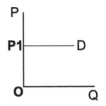

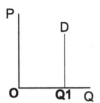

Perfectly elastic demand curve   *Perfectly inelastic demand curve*

Answers from page 64.

Q15: If a good has many close substitutes, the demand for it will be price *elastic*.

Explanation - if a good has many close substitutes, a rise in its price will cause many consumers to switch to a (now) cheaper substitute. If it falls in price, many consumers will start to buy that good instead of its (now) dearer substitute.

Q16: The more essential or habit forming a good is, the more price *inelastic* the demand for it will be, e.g. salt, cigarettes.

Q17: If it is fashionable to consume a particular good the demand for it will not only be high, it will also be price *inelastic*.

Q18: If a good is very cheap, relative to average incomes, the demand for it will tend to be price *inelastic*, e.g. the demand for bread is much more price *inelastic* than the demand for cars.

Q19: The more frequently something is bought, the more price *elastic* demand will be.

Explanation: if a good is bought frequently, consumers will be aware of any change in its price and might therefore alter their demand for it. If a good is bought infrequently consumers might not even remember what they paid for it the last time they bought it and will therefore not react to any change in its price.

Q20: The demand for a pot of glue is likely to be price *inelastic* because it tends to be bought infrequently.

Q21: If a product is a relatively small but vital part of something else the demand for it will be price *inelastic*.

Explanation: if the small item is not bought because its price has increased the large item will be useless, e.g. a battery for an expensive watch.

Determinants of PED (page 64)

Q22: b) Price inelastic

Q23: b) Price inelastic

Q24: b) Price inelastic

Q25: a) Price elastic

Q26: There are no close substitutes for petrol, e.g. you cannot put diesel in a petrol engine, but there are many close substitutes for any one brand of petrol, e.g. BP petrol is a close substitute for Shell petrol.

Total revenue (page 66)

Q27: a) The revenue gained from selling 80 goods at £30 rather than £25.

Q28: b) The revenue lost from only selling 80 goods instead of 100.

Q29: The total revenue is £2,500 when P = 25 is and £2,400 when P = 30.

Q30: The TR from the sale of Good X increases but the TR from the sale of Good Y decreases.

Q31: The revenue gained (rectangle A) is greater than the revenue lost (rectangle B).

Q32: The revenue lost (rectangle B) is greater than the revenue gained (rectangle A).

Q33: If the demand for a good is price inelastic, producers of the good will gain revenue if its price *increases*. If the demand for a good is price elastic, producers of the good will *lose* revenue if its price increases.

Q34: If the demand for a good is price elastic, price and TR move in *opposite directions* directions, i.e. an increase in price leads to a *decrease* in TR and vice versa.

The importance of PED (page 68)

Q35: Firms will tend to increase the price of goods whose demand is price *inelastic* and reduce the price of those goods whose demand is price *elastic*.

Q36: This helps explain why holidays, travel, etc. are cheaper at off-peak times - demand is not only smaller, it is also more price *elastic*.

Q37: It also helps explain why firms spend so much money on advertising. The aim is not only to increase demand, but also to make it more price *inelastic*. This will enable them to increase price without losing too many *customers*.

Q38: The demand for all of these goods (tobacco, alcohol and petrol) is highly price *inelastic*.

End of Topic 5 test (page 70)

Q39:

$$PED = \frac{\text{percentage change in demand}}{\text{percentage change in price}}$$

$$0.8 = \frac{?}{20} = \frac{16}{20}$$

Therefore, because the price fell, demand would increase by 16% i.e. from 100 to **116**.

Q40:

$$PED = \frac{\text{percentage change in demand}}{\text{percentage change in price}}$$

$$0.7 = \frac{?}{20} = \frac{14}{20}$$

Therefore demand would increase by 14% i.e. from 100 to **114**.

Q41: d) -2.0

Q42: d) If the demand for your product is price inelastic, you should increase the price.

Q43: a) An increase in its price will result in fewer of the good being sold but its sales revenue rising.

Q44: a) A large number of substitutes. Consumers will easily change between alternatives in response to price changes.

Q45: a) No close substitute exists and b) The product costs just a few pence. Few consumers will be able or willing to switch if there is no close alternative. If the product is very cheap then an increase of several per cent will have little effect on sales. Luxuries are a large part of a consumer's overall spending and can be done without.

Q46: a) BP petrol. Many other brands of petrol are close substitutes and can be switched to. The Guardian newspaper is differentiated from others and most buyers would see it as very different from, for example, the Times, the Telegraph or The Sun. Matches are so cheap that a price rise will be ignored by most buyers as insubstantial.

Q47: d) 0.5 and the revenue will rise.

Q48: a) elastic and the revenue increases. Profits II and III are uncertain because we have no information about costs. For example if the average cost per car was £19,001 then a loss of £1 per car would be made, even though revenues have increased.

The equation for PED gives an answer of 2 which is elastic as it is greater than 1. If in doubt, refer to *5.2 Price elasticity of demand (PED)*.

Topic 6: Production

The factors of production (page 75)

Q1: c) Rent

Q2: a) Wages

Q3: d) Interest

Q4: b) Profit

Short-run and long-run (page 76)

Q5: b) Variable

Q6: a) Fixed

Q7: a) Fixed

Q8: b) Variable

The law of diminishing returns (page 79)

Q9:

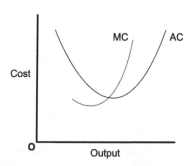

Q10: c) the rent paid for the use of the factory.

Q11: c) fixed cost per unit becomes less.

End of Topic 6 test (page 81)

Q12: a) a football team employs its first goalkeeping coach.

Q13: a) the cost of flour.

Q14: a) experiencing diminishing returns.

Q15: d) as the quantity of one of the factors employed is increased, eventually the output ceases to rise in proportion.

Q16: The short-run average cost curve first falls because of increasing returns to the fixed factor. *(1 mark)* This means that the fixed factor is used more and more efficiently *(1 mark)* until it best combines with the number of variable factors used. *(1 mark)* For example, a machine now has enough workers to make sure it is continuously running. *(1 mark)* Reaching the lowest point in the average cost curve is the optimum output level and represents technical efficiency (maximum output from minimum input). *(1 mark)*

The short-run average cost curve then begins to rise. *(1 mark)* Continuing to add variable factors will not increase efficiency *(1 mark)* beyond the optimum point. For example, adding even more workers to the one machine, may increase output a bit more. However, the wages of the added workers who make such a small contribution to output will force average cost up. *(2 marks)*

The solution is usually to expand to new premises, or to buy more machines. *(1 mark)* This can only happen in the long-run, when all factors can be varied. *(1 mark)*

(maximum of 9 marks)

Topic 7: Costs

Fixed and variable costs (page 85)

Q1:

Fixed	Variable
manager's salary	workers' wages
factory rent	designer royalties
fire insurance	wood for the tables

Fixed, variable and total costs (page 85)

Q2:

Output (units)	Fixed costs (£)	Variable costs (£)	Total costs (£)
0	*25*	0	25
1	25	30	*55*
2	*25*	*45*	70
3	25	*60*	85

Average cost (page 86)

Q3:

Output (units)	Fixed costs (£)	Variable costs (£)	Total costs (£)	Average costs (£)
0	100	0	100	-
10	*100*	90	190	19
20	100	*160*	260	*13*
30	100	230	*330*	*11*

Marginal cost (page 87)

Q4:

Output (units)	Fixed costs (£)	Variable costs (£)	Total costs (£)	Marginal costs (£)
0	200	0	200	-
1	200	120	320	*120*
2	200	210	410	*90*
3	200	290	490	*80*
4	200	360	560	*70*

Summary of costs (page 88)

Q5:

Output (units)	Fixed cost (£)	Variable cost (£)	Total cost (£)	Marginal cost (£)	Average cost (£)
0	20	0	20	n/a	n/a
1	20	18	*38*	*18*	*38*
2	20	34	*54*	*16*	*27*
3	20	46	*66*	*12*	*22*
4	20	56	*76*	*10*	*19*
5	20	65	*85*	*9*	*17*
6	20	70	*90*	*5*	*15*
7	20	92	*112*	*22*	*16*
8	20	124	*144*	*32*	*18*

Average fixed costs (page 89)

Q6:

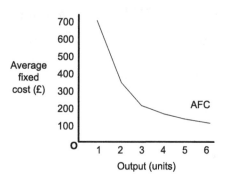

Average variable costs (page 91)

Q7:

Output (units)	Fixed cost (£)	Average fixed cost (£)	Variable cost (£)	Average variable cost (£)	Total cost (£)	Average total cost (£)
0	24	n/a	0	n/a	24	n/a
1	24	24	16	16	40	40
2	24	12	30	15	54	27
3	24	*8*	42	*14*	*66*	*22*
4	24	*6*	48	*12*	*72*	*18*

Internal economies of scale (page 93)

Q8:

Description	Internal economy of scale
Merging a hotel chain with an airline	*Risk-bearing*
Obtaining a 15% discount on an order for 100,000 televisions	*Purchasing*
Replacing two small secondary schools with one larger one	*Technical*
Advertising on local radio for a local chain of bakers with ten retail shops	*Marketing*
Employing a Human Resource Manager to take care of hiring staff	*Managerial*
Receiving a favourable interest rate on a loan from a bank	*Financial*
Processing a single order for the sale of 100,000 televisions	*Administrative*
Developing an ironing machine to reduce ironing time by 50%	*Research and development*

Q9: c) replacing three smaller ships with a super tanker.

Q10: d) reductions in average costs as a firm grows.

External economies of scale (page 95)

Q11:

Description	External economy of scale
Tyre manufacturer sites nearby	*Local suppliers*
Local university obtains grant to research crash safety	*Research centres*
Places on engineering courses available	*College courses*
Many qualified applicants for vacancies	*Locally skilled labour*
Local council improves road linking to nearby motorway	*Infrastructure improvement*

Revenues (page 98)

Q12:

Units sold (£)	Sales price (£)	Total revenue (£)	Marginal revenue (£)	Average revenue (£)
1	20	20	20	20
2	20	40	20	20
3	20	60	20	20
4	20	80	20	20
5	15	95	15	19

End of Topic 7 test (page 100)

Q13: b) addition to total cost caused by producing one more unit.

Q14: c) The managing director's salary.

Q15: b) £18

Q16: a) maximise profits.

Q17: c) 300

Q18: d) several firms in the industry benefit from being located near to each other.

Q19: c) £75

Q20: The long-run is defined as that period of time when all factors can be varied. *(1 mark)* For a firm this may mean finding new land and building a bigger factory, for example. *(1 mark)*

Economies of scale is a term that covers the advantages large firms have over small firms. *(1 mark)* These long-run advantages usually give the large firms an average cost advantage. They reduce the long-run average cost (cost per item). *(1 mark)* Now give examples of economies of scale (two examples well explained is enough) *(3 marks)*

Very large firms can suffer from diseconomies of scale. *(1 mark)* In the long-run, average costs begin to increase. *(1 mark)* The firms become slow-moving, lumbering giants encumbered by bureaucracy *(1 mark)* and layers of middle management. They respond more slowly to changing market conditions *(1 mark)* than their smaller rivals.

Optional - you may choose to explain how the long-run curve is made up of successive short-run curves. This has some relevance, but you won't achieve a high mark without covering economies and diseconomies of scale.

As a firm grows, it will move to an entirely new short-run average cost curve. This happens as it increases the scale of production, having been able to change a fixed factor in the long-run. Indeed, as the firm grows it will move on to successive new short-run average cost curves. Each curve will represent a new lower cost position than the previous one, until diseconomies of scale set in.

Maximum of 9 marks. You can expect some credit for defining the long-run, and again a diagram may acquire a mark. The key part of your answer (that is essential to obtaining the highest mark) is the explanation of economies of scale reducing average costs, and the potential for diseconomies of scale to occur and raise average costs after a point.

Topic 8: Supply

Answers from page 104.

Q1: The theory of demand attempts to explain **consumer** behaviour.

Answers from page 104.

Q2: To go from individual to market supply, we **add up** all the individual supplies.

Answers from page 105.

Q3: When a firm adds to its stock of goods, output will be **greater than** supply. When a firm uses its stock of goods to help meet demand, output will be **less than** supply.

Answers from page 106.

Q4: b) a direct

Supply curve (page 106)

Q5:

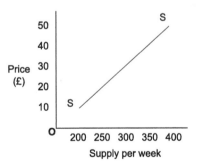

Answers from page 106.

Q6: Supply curves, like demand curves, are drawn on the basis of **ceteris paribus**.

End of Topic 8 test (page 108)

Q7: d)

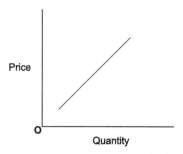

Q8: Output is the production in a time period but you can sell (supply) more than this by reducing your stocks.

Conversely, if you supply to the market less than you produced (output) then your stock will increase.

Q9: Suggested reasons:

- existing producers seeking to maximise their profits will move as many resources as possible into this good;

- existing producers may be able to overcome additional overtime costs and increase the level of profitable production;

- less efficient (higher cost) producers will enter or re-enter the market as they can now make a profit by producing the good;

- entrepreneurs (new suppliers) will move into the production of goods that now offer above normal profits.

Topic 9: Determinants of supply

Determinants of supply (page 110)

Q1: In order to isolate the effect on supply of a change in price, we must again assume that all other determinants, i.e. the conditions of supply, are not changing. Therefore we must assume *ceteris paribus*.

Change in profit (page 110)

Q2: As profit = revenue - costs, it will increase if something happens which results in *an increase* in revenue or *a decrease* in costs.

Effect of changes in costs (page 111)

Q3:

Change in costs on supply schedules	Effect on supply curve
Efficiency gains due to new technology	*right*
Higher wages	*left*
Rising price of components	*left*

Relationship between costs and supply (page 111)

Q4: A decrease in the cost of wood will increase the supply of wooden tables because the profit made on each table will *increase*.

The prices of other goods (page 112)

Q5: Increase the supply of red t-shirts and produce fewer blue t-shirts.

Government intervention (page 113)

Q6: a) a decrease

Q7: b) an increase

Increases in productivity (page 113)

Q8: b) 180 units, 15 workers

The weather (page 114)

Q9: For example, a very dry summer may lower some crop yields and a period of bad weather may delay outdoor work on construction sites.

An increase in supply (page 114)

Q10:

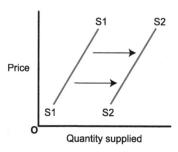

Q11: If the supply of a good increases, the supply curve will shift **to the right**.

Causes of an increase in supply (page 115)

Q12: a) an increase

Q13: b) a decrease

Q14: b) a decrease

Q15: b) a decrease

Q16: a) an increase

Q17: A decrease in price will cause a movement along the supply curve, not a shift of the curve.

Q18:

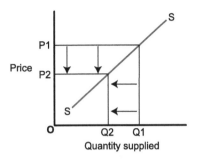

The decrease in price results in a decrease in the quantity supplied (Q1 to Q2) but does not result in a new supply curve.

A decrease in supply (page 116)

Q19: b) less

Q20: b) higher

Q21: Five causes of a decrease in supply are:

- a decrease in productivity;
- an increase in the costs of producing the good;
- an increase in the price of other goods the producer is making;
- an increase in the tax placed on the good;
- a decrease on the subsidy producers receive for producing the good.

End of Topic 9 test (page 118)

Q22: Supply will fall because the cost of producing plastics will have increased. There will be a leftwards shift in the supply curve.

Q23: a) True

Q24: b) False

Q25: b) False

Q26: b) False

Q27: a) True

Q28: b) False

Q29: a) True

Q30: a) True

Q31: b) False

Topic 10: Markets

Goods, services, resources and money (page 124)

Q1:

Goods	Services	Resources	Money
cars	haircuts	labour	foreign currency
sweets	education	raw materials	

Forms of price (page 125)

Q2:

- The price of labour is **wages**.
- The price of foreign currency is its **exchange rate**.
- The price of land is **rent**.
- The price of borrowing money is **interest**.

Q3: The entry requirements.

Equilibrium price (EP) (page 125)

Q4: At the equilibrium price, the amount consumers wish to buy equals **the amount producers wish to sell**.

Q5: At the equilibrium price there are neither **shortages** nor **surpluses**.

Market price (page 127)

Q6: There will be a surplus, i.e. excess supply (supply > demand).

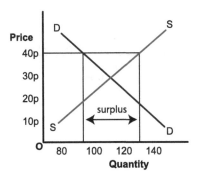

Q7: Reduce the price. If the market price is above the equilibrium price, there will be a surplus of the good on the market. In order to get rid of this surplus, the sellers will reduce the price.

Q8:

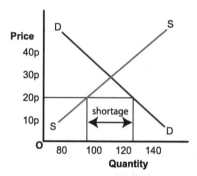

If the market price is below the equilibrium price, there will be a shortage of the good on the market. Consumers will compete with each other to get the good and will bid up the price.

If, at any moment in time, the price of a good (in a free market) is not at the equilibrium level, the forces of the market will push it back towards the equilibrium level. Therefore, in a free market, the equilibrium price (and quantity) will eventually be established.

Changes in supply or demand 1 (page 128)

Q9:

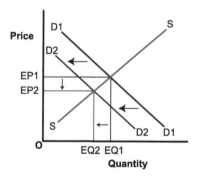

Q10:

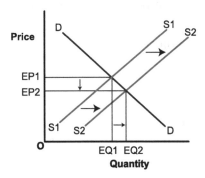

Q11:

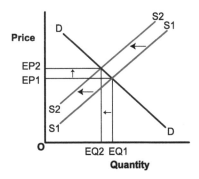

Changes in supply or demand 2 (page 128)

Q12: An increase in demand will cause *an increase* in the equilibrium price and *an increase* in the equilibrium quantity.

Q13: A decrease in demand will cause *a decrease* in the equilibrium price and *a decrease* in the equilibrium quantity.

Q14: An increase in supply will cause *a decrease* in the equilibrium price and *an increase* in the equilibrium quantity.

Q15: A decrease in supply will cause *an increase* in the equilibrium price and *a decrease* in the equilibrium quantity.

Changes in supply or demand 3 (page 129)

Q16: The EP will fall but the EQ might rise, fall or stay the same.

Q17: The EQ will increase but the EP might rise, fall or stay the same.

Q18: The EQ will decrease but the EP might rise, fall or stay the same.

Joint or complementary demand (page 130)

Q19:

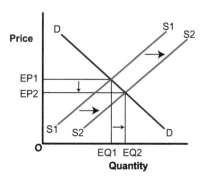

Q20:

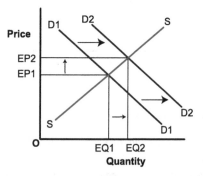

Q21: The increase in the supply of cars reduces the price of cars which increases the amount of cars sold, i.e. the *quantity* demanded of cars increases. The fact that more cars are being bought will increase the demand for petrol and increase its price.

Competitive demand (page 131)

Q22:

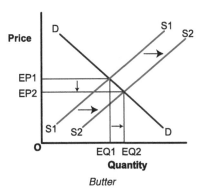

Butter

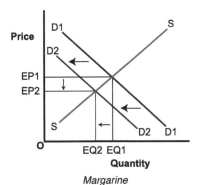

Margarine

An increase in the supply of butter will reduce the price of butter. A fall in the price of butter will reduce the demand for margarine as some consumers will switch from buying margarine to buying butter. The fall in the demand for margarine will reduce its price.

Joint supply (page 131)

Q23: If farmers increase the number of cows they own in response to the increased demand for milk, the supply of meat will increase some time later. This increase in supply will cause the price of meat to fall.

End of Topic 10 test (page 133)

Q24: c) It will rise.

Q25: c) The price of good X would decrease.

Q26: d) It would increase.

Q27: d) An increase in the supply of good X.

Q28: c) Both of the above.

Q29: a) A decrease in the price of golf clubs.

Q30: b)

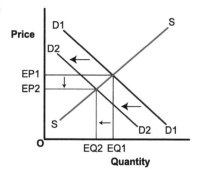

Q31: The effect of the increase in supply *(1 mark)* must have been **outweighed** by an increase in demand *(1 mark)*.

Topic 11: Market intervention

Market failure (page 140)

Q1:

Government action	Market failure
Use tax revenue to pay completely for the good or service	*Public good*
Use high taxes to discourage excess consumption and production.	*Demerit good*
Introduce strict laws and regulations covering the industry	*Externalities (negative)*
Subsidise the companies to cover the losses made	*Externalities (positive)*
Supply some of the good or service, paid from taxes	*Merit good*
Create a Competition Commission to monitor mergers and take-overs	*Monopoly*

Maximum price (page 141)

Q2: b) high

Q3:

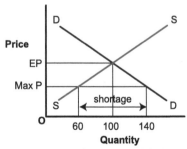

As the maximum price is below the EP, demand will be greater than supply, i.e. there will be a shortage of the good in the market.

The minimum wage and unemployment (page 141)

Q4: A minimum wage set *above* the equilibrium wage in an industry would *reduce* the *demand* for workers in that industry. Although more people would now be *willing* to work in the industry, i.e. the *supply* of workers would *increase*, employers *would not* be willing to employ as many as before, i.e. there would be a *surplus* of workers.

Minimum price (page 142)

Q5: a) above

Q6:

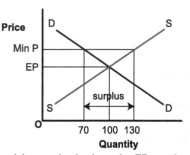

As the minimum price is above the EP, supply will be greater than demand, i.e. there will be a surplus of the good in the market.

Imposing expenditure taxes (page 143)

Q7: c) P2 to P3

Q8: b) P2

Q9: c) P3

Q10: a) P1 to P2

Q11: b) P1 to P3

Q12: b) inelastic

Granting subsidies (page 144)

Q13: b) P2

Q14: c) P2 to P3

Q15: c) P3

Q16: a) P1 to P2

Q17: b) P1 to P3

Q18: b) producer

Types of market (page 147)

Q19: In the real world, all markets are, to a greater or lesser extent, *imperfect*.

Perfect markets (page 147)

Q20: In a perfect market there can only be *one* price for the good at any moment in time.

Imperfect markets (page 148)

Q21: a) greater

Q22: a) greater

Q23: b) lower

Q24: b) lower

Q25: b) lower

Monopoly (page 149)

Q26: A monopolist, if he/she is to have any significant power, must control the supply of something with no close *substitutes*.

Oligopoly (page 150)

Q27: Examples of non-price competition include:

- home delivery service;
- 24 hour shopping;
- loyalty cards;
- discounted petrol;
- in-store chemists, restaurants, and creches;
- innovative technology e.g. cost as you go;
- internet shopping.

Market types (page 150)

Q28: c) Monopolistic competition

Q29: c) Monopolistic competition

Q30: a) Monopoly

Q31: b) Oligopoly

Q32: c) Monopolistic competition

Q33: b) Oligopoly

End of Topic 11 test (page 154)

Q34: b) O to Q3

Q35: a) An increase in the tax on good X, and d) a decrease in the subsidy on good X.

Q36: b) False

Q37: a) True

Q38: b) False

Q39: b) False

Q40: a) True

Q41: b) False

Q42: a) True

Q43: b) False

Q44: b) False

Topic 12: End of unit test

End of Unit 1 test (page 158)

Q1: In Economics, scarcity refers to the fact that there are not enough resources in the world to produce enough goods and services to completely satisfy everyone.

It comes about because, although our wants for goods and services are unlimited, the resources we need to produce the goods and services are limited.

It is the basic economic problem because all other economic problems are a result of scarcity. If nothing is scarce, there is no need to choose or economise and Economics would cease to exist!

Q2: Opportunity cost is the sacrifice of the next best alternative choice and occurs every time a choice is made. Technical efficiency occurs when a producer is getting the maximum output from his/her inputs. It is the output where average total cost is at a minimum, i.e. optimum output.

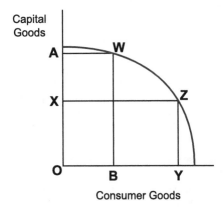

All points on the boundary, e.g. W and Z, represent technically efficient combinations of capital and consumer goods. Opportunity cost is shown by any movement along the boundary. For example, if an economy is producing at point W and wants to produce BY more consumer goods it will have to sacrifice AX capital goods.

Q3: Any two of the following three options:

- existing consumers of the good experience a rise in their real income, i.e. they can buy their usual amount of the good but will have some income left over. With this 'extra' income they might buy more of the good;
- it may become cheaper than its substitutes and some consumers might therefore switch their consumption;
- it becomes a better buy, i.e. consumers get the same amount of satisfaction for less money.

Q4: Any one of the following four options:

- Speculation - Consumers are expecting the price to rise even further;
- Quality - Higher prices can be taken as an indication of higher quality;
- Ostentatious buying - Higher prices can make goods more exclusive and therefore more desirable;
- Giffen goods - If the price of a staple food, e.g rice, rises some poor people might buy more because they can now no longer afford to buy any dearer food.

Q5: Price elasticity of demand (PED) measures the responsiveness of the demand for a good to a change in its price, i.e. the extent to which the quantity demand for a good changes when its price changes.

The formula is:

$$PED = \frac{\text{the \% change in the quantity demanded of good X}}{\text{the \% change in the price of good X}}$$

Q6: If the demand for a good is price inelastic, when its price changes by $x\%$ the demand for the good will change by less than $x\%$. Therefore, if its price rises the revenue from the sale of the product will also rise as the revenue gained from the higher price will be greater than the revenue lost from the fall in sales. If its price falls total revenue will also fall.

If the demand for a good is price elastic, when its price changes by $x\%$ the demand for the good will change by more than $x\%$. Therefore, if its price rises the revenue from the sale of the product will fall as the revenue gained from the higher price will be less than the revenue lost from the fall in sales. If its price falls total revenue will rise.

Q7: Marginal cost is the increase in total cost when one more good is produced, i.e. the extra cost of producing one more good.

Average total cost is average cost of producing one good. It is calculated by dividing the total cost of producing a good by the number produced.

Q8:

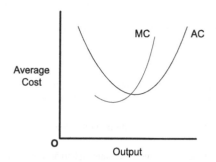

Q9: The market clearing price is the price where demand equals supply (also known as the equilibrium price). At that price, the amount consumers wish to buy equals the amount producers which to sell. It is the price which clears the market and there is no unsold stock (surpluses) nor any unsatisfied demand (shortages). In the following diagram the market clearing price is P1.

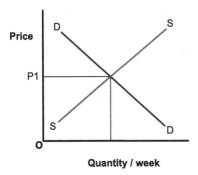

Quantity / week

Q10: An exceptionally good strawberry harvest will increase the supply of strawberries (the supply curve will shift to the right) which will reduce the price of strawberries.

The fall in the price of strawberries will increase the demand for fresh cream as cream and strawberries are complementary goods. The increase in the demand for fresh cream will increase its price.

Q11: If, because of a fall in demand, a firm is not earning enough to cover its costs, and is making a loss, it has two basic courses of action. It can shut down temporarily and start up production some time later, when demand has picked up, or it can continue to produce.

The only costs that are saved by temporarily closing down are variable costs, i.e wages, raw materials. Fixed costs, e.g. rent, interest, salaries, still have to be paid even when the firm is not producing anything. Therefore, if the firm is earning enough revenue to cover its variable costs, there is no reason to shut down - and by staying in production it will be maintaining its workforce and the loyalty of its customers. This only applies to the short run as, in the long run, a firm must cover all its costs.

Q12: Any two of the following six options:

* A perfect market has many firms; a monopoly market has only one firm;
* The firms in a perfect market are small; in a monopoly the firm can be very large;
* A perfect market has no entry barriers; a monopoly has high entry barriers;
* The firms in a perfect market are price takers; the firm in a monopoly can set their price;
* In a perfect market super-profits can only exist in the short run; but in a monopoly in the long run, super-profits can continue to be made;
* In a perfect market the price equals the average cost (cost includes the return of a normal profit); but in a monopoly price will be above average cost. This implies that the consumer may be getting a poor deal from the monopoly.

Answers to questions and activities for Unit 2

Topic 1: Government finance

Government revenue (page 166)

Q1: Income Tax, VAT and National Insurance. Note that 'Borrowing' is not a tax, and 'Other revenues' is a combined entry including several smaller revenue sources.

Q2: 15

Q3: 36

Q4: 21

Q5: Speeding fines and prescriptions.

Q6: If spending is greater than revenue (this will be covered later in this unit).

Effect of taxation on individuals and firms (page 168)

Q7: Regressive. The lower income groups are paying a bigger percentage of their income in tax than the larger income groups.

Q8: b) False

Q9: a) True

Q10: b) False

Q11: a) True

Q12: a) True

Public and merit goods (page 169)

Q13:

a) Public
b) Public
c) Merit
d) Public
e) Merit
f) Public

Government spending (page 170)

Q14:

Area of government spending	Amount (in £bn)
Defence	*40*
Education	*97*
Transport	21
Public Order and Safety	31
Health	*137*
Industry, Agriculture and Employment	16
Housing and Environment	23
Debt Interest	*51*
Personal Social Services	31
Social Protection	*220*
Other	53

Q15: *Social protection* and *law and order*. More people would claim Jobseeker's Allowance and the crime rate might increase.

Q16: *Health* and *social protection*. More old people would be in care and claiming a state pension.

Q17: *Law and order* and *defence*. More police and soldiers would be required.

Q18: *Education*. There would be fewer pupils in state schools and spending could fall.

Q19: *Law and order*. More money would be required to pay salaries.

Public Sector Net Cash Requirement (PSNCR) (page 173)

Q20:

Government Revenue (in £bn)	Government Spending (in £bn)	PSNCR (in £bn)
10	12	2
15	14	*£ -1 bn*
20	20	*£0*
£35 bn	40	5
13	*£10 bn*	-3
£72 bn	60	-12

End of Topic 1 test (page 175)

Q21: a) direct and progressive.

Q22: c) paying teachers' salaries.

Q23: b) old age pensions.

Q24: d) government spending exceeds government revenue.

Q25: c) both of the above.

Q26: *Income Tax* is the only tax to meet all four criteria. Indirect taxes like VAT and excise duties take no account of ability to pay but are relatively cheap to collect. Council Tax takes no account of ability to pay but is certain and relatively convenient to pay. Corporation Tax is certain but takes the same percentage of all sizes of profits.

Topic 2: Government aims - inflation

Test your prior knowledge (page 179)

Q1: The prices you have to pay for goods and services.

Q2: The goods and services you can buy with your income.

Price of leather (page 181)

Q3: It is a cost of production. To maintain profits, firms will increase the price of suites.

Prices/wages spiral (page 184)

Q4: One worker's wage award leads to price increases so more workers seek wage increases and the process continues.

Money supply (page 185)

Q5: In a modern economy money consists of:

- coins and notes in circulation;
- bank deposits.

Bank deposits are entries in bank accounts which are created when a customer deposits money or when a bank gives a loan. Bank deposits can be spent using Switch, direct debit and transfers between accounts.

Inflation record (page 186)

Q6: Inflation has remained low and steady in the UK in recent years due to:

- good fiscal prudence on the part of the UK Government with control of public spending and public sector pay awards;
- appropriate and careful use of interest rates to control aggregate demand where necessary;
- a strong pound keeping the price of imports low;
- strong competition from the "tiger economies" of South Eastern Asia making sure we keep our prices steady to remain competitive;
- a rise in labour productivity keeping costs low;
- relatively steady world oil prices which keep costs of production in many industries steady too;
- the absence of any prices/wages spiral leading to realistic pay awards in both the public and private sectors;
- globalisation delivers cheaper clothing and manufactures mainly from Asia;
- trade unions find it harder to engage in successful industrial action on wages;
- business costs are reduced by increasing use of zero-hour and temporary contracts;
- raw material (commodity) prices have eased as world demand slowed following the banking crisis;
- since the banking crisis, low UK demand has held back inflation.

Price index weight (page 188)

Q7: Order of weight on the price index:

1. Food;
2. Clothing;
3. Hair products;
4. Newspapers.
5. Gardening products;

Percentage change (page 188)

Q8:

	Year 1 (base)		Year 2	
	Price	Index	Price	Index
Food	£120	100	£132	110
Clothing	£50	100	£51	102
Hair products	£20	100	£25	125
Newspapers	£10	100	£10	100
Gardening products	£5	100	£4	80

Newspaper article (page 190)

Q9: Mortgages and food are a big proportion of a family's income and so would have a large weight in the calculation of inflation of RPI.

Q10: The Retail Price Index excluding mortgages (RPIX) and the Consumers Price Index (CPI).

Q11: The RPIX does not include mortgages and the CPI excludes mortgages and council tax and house insurance.

Q12: Usually pensioners and people on benefit and students.

Q13: Anything we buy from US will be dearer putting up our cost of living, e.g. Chrysler cars. Any oil we buy from US to use in production will put our costs of production up so our goods will be dearer.

Government spending statements (page 191)

Q14: b) False

Q15: a) True

Q16: a) True

Q17: a) True

Inflation - summary (page 192)

Q18:

1. Inflation has the effect of *reducing* the purchasing power of money.
2. Real interest rates are *nominal* interest rates less *the inflation rate*.
3. Inflation in the UK makes our exports *less* price competitive.
4. People on *fixed* incomes face a drop in *real* income because of inflation.
5. Inflation in the UK makes our imports *more* price competitive.

End of Topic 2 test (page 193)

Q19: c) 2%

Q20: d) Index

Q21: b) prices on average are rising more slowly.

Q22: a) borrowers.

Q23: c) Pay rises that are greater than productivity gains.

Q24: The consumer price index takes a basket of about 600 goods and services that are representative of the purchases of an average household and monitors them every month to give an indication of the price rises. The items in the basket do not all have the same weighting. Weighting depends on the proportion of income spent on the items.

Q25: This was a period when manufacturing moved to low wage economies with a reduction in the costs of production. An example of this is cheaper clothing from Asia as sold by brands such as Primark.

The influence of trade unions in pushing for higher wages had been greatly reduced by the laws limiting their power in industrial disputes (introduced in the 1980s). As a result, pay rises were generally in line with rises in productivity which held back wage-cost inflation. In addition, competition from low wage economies abroad lead to lower wage increases to allow UK firms to compete.

Membership of trade unions fell substantially and the pay negotiating position of many workers became weaker.

Globalisation delivered new synergies from the rapid expansion of international trade and the ensuing cost reductions and productivity gains reduced prices.

The recent recession caused a fall in demand which led to lower demand pull inflation.

Topic 3: Government aims - unemployment

Definition of unemployment (page 196)

Q1: Anything used in the production of goods and services.

Q2: Land, labour, capital and enterprise.

Groups in society (page 196)

Q3:

Working population	Dependent population
soldier	student
bank employee	child under school age
unemployed job seeker	househusband / housewife
café owner	pensioner

Rate of unemployment (page 197)

Q4: 5

Q5: 2.5

Q6: 6.67

Q7: 15

Q8: 10

Causes of unemployment (page 200)

Q9: Structural unemployment

Q10: Cyclical, general or mass unemployment

Q11: Geographical immobility of labour prevents workers from moving from one *area* to another.

Q12: Technological unemployment

Q13: Occupational immobility

Effects of rising unemployment (page 202)

Q14: Four ways that rising unemployment affect government finances are:

* less money taken in income tax, VAT and corporation tax;
* more government spending on benefits;
* more government spending on training courses;
* less money available for education and other public services.

Measures taken to increase employment (page 204)

Q15: Measures taken include:

* increase public spending;
* encourage entrepreneurs;
* incentivise work by cutting income tax;
* reduce trade union power to increase flexibility in the labour market.

Trends in unemployment (page 205)

Q16: a) True

Q17: a) True

Q18: a) True

Q19: a) True

Q20: b) False

Standards of living (page 206)

Q21: d) 1, 2 and 3

End of Topic 3 test (page 208)

Q22: a) recession.

Q23: c) both of the above.

Q24: d) the percentage of the working population (registered or unregistered) who are unemployed.

Q25: a) average standards of living.

Q26: d) Increases in consumer spending.

Q27: Any four from:

- they have less ability to purchase goods (their standard of living falls substantially);
- they may go into debt as a consequence;
- their house may be re-possessed;
- their skills may quickly become outdated;
- they may need to seek re-training to increase occupational mobility;
- they may need to move for work (geographic mobility);
- they may encounter stress and stress related illnesses.

Two developed answers can be enough for four marks but it is equally valid to offer four separate points with less description.

Q28: Economic growth is an increase in the output of goods and services. Sustainable economic growth is a rate of economic growth (probably no more than 3% for an advanced economy) that occurs without rising inflation. New technology can allow supply to match this increase in demand in the economy. As prices are not soaring, governments do not need to take action to slow down demand.

Marks are awarded for the overall quality of the answer. Up to two marks could be awarded for a clear definition of economic growth. A clear understanding of the factors that can make a growth level sustainable may potentially give three marks. There is therefore more than one route to the maximum four marks.

Q29: Any four from:

- a healthy work-life balance;
- commuting to work time;
- low crime rates;
- a sense of community;
- levels of pollution and congestion;
- interesting or stimulating employment;
- the weather (should you let it!).

Four marks can come from, ideally, giving four straightforward points. However, if there is some overlap and the answer becomes descriptive then the marker may go with the flow and find four distinct points of value.

Topic 4: Government policy

Test your prior knowledge (page 212)

Q1: Money spent by central and local government in the economy.

Q2: It is financed mainly by taxation.

Fiscal policy (page 215)

Q3:

Statement	Description
Contradictory fiscal measures	Raising corporation tax and cutting government spending
Examples of current spending by government	Teachers' wages and medicines for NHS (there are many others)
A definition of fiscal policy	Use of public spending and taxation to alter aggregate demand
Examples of capital spending by government	New state schools and hospitals (there are many others)
Macroeconomic objectives of government	Low inflation, high employment, sustained economic growth and a balanced trade position
Who the Golden Rule says should pay for current spending by government	This present generation of taxpayers
Expansionary fiscal measures	Cutting income tax and increased government spending
Concept of aggregate demand increasing by more than the amount of government injection	The multiplier
Type of government spending that can justify government borrowing	Capital spending

Economic policy (page 217)

Q4: Due to the increased use of credit buying and home ownership.

Monetary policy (page 218)

Q5:

Statement	Description
A definition of monetary policy	The manipulation of interest rates and the money supply to achieve macroeconomic objectives
Responsible for setting interest rates	The Monetary Policy Committee of the Bank of England
An expansionary monetary policy	Lower interest rates
A contractionary monetary policy	Raise interest rates
What macroeconomic objectives monetarists regard as the most significant	Low and steady inflation

Answers from page 220.

Q6: The government reducing its control and regulation of the private sector of the UK economy.

The labour market and supply-side policies (page 221)

Q7: A product market is where a particular good or service is exchanged. The labour market is the demand for and supply of workers.

Q8: It means people keep a bigger proportion of their wage so people will be encouraged to take jobs.

Q9: The introduction of the *minimum* wage will encourage workers to take jobs they previously would not have taken.

Q10: The *privatisation* of various large state run industries was designed to encourage competition.

Q11: A *perfect (or flexible)* labour market is one that can quickly clear surpluses or shortages.

Q12: *Lower* rates of corporation tax will allow firms to keep more of their profits and also encourage higher levels of capital *investment*.

End of Topic 4 test (page 223)

Q13: a) increasing income tax rates.

Q14: b) quantitative easing.

Q15: c) 2 and 3 only

Q16: b) Decreasing income tax.

Q17: c) 2, 3 and 4 only

Q18: Low inflation, high employment, sustained economic growth and a balanced trade position. *(1½ marks each)*

Q19: The use of tax and/or public spending to influence aggregate demand.

Q20: The use of interest rates and the supply of money to influence aggregate demand.

Q21: Policies used to influence the output of goods and services in an economy.

Q22: Fiscal measures could include higher income tax and cuts in public spending. Monetary measures could include higher interest rates and restricting bank lending.

Topic 5: National income

Test your prior knowledge (page 227)

Q1: An increase in the output of goods and services in an economy.

Q2: As increase in real GNP.

The main "players" in an economic system (page 227)

Q3: Consumers, firms and government.

Factors of production (page 228)

Q4: d) Enterprise

Q5: a) Land

Q6: c) Capital

Q7: b) Labour

Flow of national income (page 230)

Q8: Households contain **consumers**. Households own **resources** which they provide to firms in return for **income**. These are spent on buying the **output of firms**. This then becomes income of firms which is then passed on to households and the process **continues**.

Circular flow of national income (page 232)

Q9: b) Decrease

Q10: b) Decrease

Q11: a) Increase

Q12: a) Increase

Q13: a) Increase

Q14: b) Decrease

Q15: c) No effect

Answers from page 233.

Q16: New technology and better management.

Q17: Productivity refers to output per input, e.g. output per worker hour.

Real national income - Scotopia (page 234)

Q18: e) A bigger volume of goods and services has been produced in Scotopia during each of the last three years.

Real national income (page 235)

Q19:

	Nominal national income (£ million)	Inflation rate (%)	Real national income (£ million)
Country A	40000	19	33613
Country B	80000	5	76190
Country C	100000	17	85470

Real and nominal national income (page 235)

Q20:

1. Using estimates of real national income to compare economic welfare internationally can be misleading because of disparities between nations in **population**.
2. During a year real and nominal national income of the UK both rose by 5%. Inflation must have been **zero**.

National income increase (page 236)

Q21: *No.* In *theory* national income could increase to infinity if, using the example above, the extra £10 billion is spent and earned continuously. However, some of this extra £10 bn income will be taxed, saved or spent on imports.

Marginal propensity to save (MPS) (page 237)

Q22: 0.1

Q23: 0.05

Q24: 0.25

Q25: 0.2

Marginal propensity to consume (MPC) (page 237)

Q26: 0.9

Q27: 0.8

Q28: 0.8

Q29: 0.5

Calculating the multiplier (page 238)

Q30: The extra income would be £200 million.
Using the formulae,

$$\frac{1}{mps} = \frac{1}{0.1} = 10$$

or, alternatively,

$$\frac{1}{1 - mpc} = \frac{1}{1 - 0.9} = 10$$

the circular flow continues until the total extra income = £20 million x 10 = £200 million. This total is added to the national income which becomes £1,200 million (or £1.2 billion).

The economy of Pictopia (page 239)

Q31:

Gross Domestic Product (GDP)	£15 billion
Add/subtract *Net property income from abroad*	+ £5 billion
Gross national product (GNP)	£20 billion
Subtract *Capital consumption*	£4 billion
National income (NNP)	£16 billion

National income statistics (page 239)

Q32: b) False

Q33: a) True

Q34: a) True

Q35: b) False

Q36: a) True

Chancellors' disagreement (page 241)

Expected answer

Q37: Your reply could include the following points:

- Ireland has a much smaller population so national income per head is higher;
- Working conditions are better in Ireland;
- Price levels are different so difficult to compare;
- Most Irish people are provided with basic necessities, e.g. housing and health;
- More luxury goods are available to the Irish population.

End of Topic 5 test (page 243)

Q38: d) £1,000m

Q39: a) the excise duty paid on tobacco.

Q40: b) the sale overseas of a Mini built in the UK.

Q41: b) the standard of living.

Q42: c) Both of the above.

Q43: UK national income is the total value of the goods and services produced by the UK over a period of one year.

Calculation difficulties include:

- Exclusion of transfer payments;
- Avoidance of double counting;
- The calculation of depreciation;
- Certain outputs difficult to value, e.g. defence and education;
- Non-recorded output (the black/hidden economy);
- Taking account of inflation.

Q44: Uses of UK national income statistics include:

- The figures show the levels of production, investment and incomes;
- They can be used to measure economic growth;
- They can be used to plan government policy;
- Comparison between countries is possible;
- Comparison between years is possible.

Q45: Some of the limitations to be considered are:

- The figures are estimates;
- Social costs of production are ignored, e.g. pollution;
- Cultural differences are not taken into account;
- Inflation can distort figures;
- Population figures can make comparison less meaningful;
- Currencies make comparison difficult;
- The spread of national income is not taken into account;
- What is being produced is not taken account of, e.g. hospital beds or tanks.

Q46: The circular flow of income shows the money flows between producers and consumers. Producers pay for the use of factors of production supplied by consumers. Consumers in turn spend to buy the goods and services produced.

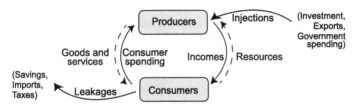

You must also show the three named injections and three named leakages in your diagram. You may choose to add the real flows of "resources" and "goods and services" but do this in a way that shows you realise they are not the same as money flows - perhaps use dotted lines or a different colour.

Q47:

a) The average propensity to consume (APC) is the proportion of all income that is spent. It is the proportion of all income that is passed on in the form of consumer spending to become income of other households in the same economy.
   If half of income is spent, the APC = 0.5.

b) The marginal propensity to consume (MPC) is the proportion of any increase in income that is spent. It is the proportion of any extra income that is passed on in the form of consumer spending to become income of other households in the same economy.
   If a household spends 40p out of every extra pound earned, then the MPC = 0.4.

Q48: When consumers receive an increase in their income caused by investment they will spend part of it depending on the MPC.

This spending becomes the income of others. A proportion of this will be spent, again becoming an increase in someone's income. Any money not spent leaks out of the circular flow. National income has increased by more than the original investment.

If half of income is spent, the APC = 0.5. The actual increase and the value of the multiplier can be calculated using the formula:

$$\frac{1}{mps}$$

or

$$\frac{1}{1 - mpc}$$

If the injection into the economy is £100 million and the MPC is 0.4 then the value of the multiplier is:

$$\frac{1}{mps} = \frac{1}{0.6} = 1.67$$

The original investment of £100 million will cause the national income to rise by the figure times 1.67, i.e. £167 million. The greater the size of the MPC the greater the size of the multiplier.

Topic 6: Place of Scotland in the UK economy

Scottish exports (page 247)

Q1: RUK (Rest of the UK), European Union and North America.

Comparing Scotland's unemployment to the rest of the UK (page 249)

Q2: South-East and East of England

Pros and cons of higher income tax accompanied by higher public spending (page 254)

Q3:

Devolved powers	Reserved powers
Construction and engineering jobs created	Disincentive to work
Improved transport infrastructure	Moving location south of the border
Less inequality	Reduced disposable incomes
More public sector jobs	

Devolved and reserved powers (page 255)

Q4:

Devolved powers	Reserved powers
Education	Employment
Environment	Immigration
Fire service	Nuclear energy
Fishing	Social security
Health	
Housing	
Justice	
Local government	

End of Topic 6 test (page 258)

Q5: a) Services

Q6: d) Rest of the UK

Q7: d) Social security

Q8: b) Education, health and public administration

Q9: c) Netherlands

Q10: Any five from:

- may lead to some higher income individuals moving their tax location from England to Scotland.;
- could encourage small businesses and entrepreneurs in taking risks, if returns are increased.;
- may act as an incentive to work;
- could lead to a reduction in the quality and quantity of public services;
- may lead to less public sector employment and those unemployed would spend less in private businesses generating a negative multiplier effect;
- increased consumer spending (higher disposable income with multiplier effect);
- poorer transport infrastructure which impacts on private business;
- fewer contracts to private firms in construction and engineering as public spending decreases;
- more inequality and social division from resulting redistribution of income.

Topic 7: End of unit test

End of Unit 2 test (page 260)

Q1: The circular flow of income shows the money flows between producers and consumers. Producers pay for the use of factors of production supplied by consumers. Consumers in turn spend to buy the goods and services produced.

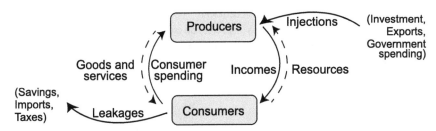

You must also show the three named injections and three named leakages in your diagram. You may choose to add the real flows of "resources" and "goods and services" but do this in a way that shows you realise they are not the same as money flows - perhaps use dotted lines or a different colour.

Q2: An injection into the circular flow, for example, from investment will increase national Income by much more than the amount of the original injection. The original injection will be passed from households to firms many times and increase national income because of these successive rounds of earning and spending.

The size of the multiplier can be measured using the formula:

$$\frac{1}{mps}$$

If we have a marginal propensity to save of 0.25 then the multiplier will be 4. An injection of £1m will increase national income by £4m.

Q3:

1. Low and steady inflation - price levels across the economy being kept in check so that real incomes and the value of money are maintained. The government has set a target of 2% (CPI) for inflation.

2. Full employment - unemployment rate of 3% or below, restricting unemployment to temporary or frictional. Government may refer to "a high level of employment" as its target, without quoting a figure.

3. Healthy trade position - a situation where imports can be paid for by the revenue from exports or a move to that position.

4. Economic growth - a real increase in GNP compared with the previous year. Note that sustainable levels of economic growth in advanced economies such as the UK are unlikely to exceed 3%, as technological progress is required to increase potential output.

Q4:

1. Fiscal policy - the use of taxation and /or public spending.
2. Monetary policy - the use of interest rates and/or bank lending.
3. Supply side policies - policies that influence the supply side of the economy, i.e. the output of goods and services.

Q5: Answers may include developments of the following points:

- Negative impact on economic growth in Scotland.
- Reduced levels of consumer spending (especially on credit).
- Reduced levels of investment because of rising cost of borrowing.
- Reduced employment (or even rising unemployment).
- Lower demand-pull price inflation.

Answers to questions and activities for Unit 3

Topic 1: Understanding global trade

UK imports - EU countries (page 265)

Q1: The following 10 EU countries are highlighted below.

1.	**Germany (4)**	11.	Japan (5)
2.	China (23)	12.	**Sweden (15)**
3.	USA (1)	13.	Hong Kong (21)
4.	**Netherlands (8)**	14.	Switzerland (9)
5.	Norway (19)	15.	Russia (27)
6.	**France (2)**	16.	**Poland (20)**
7.	**Belgium/Luxembourg (11/17*)**	17.	Canada (16)
8.	**Italy (6)**	18.	**Denmark (21)**
9.	**Ireland (7)**	19.	India (10)
10.	**Spain (3)**	20.	Turkey (19)

UK trade by category (page 270)

Q2: a) True

Q3: b) False

Q4: a) True

Q5: b) False

Q6: b) False

The advantages of trade (page 272)

Q7: Trade allows countries to obtain products that they are unable to produce themselves. In the UK that will include fruits that cannot be grown easily because the climate is unsuitable.

Trade allows countries to obtain products from the cheapest, most efficient producers. This enables citizens to increase their standard of living as the money saved can be used to purchase more goods and services.

Trade creates increased competition, and companies with international markets can cut costs by increasing economies of scale. This benefits consumers through reduced prices and improved quality.

Impact of international trade (page 272)

Q8: a) Increase

Q9: a) Increase

Q10: b) Decrease

Q11: a) Increase

Q12: a) Increase

Globalisation (page 273)

Q13: Globalisation describes the rapid expansion of international *trade*. Some developments that have contributed are the reduction in the costs of transporting goods through the development of *containerisation* and the increasing ease of modern communications using the *internet*. These developments have led to multi-national firms reducing costs by finding new *locations* for production plants and the increasing prevalence of internationally recognised *brand* names.

Before-trade and after-trade output (absolute advantage) (page 276)

Q14: 90

Q15: 80

Q16: 100

Q17: 120

Q18: a) Yes

Before-trade and after-trade output (comparative advantage) (page 279)

Q19: a) True

Q20: b) False

Q21: a) True

Q22: a) True

Q23: a) True

Trade surplus or deficit (page 282)

Q24:

Trade in goods (2006)	Trade surplus	Trade deficit
USA	Yes	
Germany		Yes
China		Yes
India		Yes
Japan		Yes

Patterns and reasons for trends in trade (page 282)

Q25: a) neighbouring

Q26: b) more

Q27: a) large

Q28: a) more

Trading nations (page 284)

Q29: c) Germany

Q30: d) Morocco

Trading nations - Japan and Ireland (page 284)

Q31: a) Ireland

End of Topic 1 test (page 287)

Q32: *The marker will be expecting about 6 developed points, or a larger number of less developed points. Marks are attached to each scoring point in the model answer. The specimen answer actually has 14 scoring points - always best to take out some insurance if you want all the marks available. Note that there are many other points that could have been made, and if you remember and can quote some figures that would impress.*

Geographically, UK trade is focussed on the EU and the USA *(1 mark)*. The EU has grown in significance as more countries have joined *(1 mark)*. As a free trade area, trade occurs without barriers such as tariffs *(1 mark)*.

The UK remains a major producer of manufactured goods (e.g. cars) *(1 mark)*. The volume of oil exports is falling but with increases in the price of a barrel the value of oil exports could continue to rise *(1 mark)*. As there are different types and qualities of oil, we also need to import oil in similar quantities *(1 mark)*. The UK has a trade in goods deficit *(1 mark)*.

In contrast UK trade in services is in surplus *(1 mark)*. This is largely due to the UK's expertise in financial services and the eminence of London *(1 mark)* and, to a lesser extent, Edinburgh.

The impact of foreign direct investment has grown greatly in recent years *(1 mark)* with the UK near the top of the world league both as a source and a beneficiary of FDI *(1 mark)*.

Scottish exports include oil and gas (although this is attributed to the UK as a whole), whisky, financial services, oil and gas service industries, office machinery and tourism *(2 marks)*.

Q33: e) United Kingdom

Q34: d) Italy

Q35: b) China

Q36: a) Canada

Q37: c) Israel

Q38: f) Zambia

Q39: As a result of trade, consumers will have more **choice**, for example, **bananas**, that cannot be easily grown in the UK. Companies will face increased **competition** and as a result will have to increase **quality** and reduce **prices** to stay in business. This will mean that consumers will have a higher **standard** of **living**.

Q40: *Advice: This question is out of 8 marks only. Under exam conditions you should allow about 12 minutes for completion. Therefore a detailed explanation of absolute and comparative advantage using efficiency tables would be excessive. Try to explain the theories in words without tables. A simple approach would be to divide the question in two and attempt to gain 4 marks on each theory.*

The theory of absolute advantage uses an example of a two-country two-product world. Initially, before trade, both countries have to make both products, as they do not have the option of trading to obtain either item. When country A is more efficient at making product X and country B is more efficient at making product Y then trade will be beneficial. By specialising in the one product and trading, the after trade outcome is that more output is produced from the same inputs. This allows both countries to gain from trade, assuming that transport costs are low.

(Note that every sentence advances the explanation another step. This means that a marker is likely to tick each sentence, and award at last 4 marks.)

Comparative advantage takes the theory of absolute advantage further. It proves that even when country A is more efficient at making both products (X and Y) and country B is less efficient for both products, trade will still offer benefits. Country A with an absolute advantage in making both products should take on the production of the product it has the greatest advantage making when compared to country B. Country B will then specialise in the product in which has the least comparative disadvantage.

(Note that again every sentence moves the explanation along, and again the answer will accumulate ticks, and at least 4 marks.)

Topic 2: Multinationals

The countries in which BP operates (page 290)

Q1: At the time of writing the website has a tab for 'BP worldwide' where you will find details of their current operations around the planet. You could repeat this task for another firm of your choosing.

Location factors (page 291)

Q2: b) Infrastructure concerns

Q3: c) Risk factors

Q4: b) Infrastructure concerns

Q5: a) Cost factors

Q6: c) Risk factors

Q7: a) Cost factors

The effects on the host country (page 293)

Q8:

Positive	Negative
creates employment	may cause pollution
improves working conditions	may switch location
increases exports	only provides low skill jobs
introduces modern technology	profits often repatriated
trains workers	undercuts local firms' prices

The effects on the home country (page 294)

Q9:

Positive	Negative
profits repatriated	deindustrialisation
survival of home-based firm	fewer exports
	jobs are lost overseas

End of Topic 2 test (page 295)

Q10: d) First Group

Q11: b) produce in more than one country.

Q12: a) the repatriation of profits.

Q13: b) the repatriation of profits.

Q14: c) political instability.

Q15: For 6 marks you will need six of the following points, or a fewer number of points with development:

- wage rates;
- land prices;
- available labour force and its skills, including level of basic literacy;
- access to raw materials;
- the road, rail, sea and air links are sufficient to allow the firm to operate efficiently and without unpredictable delays in getting goods to the market;
- the country has access to the latest information and communications systems and these systems function adequately;
- there is a framework of business and contract law that facilitates business;
- the size of the local market - developing local markets is often crucial to success, and multinationals may withdraw from markets where they cannot reach a suitable level of customer demand and are consequently unable to deliver the economies of scale that lead to profit;
- there are trade barriers that will increase costs to consider;
- the chances of a violent revolution;
- the exchange rate of the currency changing;
- an epidemic or a natural disaster such as a flood.

Topic 3: Exchange rates

Demand for currency (page 300)

Q1: a) Increase

Q2: b) Decrease

Q3: a) Increase

Q4: a) Increase

The supply of currency (page 301)

Q5: The *supply of* sterling comes from the purchase of UK *imports* by *UK* consumers and companies.

Q6: It follows that *import penetration* helps to drive the value of a country's currency *downwards*, because it increases *supply of* that currency.

Q7: 'Hot money' flows are *taken out* of pounds whenever attractive interest rates are available *outside the UK*. *Decreases* in UK interest rates can lead to an *increased supply of* pounds, because of the *diminished* returns available in UK banks.

The effect of a rising exchange rate on the economy (page 302)

Q8: £72,000

Q9: £60,000

The effect of a rising exchange rate on inflation, economic growth and employment (page 304)

Q10: A rising exchange rate makes our exports more *expensive*, and our imports *cheaper*. This *increases* unemployment because UK goods are *less* price competitive in world markets. With less output economic growth *decreases*, and combined with a *negative* multiplier effect, there is a danger of *recession*.

The effect of a falling exchange rate (page 304)

Q11: A falling exchange rate for the pound will make our *exports* cheaper and our *imports* more expensive. This will make UK exporters *more* price competitive. In the UK market foreign firms will be under pressure to *raise* prices. As a result UK firms may increase sales and output thus increasing economic *growth*. This will create more *employment* in the UK. However the cost of imports will make *inflation* higher.

Fixed exchange rates (page 306)

Q12: Fixed exchange rates allow firms to trade with *certainty* that exchange rate movements will not affect the *profitability* of international contracts. For long periods, *speculation* will not take place because *central* banks will successfully maintain the currency value.

Floating exchange rates (page 308)

Q13: Floating exchange rates *automatically* adjust to prevailing economic conditions. No *intervention* by central banks means that large *reserves* of foreign currency are not required and *speculators* find it difficult to spot an inappropriate exchange value to *profit* from when the rates reflect prevailing economic conditions.

Exchange rate systems (page 308)

Q14: a) Advantage for fixed exchange rate

Q15: b) Advantage for floating exchange rate

Q16: b) Advantage for floating exchange rate

Q17: a) Advantage for fixed exchange rate

Trends in the pound to dollar exchange rate (page 310)

Q18:

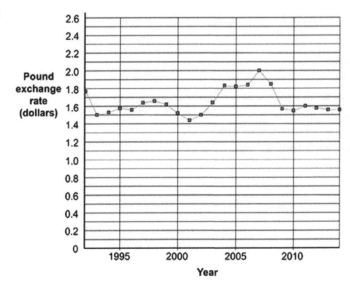

End of Topic 3 test (page 312)

Q19: a) exports from the UK increase.

Q20: d) increase exports.

Q21: a) as economies grow at different rates, they become unsustainable.

Q22: d) interest rates.

Q23: c) Both of the above.

Q24: You should provide an explanation of how the demand for sterling is determined by:

- the demand for UK exports;
- the level of FDI in the UK;
- the amount of tourists visiting the UK;
- hot money inflows.

(1 mark for each determinant and 1 mark for each explanation)

Full marks can also be gained for explaining the factors which influence the determinants, e.g. relative inflation rates, the UK rate of interest, and the state of the UK economy.

Q25: *"Discuss" means discuss points in favour and points against. Some points made here can be quite complex and if well discussed and might be worthy of 3 marks. Try to explain at least two advantages and two disadvantages to target full marks.*

The advantages include:

- no need to defend a particular exchange rate;
- can adopt an independent monetary policy;
- possible automatic adjustment to the Balance of Payments (Marshall Lerner).

(Maximum 6 marks)

The disadvantages include:

- fluctuating exchange rates - therefore trade becomes more risky;
- greater risk of high inflation;
- can lead to a depreciation/inflation spiral;
- greater scope for currency arbitrage.

(Maximum 6 marks)

Q26: *This answer to this question can extend beyond the current section. However you can start by developing the first part of your answer along the lines of how a fall in interest rates reduces the exchange value of sterling and go on to explain how this can impact on inflation through rising import prices.*

The main problem is the risk of overheating with the consequent rise in demand-pull inflation, trade deficits - so look for a detailed explanation of why AMD will rise, e.g. borrowing cheaper, saving less rewarding, marginal investments now viable, and increased real income of mortgage holders.

This is all that is required for full marks but other reasons include the fall in the value of sterling because of hot money outflows leading to an increase in the price of imports and cost-push prices, a large increase in house prices (because of cheaper mortgages) and an increase in consumer debt.

(Maximum of 2 marks each)

Topic 4: The balance of payments

Visible or invisible (page 318)

Q1: a) Visible

Q2: b) Invisible

Q3: b) Invisible

Q4: a) Visible

Visibles (page 319)

Q5:

Year	Export of goods (£ billion)	Import of goods (£ billion)	Visible balance (£ billion)
2010	271	368	-97
2011	309	406	-97
2012	305	414	-109
2013	307	419	-112
2014	292	412	-120

Q6:

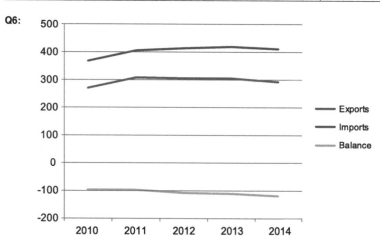

Invisibles (page 319)

Q7:

Year	Export of services (£ billion)	Import of services (£ billion)	Invisible balance (£ billion)
2010	176	116	60
2011	190	118	72
2012	196	121	75
2013	209	130	79
2014	208	123	85

Q8:

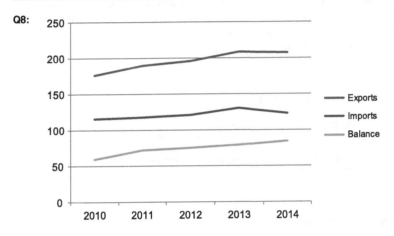

Surpluses and deficits (page 321)

Q9:   The UK has a *deficit* in trade in goods, but a smaller *surplus* in trade in services. Taken together the overall UK *current* account is in deficit. Two factors causing this are low *wages* overseas and a £ exchange rate that for periods can be *high*. Fortunately the UK enjoys net *capital* inflows and has a strong *financial services* sector based around the pre-eminence of *London*.

444

Costs and benefits of foreign direct investment (page 323)

Q10: Your answer could develop several of the following points:

- jobs are created by the investment in construction and then in operations;
- the multiplier effect further increases the employment effects in the local community;
- the jobs are often on the assembly line with few higher paid posts for locals;
- multinationals show little loyalty in recessions and branch plants often close first;
- multinationals are footloose and may move on after a few years to a cheaper location;
- management skills from abroad are introduced;
- the investment counts towards the balance of payments as a credit;
- the multinational will be keen to export from Scotland to the EU improving the trade balance;
- wages and working conditions may be more attractive in these multinationals and local firms face higher costs to match them, or struggle to find staff;
- the tax base for local authorities in Scotland will increase and this provides funds for local authority services.

Trends in the current account (page 324)

Q11: Combined, the trade in goods and services have moved from a small surplus in 1997 to a significant deficit of between £30bn and £40bn in recent years to 2013.

Q12: The current account balance has moved into greater deficit since 1998, from less than £5bn to more than £70bn in 2013. As a percentage of GDP it has moved from less than 1% in 1998 to more than 4% in 2013.

Trends in the trade in goods and services (page 325)

Q13: The trade in services surplus has increased from less than £20bn before 2003 upwards to a surplus of nearly £80bn in 2013. The trade in goods deficit has widened from less than £20bn in 1997 to £110bn in 2013.

End of Topic 4 test (page 326)

Q14: c) trade in services.

Q15: c) show a deficit for goods and a surplus for services.

Q16: c) Both of the above.

Q17: c) foreign direct investment.

Q18: a) visibles and invisibles.

Q19: *The development of the answer with examples is probably not essential with only 4 marks at stake. However it is included because you will not be sure what the markers' instructions are, so it is safer to add some relevant details or examples to most answers.*

A trade in goods deficit means that exports of goods (e.g. tangible items such as cars) are less than imports of goods. The UK has a substantial deficit in goods.

A budget deficit describes the government spending more (e.g. on the NHS) than it takes in through tax revenue (e.g. income tax) in a year. The government has to borrow to make up for the shortfall.

Q20: Budget deficits speed up the economy. The government is putting more money in as government spending than it is taking out in taxes. This will lead to decreased unemployment. Companies receiving government contracts will have to hire more staff. The government will also directly employ more teachers, doctors, etc. in the public sector. When the newly employed spend their incomes there will be a multiplier effect and a new round of jobs created.

When the UK economy grows fast, the demand for goods and services begins to exceed the supply. Especially as full employment is reached, increases in supply become difficult to achieve. As a result more and more imports are sucked in to satisfy the demand from UK consumers. Imports will exceed exports. Thus a budget deficit leads to a trade deficit.

Q21: At times the exchange rate of the pound sterling has been relatively high against the currencies of our major trading partners. This makes our exports less price competitive in foreign markets, and at home imports will be cheaper. Sales of foreign goods increase as they are substituted for the higher priced UK goods. This led to a growing trade deficit.

Labour costs in much of the world are cheaper than in the UK. The rapidly growing economies such as those of Eastern Europe and of China are producing more and more manufactured goods. These goods are priced at less than those made in the UK, so UK firms are losing customers in home and foreign markets. For example, shoe manufacturing in the UK has declined in the face of cheap imports. This leads to a growing trade in goods deficit.

Topic 5: Understanding the impact of the global economy

The eurozone (page 331)

Q1: Eurozone countries

Austria	Belgium	Cyprus	Estonia
Finland	France	Germany	Greece
Ireland	Italy	Latvia	Lithuania
Luxembourg	Malta	Netherlands	Portugal
Slovakia	Slovenia	Spain	

Joining the euro - advantages and disadvantages for the UK (page 333)

Q2:

Advantages of joining the euro	Disadvantages of joining the euro
Easier for consumers to compare prices in different countries	One interest rate set for all of eurozone
No commission on changing currency	Devaluation of pound no longer possible
Exchange rate certainty for firms within eurozone	
Multinational investment in UK more likely	

Enlargement of the EU - benefits and problems for the UK (page 336)

Q3:

Benefits of enlargement for the UK	Problems of enlargement for the UK
Wider markets for UK goods	Additional EU budget costs for the UK
Increased choice for UK consumers	Multinationals move to cheaper locations
Skilled workers from abroad to fill vacancies	

Human Development Index (HDI) of the countries of the world (page 337)

Expected answer

You will find many of the highest ranked countries in Europe and North America. Parts of Africa will feature among the lowest ranked countries.

Levels of development (page 337)

Q4:

Nation	Income per person ($)	Life Expectancy (years)	Literacy Rate (%)	Developing/ Emerging/ Developed
Malawi	900	60	75	Developing
India	4,000	68	63	Emerging
Bangladesh	2,100	71	58	Developing
Japan	37,100	84	99	Developed
South Africa	11,500	50	93	Emerging
Sweden	40,900	82	99	Developed
Chad	2,500	49	35	Developing
United Kingdom	37,300	80	99	Developed
Brazil	12,100	73	90	Emerging

Note: The answers are not always clear-cut. For example, South Africa has a life expectancy more in keeping with a developing country than an emerging country.

World Factbook (page 338)

Expected answer

There is no definitive solution to this task - it depends on your choice of countries.

Developing countries (page 339)

Q5:

Land	Labour	Capital
Droughts leading to crop failure	Low literacy rates	Lack of modern technology
Few natural resources	Poor health	Little is saved
Seasonal flooding	Unskilled workers	Poor transport infrastructure
		Weak banking system

Senegal (page 342)

Q6: b) 61

Q7: a) 50%

Q8: b) $2,100

Q9: c) 54%

Q10: c) 78%

Q11: b) 43%

Aid versus trade (page 344)

Q12:

Type of aid	Description	Problem
Bilateral aid	From one country to another	Tied to buying from donor country
Multilateral aid	From international organisation	Economic "strings" attached (e.g. balanced budget)
Emergency aid	Disaster relief (food and medicine)	May encourage dependency
Soft loans	Low interest finance to assist development	Increases debts

Emerging economies (page 345)

Q13: Emerging economies such as *Brazil* no longer depend on *primary* production. They tend to have *high* levels of spending on infrastructure. Literacy rates are *over* 50% as a result of these spending levels on education. *High* levels of foreign investment occur, encouraged by political *stability*. GDP per capita, for example, could be *$10,000* per annum and standards of living are *rising*. With *increasing* levels of birth control, the age structure of emerging economies shows more people in the *working* age categories.

Malaysia (page 347)

Q14: b) 75

Q15: c) 93%

Q16: b) $17,500

Q17: a) 4%

Q18: a) 11%

Q19: c) 29%

End of topic test (page 350)

Q20: b) monetary policy.

Q21: b) Malawi, India, Japan.

Q22: c) Free trade with EU members.

Q23: b) It may have to be spent with the donor country.

Q24: d) Slovenia, Germany, Norway.

Q25: The UK trades mainly with the EU because there are no trade barriers such as tariffs between EU countries. This means that the prices of traded goods are not subject to taxes as they cross frontiers and can compete fairly in foreign markets.

The EU has a large population and is a single market of over 400 million consumers. Paperwork and frontier delays have been reduced making it easier to export and import.

The EU consumers have high incomes and spend a lot on goods and services. They are also close to the UK so that transport costs on goods are less, and share a similar culture and tastes. This makes exporting to them more likely to be successful.

Q26: *Advantages*

Shortages in the labour market will be filled by immigrants from the new members seeking the higher wages of the UK. This will benefit firms who would have production problems if they could not find the appropriate applicants among UK citizens.

Wage inflation that would result from skill shortages will be far less likely to occur. Employers will no longer have to attract workers from other firms by outbidding them on wages. This will help the UK economy to meet its 2% inflation target.

Enlargement provides a bigger single market for UK firms and they may increase economies of scale. Faced with more competition they will need to be more innovative and to hold down prices for consumers.

Disadvantages

The low-wage new members may attract multi-nationals to invest away from the UK, creating unemployment. Low priced imports may attract consumers away from UK produced goods and this will reduce profits and dividends, and increase unemployment.

The new members will be eligible for EU funds to develop their economies and support their farmers. The UK will be a net contributor to this growing bill.

Q27: Economic costs to the UK would include the large initial expense of changing all the coins and notes, and the changes required to slot machines.

If the UK joined the euro then the option of devaluing our currency would be lost from our economic policy options. If the economy suffered from low productivity or our exports were difficult to price competitively because of UK inflation it would no longer be possible to boost the economy through devaluation.

The interest rate set by the European Central Bank for the eurozone may not always be appropriate to the needs of the UK. If the UK is moving into recession it may benefit from lower interest rates but cannot be sure that the ECB will lower the eurozone interest rate. The UK economy might move into recession as a direct result of this. The UK would lose control of monetary policy, although it would keep some influence on the eurozone rate.

Benefits include the greater certainty for companies that they will not lose profit because of adverse exchange rate movements. Foreign direct investment in the UK may increase because of this, creating jobs.

The absence of currency conversion costs will also attract them as costs are lowered.

Q28: *Note the use of "discuss" which means that both positive and negative aspects of aid must be dealt with. If you are able to develop 4 points thoroughly you may well be awarded all 12 marks. Another approach is to provide 6 points and develop them to an extent.*

Solution: Here are a selection of points that you could discuss in your answer, they are in note form. You would need to develop them in your answer.

Type of aid: emergency relief - e.g food aid. Positive effect: saves lives. Negative effect: risk of dependency, undercuts local farmers.

Type of aid: infrastructure projects - e.g. dams. Positive effect: generally advantageous, e.g. increased crop yield. Negative effect: not good for communities cleared to make way.

Type of aid: providing university education in developed countries. Positive effect: graduates return with skills to assist progress. Negative effect: some may remain abroad, but generally positive.

Type of aid: "soft loans" - made at below commercial interest rates. Positive effect: used for investment in infrastructure. Negative effect: corruption may siphon off money from intended use.

Type of aid: tied aid - i.e. buy from donor country. Positive effect: receive equipment as a result of tied aid. Negative effect: no choice - may not get best value or most suitable.

Type of aid: multilateral aid - e.g. from World Bank. Positive effect: funds to develop economic infrastructure. Negative effect: expected to find market solutions, curb public spending.

Q29: *This specimen answer indicates some scoring points - 18 marks in all. Don't be put off by this. You can obtain the full 8 marks from a less detailed response. Remember that "discuss" requires you to consider the pros and cons.*

Allowing LDCs access to markets such as the EU's without facing tariff barriers and unfairly subsidised EU food will lead to greater orders for farmers in the LDC *(1 mark)*. As cheap producers they have a comparative advantage in the production of some primary products *(1 mark)*. Free trade will lead to higher revenues, more employment, better wages and investment in agriculture *(2 marks)*. This will have positive multiplier effects on all other sectors of the economy *(1 mark)*. Economic growth will increase *(1 mark)*. This will develop the ability of the LDC to sustain itself without aid *(1 mark)*. It will contribute export revenues to help the trade balance *(1 mark)*. It will increase the government's tax revenues *(1 mark)* and they can be invested in infrastructure such as health, education and transport *(1 mark)*.

Aid can only provide temporary relief *(1 mark)*. It may encourage dependency *(1 mark)* as it is difficult for local enterprise to compete with free hand-outs *(1 mark)*. If you cannot make a profit you may not plant the seed *(1 mark)*.

However, aid is valuable in times of flood or drought *(1 mark)*. It keeps people alive, at least in the short term *(1 mark)*. Grants for infrastructure projects (e.g. water and sanitation) can also help to develop the economy *(1 mark)*. Both aid and trade can be helpful, but the long-term solution may come from free trade *(1 mark)*.

Topic 6: End of unit test

End of Unit 3 test (page 354)

Q1:

Description	Nation
Major export market for UK	USA
Major source of UK imports	China
Uses the yen as currency	Japan
Uses the euro as currency	Malta
Example of emerging economy	Brazil
Example of developing economy	Malawi
Example of developed economy	Canada
European nation not in EU	Norway

Note: It is also true that the USA is a significant source of UK imports. However, none of the other examples are in the top export markets. USA should therefore be the choice for the major export market for UK.

Q2: Trade barriers (6 marks)

Any three of the following trade barriers - worth 2 marks each. Always give examples if you can, they can help you to get the full marks if your description is weak.

A quota is a limit by value or volume on imports. There are many examples of quotas around the world. In the past the EU has placed a limit on the import of textiles from China. (2 marks)

An embargo is a total ban on imports, perhaps because of political or military conflict. It can also happen for health reasons so British beef was subject to an embargo when BSE affected the herd. American beef is also the subject of embargoes because of their use of growth hormones in the feed. (2 marks)

A tariff is a tax on imports that increases the price of the import and therefore reduces sales and advantages home produced goods. For example Scotch whisky faces high tariffs in many markets e.g. India. In 2006 imported leather shoes from China were subjected to a 19% tariff entering the EU. (2 marks)

A subsidy is assistance that gives home producers a cost advantage over imports. This government financial help can take many forms, but essentially allows a less efficient home-based company to charge less and continue competing against efficient importers. The Common Agricultural Policy of the EU is an excellent example of subsidies to home producers enabling them to compete with cheap imports. (2 marks)

An administrative delay is an artificially created bureaucratic (paperwork) hold-up, that adds to the importer's costs. Any delay in getting goods on the shelf adds to costs, and there is always the chance that importers may look to find easier opportunities in other countries. (2 marks)

Justifications (4 marks)

Any two of the following justifications - worth 2 marks each.

Avoiding job losses - imports take custom away from home producers of the same good or service. This would lead to job losses, that may be concentrated in one region with negative multiplier effects. (2 marks)

The Infant Industry Argument is a strong one when properly applied. It protects a new industry's home market until it is large enough to enjoy economies of scale and compete freely on world markets. (2 marks)

Retaliation is a reaction to unfair trade by another country. For example "dumping" items below cost price may lead to tariffs as retaliation. (2 marks)

Trade deficits can be corrected by reducing imports. This assumes that there is no retaliation against the country imposing the initial trade barrier. (2 marks)

Q3: UK firms:

Exporting firms will find it difficult to compete in foreign markets. The high exchange rate forces them to increase prices abroad or accept a substantial cut in profit margins. *(2 marks)*

Example: a Jaguar car selling for £30,000 in the UK will at £1 = $2 be priced at $60,000 in the USA. If the pound gets stronger (£1 = $2.50) then the price in dollars would be $75,000. *(2 marks)*

This price rise will cause demand to fall, and when fewer are sold, then profits will fall. Alternatively they need to increase productivity and lower their average costs so that they can regain competitive prices. *(2 marks)*

Goods imported into the UK will be cheaper. This will increase price competition for import-competing UK firms. Sales and profits will be reduced. Some may go bankrupt. Alternatively they need to increase productivity and lower their average costs so they can be competitive on price once more. *(3 marks)*

Firms that use imported raw materials and components will gain from cheaper input prices. They still face stiffer price competition with foreign firms as a result of the higher exchange rate, but at least a reduction in some of their costs will help. *(2 marks)*

In summary UK firms will need to increase productivity to compensate for the loss of competitiveness. They could also seek to differentiate their products so that they have fewer substitutes and have lower price elasticity. *(2 marks)*

UK consumers:

If you are consuming a holiday abroad the strong pound will make it cheaper. If your hotel was going to charge you $900, then at £1= $2, this would be £450. If the pound strengthens to $3 and buys more dollars then your hotel may only charge you £300. *(2 marks)*

Imported products will be cheaper. Home-based firms may lower prices to be competitive. Inflation is reduced and your salary will buy more goods and services - an increase in your standard of living. *(3 marks)*

Q4: Advantages:

Joining the euro increases price transparency for UK consumers, allowing prices to be compared without exchange rate fluctuations clouding the issue. *(2 marks)*

Currency conversion costs for UK firms and consumers are eliminated when dealing with other eurozone countries. This may make the UK more attractive for foreign investment as multinationals can locate in the UK and export to the eurozone at lower cost. Costs for import/export are reduced and therefore prices should fall. This increase the standard of living as a price cut has the same effect as a pay rise. *(4 marks)*

There is certainty for businesses dealing with the eurozone that adverse currency fluctuations will not reduce their profits. This may attract multinationals to set up in the UK (foreign direct investment) and use it as a base for exporting to the eurozone. *(2 marks)*

There is an argument that the European Central Bank will take a strong line on controlling inflation, although the Bank of England has been given independence to do the same so this argument is now weaker. *(1 mark)*

Disadvantages:

One currency means one interest rate. The euro interest rate is set for the entire eurozone. It may not suit the needs of the UK economy if we are not at the same point in the business cycle as other euro economies. We may want a high rate to slow inflation and they may need a low rate to cure unemployment. *(3 marks)*

The UK can no longer set an independent economic policy. With limited influence over interest rates, the government will need to use fiscal policy to adjust the economy. The ability to devalue or depreciate the currency to solve a balance of payments deficit is also lost. It would now be necessary to have a budget surplus and squeeze the economy with higher taxes and cuts in government spending in order to cut imports. *(4 marks)*

Q5: *A "compare and contrast" question needs careful handling. You should compare points alongside each other. This solution consists of paragraphs with mark allocations. You do not have to include all the points in your answer.*

Developing countries have lower GDP per capita than emerging economies. They are far poorer. Typically a developing country like Malawi may have $800 per annum average income, but an emerging economy may have $5,000 or more per annum average income. *(2 marks)*

As a result a developing country's poverty leads to lower life expectancies and poorer health. This impacts on the ability of developing countries to produce at the same level as emerging economies. *(2 marks)*

Both developing countries and emerging economies tend to have international debts. However emerging economies have greater ability to pay the interest on the debt. Emerging economies borrow to invest in infrastructure projects such as roads and harbours that help to attract multinational investment. Developing countries are more likely to use the loans for crisis management in their struggling health and education services, or to pay for clean water projects or just for imported oil. *(3 marks)*

Developing countries have a higher percentage of the population employed in primary production, especially agriculture. Emerging economies have a more diverse employment profile with far more people employed in factories and services in their growing urbanisation. *(2 marks)*

Developing countries may rely heavily on the world price of one major export, often a crop. Emerging economies export a range of manufactured goods as well as crops. *(2 marks)*

Emerging economies have high rates of economic growth (e.g. China, Brazil, India). Rates of 8% growth and more have been known. However developing countries can struggle to make any growth - their agricultural economies can be hit by flood and drought. Developing countries do not produce a surplus to invest in the future. This limits their growth as does a weak banking system. *(4 marks)*

Developing countries tend to be more politically unstable than emerging economies and this does not make them safe for foreign investors. Military spending can be high relative to the economy, and corruption has a bigger impact on developing countries. Emerging economies flourish under strong leadership with an enterprise bias and democratically elected governments, e.g. Singapore. *(2 marks)*

BV - #0003 - 030919 - C0 - 210/148/25 - PB - 9781911057406